Children's Interpersonal Trust

Ken J. Rotenberg
Editor

Children's Interpersonal Trust

Sensitivity to Lying, Deception,
and Promise Violations

Springer-Verlag
New York Berlin Heidelberg London
Paris Tokyo Hong Kong Barcelona

Ken J. Rotenberg
Department of Psychology
Lakehead University
Thunder Bay, Ontario P7B 5E1
Canada

With four illustrations.

Library of Congress Cataloging-in-Publication Data
Children's interpersonal trust: sensitivity to lying, deception, and
    promise violations / Ken J. Rotenberg, editor.
        p.   cm.
    Includes bibliographical references.
    ISBN 0-387-97511-X (alk. paper)
    1. Trust (Psychology) in children.   2. Truthfulness and falsehood
in children.   3. Truthfulness and falsehood.   4. Deception.
    5. Promises.   I. Rotenberg, Ken J.
BF723.T78C55   1991
155.4'18—dc20   90-25448

Printed on acid-free paper.

Typeset by Best-set Typesetter Ltd., Chai Wan, Hong Kong.
Printed and bound by Edwards Brothers, Inc., Ann Arbor, Michigan.
Printed in the United States of America.

9 8 7 6 5 4 3 2 1

ISBN 0-387-97511-X Springer-Verlag New York Berlin Heidelberg
ISBN 3-540-97511-X Springer-Verlag Berlin Heidelberg New York

Contents

Contributors vii

1. Children's Interpersonal Trust: An Introduction   1
   KEN J. ROTENBERG

2. What is a Lie? Children's Use of Intentions and Consequences
   in Lexical Definitions and Moral Evaluations of Lying   5
   CANDIDA C. PETERSON

3. Young Children's Verbal Misrepresentations of Reality   20
   MAGDA STOUTHAMER-LOEBER

4. Children's Cue Use and Strategies for Detecting
   Deception   43
   KEN J. ROTENBERG

5. Children's Responses to Authentic Versus Polite Smiles   58
   DAPHNE BLUNT BUGENTAL, HAL KOPEIKIN AND LINDA LAZOWSKI

6. Children's Deception Skills and Social Competence   80
   ROBERT S. FELDMAN AND PIERRE PHILIPPOT

7. Children's Trustworthiness: Judgments by Teachers, Parents,
   and Peers   100
   JOHN M. WILSON AND JAMES L. CARROLL

8. Betrayal Among Children and Adults   118
   WARREN, H. JONES, MIRAMAR G. COHN, AND CURTIS E. MILLER

9. Trust and Children's Developing Theories of Mind   135
   MICHAEL CHANDLER AND SUZANNE HALA

10. The Trust-Value Basis of Children's Friendship   160
    KEN J. ROTENBERG

Contributors

DAPHNE BLUNT BUGENTAL   Department of Psychology, University of California, Santa Barbara, Santa Barbara, California 93106, USA

JAMES L. CARROLL   College of Education, Wichita State University, Wichita, Kansas 67208, USA

MICHAEL CHANDLER   Department of Psychology, University of British Columbia, Vancouver, BC Z6T 1W5, Canada

MIRAMAR G. COHN   Department of Psychology, University of Tulsa, Tulsa, Oklahoma 74104, USA

ROBERT S. FELDMAN   Department of Psychology, University of Massachusetts at Amherst, Tobin Hall, Amherst, Massachusetts 01003, USA

WARREN H. JONES   Department of Psychology, University of Tennessee, Knoxville, Tennessee 37996-0900, USA

HAL KOPEIKIN   Department of Psychology, University of California, Santa Barbara, Santa Barbara, California 93106, USA

LINDA LAZOWSKI   Department of Psychology, University of Indiana, Bloomington, Indiana 47401, USA

CURTIS E. MILLER   Department of Psychology, University of Tulsa, Tulsa, Oklahoma 74104, USA

CANDIDA C. PETERSON   Department of Psychology, University of Queensland, St. Lucia, Brisbane, Queensland 4067, Australia

PIERRE PHILIPPOT   Department of Psychology, University of Louvain, Louvain-La-Neuve, Belgium

KEN J. ROTENBERG   Department of Psychology, Lakehead University, Thunder Bay, Ontario P7B 5E1, Canada

MAGDA STOUTHAMER-LOEBER   University of Pittsburgh, Western Psychiatric Institute and Clinic, Pittsburgh, PA 15213-2593, USA

JOHN M. WILSON   Tempe Elementary School, P.O. Box 27708, Tempe, Arizona 85285, USA

1
Children's Interpersonal Trust: An Introduction

KEN J. ROTENBERG

Social philosophers during the course of history (i.e., Hartmann, 1932) and modern-day researchers (i.e., Deutsch, 1973; Rotter, 1971, 1980) have expressed the belief that interpersonal trust is essential for the achievement of harmonious and cooperative social relationships among people. Interpersonal trust has been considered to be the social "cement" that binds interpersonal relationships in society and is necessary for its survival. As part of this recognition, social philosophers and researchers have been concerned with children's interpersonal trust. Often, this has been guided by the notion that the interpersonal trust of adults, and therefore society, has its origins in the interpersonal trust formed during childhood. The belief held is that insight into the strength of the adults' interpersonal trust is provided by understanding the formation of interpersonal trust during childhood. This rationale served as one impetus for this book. In addition, however, the book is guided by the notion that it is important to understand interpersonal trust in children for its own sake. Children are part of society and, as a consequence, it is important to determine the factors that affect their interpersonal trust.

The purpose of this book is to present the current theory and research on children's interpersonal trust. A wide span of childhood is considered, from the beginning of toddlerhood (2 years) through early adolescence (12 years). Interpersonal trust is conceptualized as a child's confidence that a person's verbal and nonverbal communications accurately represent, or correspond to, internal states and external events. That confidence, and hence trust, is viewed as a continuum (trust to distrust) that can be shown by children through verbal or overt behavior. In addition, children's lack of confidence and, hence, distrust reflect the degree to which they believe that the misrepresentation or distortion in communication is intentional. This latter facet of interpersonal trust depends, however, on children's sophistication in understanding and use of intentionality to define lying, which has been found to increase with age (see Chapters 2 and 3). The present definition of interpersonal trust is an integration of those found in the literature (Giffin, 1967; Johnson-George & Swap, 1982; Rotter, 1967, 1971; Schlenker, Helm, & Tedeschi, 1973).

According to the definition, children's interpersonal trust includes their sensitivity to lying, deception, and promise violations. Promise violations may be regarded as having a distinct quality; the external event is the communicator's own behavior and is perceived to be under his or her control. Sometimes, researchers address these phenomena without reference to interpersonal trust per se. Considering them under the rubic of interpersonal trust is useful, however, because it offers greater explanatory power and opportunities for research. In particular, interpersonal trust may serve as a psychological dimension on which the different phenomena or "domains" map. For example, by adopting this approach, researchers may embark on assessing children's generalizion across their experiences with lying, deception, and promise violations. Furthermore, this may reveal whether, and if so how, children adopt a trusting or distrusting *orientation* toward others. Also, when considering children's trusting (as identified previously), researchers frequently address what may be considered the opposite side of the coin, that of children's trustworthiness (see Chapters 7 and 8). From the present perspective, (un)trustworthiness comprises children's tendency to engage in lying, deception, and promise violations.

This book is concerned with four related themes that have historical significance in the field of psychology. First, there is a long history of interest in children's conceptualization of lying and the qualities of communucation that define it. Perhaps best known is Piaget's (1932) book on moral development that included this topic. In the present book, Candida Pederson (Chapter 2) describes cross-cultural research on developmental changes in children's criteria for defining lying. To some extent, this issue is dealt with by Magda Stouthamer-Loeber (Chapter 3), although her research extends this issue to examine young children's verbal misrepresentations of reality and their parents' reactions to those misrepresentations.

Second, researchers have been interested in children's ability to understand deception. This continues a tradition of assessing children's social cognitive ability to understand the thoughts, beliefs, and emotions of people (see Astington, Harris, & Olson, 1988). In the present book, Michael Chandler and Suzanne Hala (Chapter 9) discuss the relevance of children's "theories of mind" to their understanding of deception and focus on controversy of whether children understand deception early (at 2 to 3 years of age) or later (at 5 to 6 years of age) in development.

Third, researchers have been interested in the children's use of cues to detect deception (e.g., Zuckerman, Blanck, DePaulo, & Rosenthal, 1980). In the present book, Daphne Blunt Bugental, Hal Kopeikin, and Linda Lazowski (Chapter 5) describe research on young children's differential response to authentic as opposed to polite smiles by adults. Furthermore, Bugental and her colleagues explored the differences in those processes between children from abusive and those from nonabusive families. In Chapter 4, I describe an investigation of children's reports of the cues they use to detect deception and the strategies they engage in to detect it. Robert S. Feldman and Pierre Philippot (Chapter 6) describe research supporting the conclusion that children's ability to detect deception is an integral part of their social competence. Finally, John M. Wilson and James L. Carroll (Chapter 7) have found that children are sensitive to their peers' lying and deception and that their perceptions can serve as a valuable measure of peers' untrustworthy communications.

Fourth, children's interpersonal trust has been investigated over the past two decades (Imber, 1973; Rotenberg, 1980), largely in terms of children's beliefs that others fulfill their promises. I have assessed the role of promise fulfillment and secret keeping as bases of children's peer friendship (Chapter 10). Children's reactions to promise violations as well as lying and deception are evident in Warren H. Jones, Miramar G. Cohn, and Curtis Miller's (Chapter 8) research on betrayal among children and adults.

Woven throughout the chapters are the researchers' concerns over (a) developmental changes in children's cognitive *abilities* that permit them to comprehend or define lying and deception (Chapter 2) and (b) the role that social agents play in forming children's trust—a concern that has its origins in Erikson's (1963) writings (Chapter 9).

There is a growing body of research on children's interpersonal trust; unfortunately, however, this has been scattered throughout the literature. This book is designed to bring the research "together" to provide an integrated and insightful view of this important aspect of children's social functioning. It is hoped that this integrated presentation will stimulate further theory and research on children's interpersonal trust.

References

Astington, J.W., Harris, P.L., & Olson, D.R. (1988). *Developing theories of mind.* Cambridge, UK: Cambridge University Press.

Deutsch, M. (1973). *The resolution of conflict: Constructive and destructive processes.* New Haven, CT: Yale University Press.

Erikson, E.H. (1963). *Childhood and society* (2nd ed.). New York: W.W. Norton.

Giffin, K. (1967). The contribution of studies of source credibility to a theory of interpersonal trust in communication process. *Psychological Bulletin, 68,* 104–120.

Hartmann, N. (1932). *Moral values: Vol. 2. Ethics.* New York: Macmillan.

Imber, S. (1973). Relationship of trust to academic performance. *Journal of Personality and Social Psychology, 28,* 145–150.

Johnson-George, C., & Swap, W.C. (1982). Measurement of specific interpersonal trust: Construction and validation of a scale to assess trust in a specific other. *Journal of Personality and Social Psychology, 43,* 1306–1317.

Piaget, J. (1932). *The moral judgment of the child*. London: Routledge & Kegan Paul.

Rotenberg, K.J. (1980). "A promise kept, a promise broken:" Developmental bases of trust. *Child Development, 51*, 614–617.

Rotter, J.B. (1967). A new scale for the measurement of interpersonal trust. *Journal of Personality, 35*, 651–665.

Rotter, J.B. (1971). Generalized expectancies for interpersonal trust. *American Psychologist, 26*, 443–452.

Rotter, J.B. (1980). Interpersonal trust, trustworthiness and gullibility. *American Psychologist, 35*, 1–7.

Schlenker, B.R., Helm, B., & Tedeschi, J.T. (1973). The effects of personality and situational variables on behavioral trust. *Journal of Personality and Social Psychology, 25*, 419–427.

Zuckerman, M., Blanck, P., DePaulo, B., & Rosenthal, R. (1980). Developmental changes in decoding discrepant and nondiscrepant nonverbal cues. *Developmental Psychology, 16*, 220–228.

2
What Is a Lie?
Children's Use of
Intentions and Consequences in
Lexical Definitions and
Moral Evaluations of Lying

CANDIDA C. PETERSON

The temptation to tell a lie is likely to arise so often in children's normal social interactions that, on the basis of frequency alone, it undoubtedly stands out from most of the other moral transgressions that children are called on to resist. Piaget (1932) argued that "lies present to the child's mind a far graver and more pressing problem than do clumsiness or even such exceptional actions as stealing" (p. 135). In addition to sheer opportunity, Piaget felt that the lie's salience as a moral temptation reflected the fact that "the tendency to tell lies is a natural and spontaneous tendency, so spontaneous and universal that we can take it as an essential part of the child's egocentric thought" (p. 135). But as if this were not enough, the adult aiming to socialize children to avoid lying is likely to have an additional problem to contend with. Most everyday instructional or punitive interventions by parents, teachers, and other adult disciplinarians are guided by the assumption that a child's understanding of words such as *lies*, *truth*, and *honesty* matches the meanings of these terms in the adult lexicon. Thus, discipline normally strives more to create the motivation to be honest than to explicate the underlying meanings of lying or telling the truth. Recent research, however, suggests that this popular assumption is flawed. This chapter will therefore survey developmental studies of the lexical meaning of lying as a basis for charting the nature and extent of the match between children's and adults' implicit definitions of the verb *lie*, along with moral evaluations of this concept.

A child's understanding of lying has also taken on special significance in recent years in the context of legal testimony. In increasing numbers, children as young as 3 years of age are being summoned to court to give evidence in complex cases ranging from divorce custody to incest and sexual violence (Berliner & Barbieri, 1984). Some very young children are even called to the stand as witnesses to their parents' homicides (Pynoos & Eth, 1984). But the admission of a child's testimony as legal evidence depends on the judge's or jury's confidence that he or she has understood, and been bound by, the oath to tell the truth. From a historical standpoint, one major impetus for the scientific investigation of children's understanding of lying was on behalf of these legal applications (Goodman, 1984; Stern, 1910). In recent years, some new breakthroughs have been made in this area. The last section of the chapter will therefore analyze the current state of knowledge about children's social cognitions of lying and truthtelling as they bear on the child's appearance in court. Areas of uncertainty and suggestions about further research needs will also be outlined.

The goals of this chapter are twofold. The first aim is to present an up-to-date survey of research into children's and adults' cognitions about what it means, both lexically and morally, to "tell a lie." Second, within this broad framework, some previously unpublished data on South Korean children's and Australian adults' lexical and moral perspectives on various lies and "pseudo-lies" will be presented. Because the subject of lying is unusually complex (Hopper & Bell, 1984; Pope & Forsyth, 1986), it may be useful to make the organizing principles and conceptual distinctions that will guide this chapter's treatment of the topic explicit at the outset. One key distinction has already been alluded to: that between lexical and moral cognitions about lying. The lexical, or definitional, dimension describes the individual's implicit answer to the question "What is a lie?" or the underlying concepts incorporated into a distinction between "lying" and being truthful. Developmental studies of this key issue are examined in the first of the chapter's three main sections. The moral meaning of lying, by contrast, describes evaluative cognitions about how right or wrong it is to deceive and about the relative goodness or naughtiness of various untrue statements. Most recent developmental studies of this question have been inspired by research Piaget (1932) conducted in the 1920s into the broad relevance of intentions and consequences to moral reasoning. Both the intentional and the consequential dimensions of lying however, are somewhat more complex than corresponding dimensions of the other transgressions Piaget studied: clumsiness and stealing. In fact, when it comes to telling a lie, *intention* can be subdivided into three separate issues (e.g., Hopper & Bell, 1984; Pope & Forsyth, 1986): (a) *deliberateness*, or whether the speaker intends to deceive versus to communicate the truth; (b) *motive*, or whether the speaker's moral intentions are selfish, Machiavellian, pragmatic, or altruistic; and (c) *intentionality of outcome*, or whether the social and material consequences produced by the lie are foreseen versus accidental. The consequences of a deceptive communication likewise can be subdivided in at least three ways: (a) *literal veracity*, or the degree of the statement's departure from objective truth, (b) *credibility*, or whether or not the listener believes the statement; and (c) *material outcome*, or whether the listener is helped, harmed, or unaffected by the speaker's statement. Unfortunately, no known published study has been ambitious enough to incorporate each of these six dimensions into one complete, balanced design. Thus, the question of their relevance to children's and adults' moral judgments of lying must be addressed piecemeal across different studies. Such a survey is attempted in the second section of this chapter, with the underlying goal of assessing how the development of moral reasoning is shaped by these six potentially influential dimensions. Finally, the third section of the chapter explores the applied significance of the theory-driven studies of lying outlined in the two previous sections. Here, the focus is on how contemporary psychological research data can assist in the legal profession's determination of the competence of a child witness to testify in court.

Lexical Research: What Does It Mean to Tell a Lie?

To appreciate the contrast with young children's lexical cognitions, it is useful to begin with the mature view of what it means to tell a lie. According to Bok (1978), most contemporary moral philosophers concur with the definition of a lie as "an intentionally deceptive message in the form of a statement" (p. 15). This excludes accidentally false utterances as well as all nonverbal forms of deceit, trickery, cover-up, and subterfuge.

Children's implicit lexical definitions are apt to be quite different. Piaget (1932, pp. 140–141) used the following interview with a 7-year-old to point out a few of the contrasts:

Adult: "What is a lie?"
Child: "Something that isn't true."
Adult: "Guess how old I am."
Child: "Twenty."
Adult: "No, I'm thirty. Was it a lie what you told me?"
Child: "I didn't do it on purpose."
Adult: "I know. But is it a lie all the same, or not?"
Child: "Yes, it is all the same because I didn't say how old you really were."

Thus, despite being fully aware that his untrue statement was an involuntary error, devoid of any motive to deceive or offend the listener, this child defined it as a lie. In general, according to Piaget, "Children of 5 to 7, while perfectly aware of the shade of difference between an intentional act and an involuntary mistake, do not tend to stress the distinction at all, and often, on the contrary, group both facts under the name of 'a lie'" (p. 139). As well as equating lies with mistaken guesses, Piaget's interviews revealed that children under the age of 8 or 9 tended to categorize fantasies, memory lapses, jokes, slips-of-the-tongue, arithmetic errors, wishful thinking, and exaggerations as lies. This way of implicitly defining the lie has been dubbed *lexical realism* (Wimmer, Gruber, & Perner, 1984). In other words, the young child equates the lie broadly with any statement that fails to convey the literal, objective truth. This is consistent with other data showing a similar tendency toward literal objectivity, or "realism." In particular, conceptual distinctions among the subjective states of knowledge inherent in mature definitions of verbs such as *to know*, *to believe*, *to guess*, and *to remember* are not observed reliably until subjects reach approximately 8 years of age (Johnson & Wellman, 1980).

Though consistent with these data, the empirical basis for Piaget's conclusion that children under age 9 adopt lexical realism to define lying is open to question. He used a clinical style of interviewing, and his questions varied from child to child. His sample was small, and his questions were, by his own admission, so unreliable that individual data were suspect, "One and the same child may give answers according to both types of responsibility" (Piaget, 1932, p. 156). Therefore, one major goal of recent investigations into the lexical meaning of lying has been to test Piaget's hypothesis that young children are lexical realists using alternative, more scientifically credible, research methodologies. At least two such studies have been published. In one of these, Wimmer, Gruber, and Perner (1984) described a series of six experiments involving groups of Austrian children aged 4 through 11 years. The basic procedure for each experiment was the same. Subjects were told stories about a character's search for a hidden object. Some included the unintentional communication of a false belief. For example, one story character was given a closed box said to contain chocolate. She believed this, and told another character so. But when the box was opened, it actually held a toy. At least 70% of $4\frac{1}{2}$-year-olds and 60% of $6\frac{1}{2}$-year-olds believed the girl character had told a "fib," despite their accurate awareness of her truthful intentions. This suggested their definition of the "fib" (in German) was based on lexical realism. Subsequent experiments confirmed that this also applied to the stronger verb "lie." Lexical realism likewise persisted in stories lacking the potential confound of the central character having herself been lied to. For example, in one story of the latter type, the chocolate was moved out of the box by an innocent third party after the central character, "Maxi," put it there. A majority of the 4- to 7-year-olds knew Maxi believed chocolate was in the box. But they defined his truthful communication of this false belief as a lie. However, although this result supports Piaget's (1932) notion that young children are lexical realists, Piaget's second hypothesis that "the identification of mistakes and lies disappears towards the age of 8" (p. 142) is not affirmed quite so consistently by the data of Wimmer et al. (1984). Three of their six experiments included subjects older than 8 years of age. While two of these suggested a decline in lexical realism with age, one (experiment 2) showed no statistically significant age change, with 55% of the $10\frac{1}{2}$-year-olds and 70% of $8\frac{1}{2}$-year-olds giving lexically realist definitions.

Additional evidence of the persistence of lexical realism in older children's implicit definitions of lying emerged when Peterson, Peterson, and

TABLE 2.1. Percentages of Australian and Korean children describing various statements as "lies."

Age (years)	5–6		7–8		9–10		11–12		Adult
Country	A	K	A	K	A	K	A	K	A
Exaggeration	60	83	85	85	88	98	95	98	50
Wrong guess (someone's age)	55	81	45	75	20	48	8	24	5
Joke	75	95	72	90	75	64	65	60	50
Accidental misinformation	90	88	69	94	65	78	48	42	30

A, Australia; K, South Korea
Note. Australian data are from "Developmental Changes in Ideas About Lying" by C. C. Peterson, J. Peterson, and D. Seeto, 1983, *Child Development, 54*, p. 1532. Copyright 1983 by Society for Research in Child Development. Korean data are from *Lexical and Moral Judgments of Deceit in Australia and S. Korea* by C. Peterson and S. Kim, 1988, Tables 1, 2, and 3. Adapted by permission.

Seeto (1983) showed videotapes depicting story characters engaging in a variety of truthful and deceptive communications to 200 West Australian students ranging in age from 5 to 57 years. As Table 2.1 indicates, exaggerations, jokes, and accidental misinformation were defined as lying by a large number of adults, as well as most children through the age of 11 years. Although their intent was not primarily deceptive, the consequences of each of these statements involved a listener being misled (e.g., not learning how big the animal was; not finding the toy, or his destination). This suggests that the transition from lexical realism to intention-based moral reasoning may not be as sudden or as absolute as Piaget's (1932) two-stage model has been taken to imply. Instead, just as adults will morally condemn well-intentioned clumsiness that results in serious damage or injury (Karniol, 1978; Peterson, 1979), they may similarly leave some room for factual inaccuracy or material consequences within a primarily intention-based lexical definition of lying. Possibly, the developmental transition is from relative domination by truth value to a relatively greater emphasis on intentions. Alternatively, lexical realism may eventually be outgrown by everyone. The process may simply take much longer for some individuals (or cultures) than Piaget's theory implied.

If a lexical realist defines the lie literally as any utterance that is factually untrue, the telling of the literal truth for deceptive reasons might not be viewed as lying. Such a statement, however, conforms to the philosopher's definition of a lie as intentional deceit. By this criterion, a large proportion of adults appear to be lexical realists, to judge by the results of a study (Peterson, 1989) in which a group of 65 Australian university students aged 18 to 62 years were shown a videotaped drama about a little boy who accidentally broke a shop window by throwing his ball through it. When his father asked "Did you kick your ball through the shop window?" the boy replied with the literal truth: "No, I did *not* kick my ball through the window" (because he had thrown it). Despite its apparently deceptive intent, the vast majority of adults (74%) judged that this statement was not a lie.

Culture and the Basis for Lexical Realism

Piaget (1932) speculated that "the inevitable constraint of the adult . . . necessarily brings about a certain moral realism which will be more or less marked according to the nature of the home" (p. 182). In other words, lexical realism should persist to older ages in households where blind obedience to adult authority is demanded, while a more egalitarian style of parental discipline should facilitate the earlier emergence of mature definitions of the lie. The same logic can be extended from individual families to cultures. If so, lexical realism should be especially pronounced in a Confucian culture such as South Korea's, where parents' authority over their children is greater than in Western society. In South Korean society, duty constrains obedience, and "Confucian duty and the expression of such duty serve to stabilize the family unit which is the framework for all relationships" (Bond, 1986, p. 287). Table 2.1 reports the results of a comparison of lexical notions of lying among children aged 5 through 12 years in urban Australia versus urban South Korea (Kim, 1986; Peterson & Kim, 1988). Dramatized versions of the list of untrue statements shown in the table were presented to the Australians on videotape and to the Koreans by means of two- or three-frame pictorial cartoon sequences with dialogue in bubbles. These were read aloud to the younger subjects in individual interviews.

Significantly more Koreans than Australians overall defined the exaggeration ($N = 350$; $X^2 = 7.3$, $p < .01$) and the wrong guess about age ($N = 350$, $X^2 = 20.1$, $p < .01$) as a lie, whereas no differences emerged for the joke or the accidental misdirection. The more evident lexical realism in Koreans' responses to the first two statements is consistent with the strong emphasis on respect for elders and authority in a culture adhering to the Confucian tradition (Bond, 1986; Song, Smetana, & Kim, 1987). In fact, in attributing the "literal character" of preschoolers' objective definitions of lies to children's overweaning respect for their elders' authority, Piaget (1932) hinted at just such a cultural contrast:

The younger child feels respect for the older, and for its parents . . . and the more simply constituted the society in which he lives, the more durable a part does this unilateral respect play in the life of an individual . . . moral realism and objective responsibility would not exist without the respect which the child feels for the adult. (p. 349)

Thus, it seems that in a culture with institutionalized respect for the elder generation, lexical realism is one of a number of possible accounts of cultural differences.

Moral Evaluations of Lying

As noted, numerous separate aspects of both intentions and consequences have been examined discretely in the research literature dealing with the moral reprehensibility of lying. No complete empirical integration, however, has been made. In his original experiments in the 1920s, Piaget (1932) included three pairwise contrasts between one intention variable, *motive* (selfish or innocent) and the consequential dimension of *literal veracity* (i.e., widely vs. only marginally discrepant from objective truth). His results indicated that children under age of 10 "ignore the liars' intention [i.e., *motive*] and [base] themselves only on the degree of likelihood of the lie" (p. 155). Lickona (1976), however, was unable to replicate this result. Instead, from as young as age 6, his North American subjects largely ignored literal plausibility and judged lies purely in relation to the speaker's selfish versus innocent motives. Along slightly different lines, Wimmer, Gruber, and Perner (1984) contrasted *communicative intention* (i.e., the speaker's deliberate plan to inform vs. deceive) with consequences entailing a true versus false message. Like Lickona, they found little support for Piaget's hypothesis that young children's moral reasoning is dominated by the truth value of consequences. In fact, of those children aged 4 through 6 years who comprehended the stories sufficiently to be tested, approximately 75% based their moral evaluations solely on the speaker's intention to speak honestly versus deceptively, while only 13% gave moral evaluations that were "governed by the truth of the message" (p. 26). Furthermore, data from another group of 6-year-olds using the same stories revealed an "almost total lack of moral realism" (p. 23). These young subjects praised speakers with truthful intentions equally highly, regardless of whether their messages proved to be true or false. They likewise perceived no significant difference in the naughtiness of an intending liar who succeeded versus one who told the truth while trying to lie. Finally, using a pair of videotaped stories that held constant all three aspects of the speaker's intentions (these were equally deliberate, selfish, and foresighted in both stories) while varying the consequential dimension of *credibility* (whether the mother believed or saw through the lie), Peterson et al. (1983) likewise failed to discover any influence at all of consequences on moral evaluations by any age group, including subjects as young as age 5.

Taken together, these results indicate that when a lie's consequences are considered in terms either of literal truth value or listener's belief, there is little contemporary support for Piaget's notion that young children are moral realists. Instead, in clear contrast to their lexical judgments (where realism is seen), very young children, like their older peers, are found to base their moral ratings of untrue statements largely on intention. Furthermore, this applies both when intent is depicted as selfish motive and when operationalized as deliberate purpose to deceive.

When the consequences of a lie, however, are depicted in another way, as material damage, a very different pattern of empirical results emerges. In his original study, Piaget (1932) included a pairwise contrast between a deliberate lie that resulted in material help (a lost tourist found his way despite the liar's intention to misdirect him) versus an unintentional deception that resulted in material harm (the tourist got lost). He found that most children under the age of 9 or 10 judged the harmful accidental lie as naughtiest. This finding has been replicated using different stories of similar format by Boehm and Nass (1962), Lickona (1976), and Peterson et al. (1983). In other words, there is evidence of moral realism when children are asked to judge lies whose consequences are materially damaging rather than more or less literally true. On the other hand, while results like these support Piaget's suggestion that the material harm caused by a lie is a more salient moral issue to young children than the liar's subjective intentions, the notion of a developmental reversal of this pattern (as implied by his two-stage model) has been challenged from another quarter. Lindskold and Waters (1983) and Lindskold and Han (1986) argued that adults are also liable to attend more closely to material consequences than to a liar's intentions when judging the moral rightness or wrongness of lying. In this research, independent groups of university students evaluated matched sets of stories about adult transgressions. One story in each pair involved a deliberate lie, whereas the other produced comparable consequences without deception. Moral ratings and perceived hierarchies of wrongness were virtually identical in each case, suggesting that the adults who judged the lies had accorded little or no importance to the wrongdoers' deceptive intentions and had based their judgments exclusively on the severity of the harm produced. Linsdkold and Han (1986) therefore concluded that "the average American college student is clearly a relativist, lacking an absolutist's unquestioning condemnation of all forms of intentional deception" (p. 130). Several other studies have compared adults' moral judgments of the intentions and outcome of lies using discrete ratings rather than story pairs. Patterson (1974) found that lies told for selfish reasons were given harsher ratings than similar falsehoods motivated by benevolent intent. Pope and Forsyth (1986) systematically varied (a) the consequences (mildly or severely harmful), (b) the deliberateness (free choice vs. coercion), and (c) the moral purpose (benign vs. selfish) of discretely presented lies and found that each of these three factors made statistically significant separate contributions to adults' moral evaluations. Maier and Lavrakas (1976) likewise found that university students rated deliberate lies causing harm (e.g., loss of money) as morally worse than comparably deliberate lies that produced less damaging consequences. These authors also interpreted the harsher moral condemnation of lies told by high-status persons (employers, politicians, etc.) than those by speakers of lower status (employee, student) in terms of the greater material harm caused by "a lie by a person with an occupation affecting many people" (p. 577). In other words, if moral realism is defined as a tendency to evaluate lies not so much by intention as in relation to the level of material damage their consequences produce, this tendency, apparently is not confined to young children in the way that Piaget's (1932) stagewise developmental progression implies. Instead, when giving moral evaluations, many contemporary adults appear to place greater emphasis on the material harm a lie causes than on deceptive intent.

Another aspect of the moral evaluation of lying relates to the philosopher Immanuel Kant's (1963) categorical premise that "a lie is a lie and is in itself intrinsically base whether it be told with good or bad intent" (p. 229). Here, two distinct aspects of intentionality are at stake: (a) deliberateness of the liar's purpose to deceive versus (b) the motive to help versus harm another person. To test Australian children's and adults' adherence to Kant's moral premise, Peterson et al. (1983) compared their moral evaluations of selfish lies compared with ratings of a lie told to protect an innocent youngster from a bully's bashing. Results indicated few age differences, with most subjects judging this "altruistic" lie to be morally superior to the selfish one. In other words, Kant's moral position earned little support. In South Korea, Kim (1986) found similar results. Again, children from as young as age 5 gave harsher moral ratings to deliberate lies told for personal gain than for altruistic reasons. In other words, in both cultures, the intentional motive to help or harm appeared to influence moral judgments of lying independently of the intentional purpose to deceive versus speak truthfully. Thus one aspect of the intention variable was again invoked at a much younger age than Piaget's (1932) two-stage model predicted.

In sum, these results suggest that both the intentions and the consequences of any lie are relevant to moral evaluations by adults as well as by young children. Many of Piaget's (1932) ideas about the basis for children's moral attitudes about lying have been called into question by this recent research. It no longer appears that younger children are "inclined to ignore intention" (p. 158) in their moral evaluations. Instead, even 5-year-olds attend to both deceptive purpose and moral motives to help or harm. Nor is there convincing empirical support at any age for the idea that perceived naughtiness is a direct function of the literal truth value of a lie, irrespective of a speaker's intentions to deceive. Finally, Piaget's notion of a sharp transition during middle childhood from one mode of moral evaluation of lying to another radically different style appears to have been replaced in the recent data by suggestions of more gradual patterns of age-related change. Although further research still is called for, these later results are strikingly consistent with a conclusion Lickona reached in 1976, that the Piagetian intentionality dimension "shows regular quantitative increases beginning at 5 to 6 years of age and extending at least as late as 17 years" (p. 229). Hence, Lickona's argument that "if growth during adolescence can be characterized equally well in terms of increasing intentionality, then such a dimension cannot be considered part of a stage that defines a particular period of development" (1976, p. 229) appears equally valid today.

Concepts of Lying and Children's Legal Testimony

The ideas children develop about what it means, both lexically and morally, to "tell a lie" have clear practical relevance to the legal profession. When child witnesses are sworn in, reactions to their testimony depend in large part on whether the lawyers, judge, or jury can accept that children fully comprehend what it means to "tell the whole truth" and whether they feel bound to do so. Piaget's (1932) theory suggested an abrupt change in comprehension of lying during middle childhood. But the more up-to-date findings reviewed in this chapter suggest a gradual developmental pattern. Some relevant concepts appear already to be in place for most children from as early as 4 years of age. But others evolve gradually, and with large individual variation, through adolescence or adulthood. Thus, Piaget's model was consistent with early common law (Goodman, 1984), which prohibited children under 7 from testifying but treated older children similarly to adult witnesses. Contemporary research findings, however, are more in keeping with modern legal practice, which, on the precedent of the landmark 1895 case entitled *Wheeler v. United States* (1895) is inclined to accept that "there is no precise age which determines the question of competency. This depends on the capacity and intelligence of the child, his appreciation of the difference between truth and falsehood as well as of his duty to tell the former" (Allison, 1986, p. 34). Thus, in "most jurisdictions" (Berliner & Barbieri, 1984), testimony from children as young as 3 or 4 years of age can be admitted, provided the court is persuaded that the child is both willing and able to tell the truth. Ordinarily, the basis for such persuasion is an oral interview by the judge, known as a "competence examination." According to Berliner and Barbieri (1984), the goals of the competence examination are threefold. The judge must prove to the court's satisfaction that "a child (a) can receive and relate information accurately, (b) can understand the difference between telling the truth and telling a lie, and (c) can appreciate the necessity of telling the truth in court" (p. 131).

Although these procedures have been used to good effect in many legal cases, the problems and inconsistencies bound up with competence examinations continue to cause concern (Allison, 1986; Goodman, 1984). As one example, Allison (1986) drew attention to the high rate of disqualification of child witnesses on the basis of undue caution or outright misinterpretation of the results of competency tests. The use of inappropriate vocabulary, confusing or leading questions, or the failure of trial judges who are "uneducated in child development" to achieve rapport with the child can cause them to "misinterpret a child's cognitive deficits and communication inabilities as the inability to testify" (p. 33). Even when a child's testimony is initially admitted, uncertainties over the reliability both of the competence test itself and of young witnesses' testimony in general very often lead to cases being overturned on appeal. Allison noted that at least "one quarter of the juvenile cases that are appealed due to questioning of the child's testimony are reversed" (p. 33).

As regards the second goal of the competence test, to establish the child witness's comprehension of the difference between lying and truthfulness, one of the court's most commonly espressed concerns (Goodman, 1984) is that young children who lack mature concepts about the meaning of lies will introduce fantasy, hearsay, or deliberate deceit into their legal testimony. However, the research examined in the first part of this chapter provides some reassurance against the likelihood of this. For, to the extent that young children's implicit "lexically realist" definitions of lying do differ from a mature, intention-based definition, the nature of the difference should equip children to be even more wary of distorting the truth than mature speakers. Lexical realism defines a lie as any objectively untrue statement, however truthfully intended. Presumably, such a definition should inhibit a child from expressing fantasies, guesses, and/or exaggerations, as well as genuine lies when bound by the promise not to tell lies to the judge. Of course, the child's ability to adhere to this resolve in practice may depend heavily on the style of questioning to which he or she is subjected while under cross-examination. As Pynoos and Eth (1984) pointed out, one of the serious dangers of leading, confusing, or intimidating interrogation strategies, over and above the problem of distorting the child's testimony, is that children who are subjected to them may leave court suffering stress or guilt over having behaved badly. To the extent that a young child equates lying with saying anything that any adult disapproves of (Piaget, 1932), such trialroom guilt may be partially unavoidable. Proper interview procedure, however, should at least limit the risks of leading children into saying things that they don't mean to and that they will regret having said once they step down from the witness stand.

Historically, the third goal of the competence test, to assure the court that the young witness was adequately motivated to refrain from lying, was achieved through religious education. As Goodman (1984, p. 13) explained, standard courtroom procedure until recent decades deemed that "unless a witness believed in divine vengeance for false statements, he or she could not be trusted to speak the truth" and would be barred from testifying. Today, a child no longer needs to mention God or "hellfire" to pass the competence test. But worries remain over whether children who promise to tell the truth in court actually feel as much obligation to do so as the adult with a thorough understanding of the penalties of perjury (Goodman, 1984). According to Berliner and Barbieri (1984), to adequately prove "the child's appreciation of the need for truth in the courtroom" (p. 131) is undoubtedly the most abstract and difficult of the three parts of the competence examination. While research on children's cognitions about lying has not dealt with this issue directly, some inferences can be drawn from studies of how lies and other related statements are evaluated morally. Presumably, a child witness who judges lying to be morally wrong will be even more reluctant to tell a lie in the tense, authority-ridden atmosphere of a courtroom than under more relaxed and familiar circumstances at home. In fact, views of the level of moral wrongness of the lie itself may vary with legal versus domestic contexts. There are no known published studies of this aspect of moral evaluation of lying. One study (Peterson & Peterson, 1990) however, of Australian children and moral judgments of films depicting child actors' lies and pseudolies lent some support to this idea. A group of 59 Australian undergraduate students and 55 primary school children aged 6 through 9 years were shown four videotaped dramas, each involving an untrue statement by a child. Two of these involved a helpful motive and the intention to tell the truth (a child witness tried but failed to correctly remember the color of another's hair and clothing). The only difference was that the character in one drama made the statement at home to her father, while the other's identical lapse of memory arose under oath in court before a judge and jury. When asked to rank these characters on a moral good–bad scale, a majority of both adults disapproved more of the memory lapse in court than at home (see Table 2.2). Similarly, most children and adults judged a deliberate lie about a broken window to be worse when told in court than at home (see Table 2.2). Research is in progress to test whether similar biases pertain to lexical judgments of lying.

TABLE 2.2. Australian children's and adults' moral evaluations of untruths told in court versus to a parent.

| | Statement type | | | |
| | Memory lapse | | Deliberate self-protective lie | |
Social context	N	Percentage	N	Percentage
Courtroom worse than domestic				
adult	41	70	41	70
child	38	69	33	60
Domestic worse than courtroom				
adult	10	17	13	22
child	17	31	22	40
Both equally good/bad				
adult	8	13	5	8
child	0	0	0	0
Total				
adult	59	100	59	100
child	55	100	55	100

Nevertheless, quite apart from any added incentive to speak truthfully in court, the fact that child research subjects from as young as 5 years of age consistently judge deliberate lies to be naughty (see the second section of this chapter) should give grounds for confidence that a witness this young is cognitively mature enough to meet the minimum legal require-ment specified by Melton (1981) that "the child have a general under-standing of the moral obligation to tell the truth" (p. 75). Furthermore, the child's own desire to avoid wrongdoing, coupled with the clear under-standing of lying as wrong, suggests that most young witnesses who are mature enough to be interviewed should possess the motivation to avoid committing this transgression in court. Of course, there may well be a gap between moral intentions and moral behavior (Goodman, 1984). This problem, however, is by no means limited to young children (Bok, 1978).

In sum, while providing suggestive evidence, the data reviewed in this chapter likewise highlight the need for further research into the important applied topic of how developmental changes in cognitions about lying may influence the young witness's competence and credibility on the witness stand. Until convincing scientific evidence is obtained, doubts over the value of competency examinations and uncertainties over how best to conduct them are likely to remain two of the most perplexing obstacles to the achievement of a fair trial in a case where a child is involved. Goodman (1984) argued:

Careful research could greatly add to our knowledge of children's abilities as witnesses, techniques for obtaining accurate testimony, the treatment of the emotional needs of child witnesses and children's perceived credibility. It is hoped that such research will improve the way child witnesses are treated by the legal system. Research also holds the potential to help save innocent people from the consequences of false accusations. . . . The fields of psychology and law share, in principle, at least one common goal—to find the truth about social events. Psychologists often pursue this goal through research, while the courts pursue it through court proceedings. It sometimes happens that a child is the only one who knows the truth. In such cases, social scientists and legal professionals must join together, turn to the child, and know when and how to listen. (p. 173)

The same conclusion could be applied equally to the studies of the growth of moral and lexical cognitions about lying reviewed throughout this chapter. Recent research has advanced our understanding of these two dimensions of social cognition well beyond the initial observations made by Piaget (1932) and the Sterns (1909) during the early part of this century. However, just as these researchers' careful listening to children's viewpoints first drew attention to the possibility that lexical and moral meanings of lying might vary with age, further research and careful listen-ing is now needed to refine our knowledge about how multifaceted inten-tion and consequence variables interact to shape the growth of children's ideas about the lexical and moral meanings of telling a lie.

References

Allison, A. (1986). Credibility of the child witness: Psychological/legal concerns. *American Journal of Forensic Psychology*, *4*(4), 33–37.

Berliner, S., & Barbieri, M.K. (1984). Testimony of the child victim of sexual assault. *Journal of Social Issues*, *40*, 125–138.

Boehm, L., & Nass, G. (1962). Social class differences in conscience development. *Child Development*, *33*, 565–574.

Bond, M.H. (1986). *The psychology of the Chinese people*. Oxford UK: Oxford University Press.

Bok, S. (1978). *Lying: Moral choices in public and private life*. New York: Pantheon.

Goodman, G.S. (1984). Children's testimony in historical perspective. *Journal of Social Issues*, *40*, 9–32.

Goodman, G.S. (1984). Child witness: Conclusions and future directions for research and legal practice. *Journal of Social Issues*, *40*, 157–176.

Hopper, R., & Bell, R.A. (1984) Broadening the deception construct. *Quarterly Journal of Speech*, *70*, 288–302.

Johnson, C.N., & Wellman, H.M. (1980). Children's developing understanding of mental verbs: Remember, know, & guess. *Child Development*, *51*, 1095–1103.

Karniol, R. (1978). Children's use of intention cues in evaluating behavior. *Psychological Bulletin*, *85*, 76–85.

Kant, I. (1963). *Lectures on ethics*. New York: Harper & Row.

Kim, S.O. (1986). *Developmental changes in the conception of lying in Korean children*. Unpublished master's thesis, Yonsei University, Seoul, S. Korea.

Lickona, T. (1976). Research on Piaget's theory of moral development. In T. Lickona (Ed.), *Moral development and behavior* (pp. 211–230). New York: Holt, Rinehart & Winston.

Lindskold, S., & Han, G. (1986). Intent and the judgment of lies. *Journal of Social Psychology*, *126*, 129–130.

Lindskold, S., & Waters, P.S. (1983). Categories of acceptability of lies. *Journal of Social Psychology*, *120*, 129–136.

Maier, R.A., & Lavrakas, P.J. (1976). Lying behavior and the evaluation of lies. *Perceptual and Motor Skills*, *42*, 575–581.

Melton, G.B. (1981). Children's competency to testify. *Law and Human Behavior*, *5*, 73–85.

Patterson, A.H. (1974, May). *Perception of manipulative behavior as a function of the manipulator, the person manipulated, and the goal of the manipulator*. Paper presented at the meeting of the Midwestern Psychological Association, Chicago.

Peterson, C.C. (1979). Severity of consequences as a factor in moral judgement. In P. Taylor (Ed.), *Piagetian theory and the helping professions* (pp. 78–82). Los Angeles: U.S.C. Press.

Peterson, C.C. (1989). *Telling the truth with deceptive intentions: Adults' lexical and moral judgments*. Unpublished manuscript, Murdoch University, Western Australia.

Peterson, C.C., & Kim, S.O. (1988). *Lexical and moral judgements of deceit in Australia and South Korea*. Paper presented at the 24th International Congress of Psychology, Sydney, Australia.

Peterson, C.C., Peterson, J., & Seeto, D. (1983). Developmental changes in ideas about lying. *Child Development, 54*, 1529–1535.

Peterson, C.C., & Peterson, M. (1990). *Children's and adults lexical and moral judgments of lies told in courtroom versus domestic contexts.* Unpublished manuscript, Murdoch University, Western Australia.

Piaget, J. (1932). *The moral judgment of the child.* London: Routledge, & Kegan Paul.

Pope, W.R., & Forsyth, D.R. (1986). Judgments of deceptive communications: A multidimensional analysis. *Bulletin of the Psychonomic Society, 24*, 435–436.

Pynoos, R. S., & Eth, S. (1984). The child as witness to homicide. *Journal of Social Issues, 40*(2), 87–108.

Song, M.J., Smetana, J., & Kim, S.Y. (1987). Korean children's conceptions of moral and conventional transgressions. *Developmental Psychology, 23*, 577–582.

Stern, C., & Stern, W. (1909). *Monographien uber die seelische Entwicklung des Kindes.* Leipzig, Germany: Barth.

Stern, W. (1910). Abstracts of lectures on the psychology of testimony and on the study of individuality. *American Journal of Psychology, 21*, 273–282.

Wheeler v. United States, 159 US 523 (1895).

Wimmer, H., Gruber, S., & Perner, J. (1984). Young children's conception of lying: Lexical realism–moral subjectivism. *Journal of Experimental Child Psychology, 37*, 1–30.

3
Young Children's Verbal Misrepresentations of Reality

MAGDA STOUTHAMER-LOEBER

Interpersonal communication is based on the premise that verbal messages are relatively accurate and are understood in the same way by the listener as by the speaker (Bok, 1978). This accuracy of communication often is lacking in young children, because of their limited cognitive abilities. An important developmental task for young children therefore is learning to reduce unintentional verbal misrepresentations of reality. Hand in hand with acquiring the skills and rules for accurate reporting comes the awareness of the perils of always practicing it and the benefits of intentionally obscuring events, that is, lying. This dual development makes it difficult for adults to always clearly distinguish between children's intentional and unintentional misrepresentations of reality. Perhaps as a consequence, little is known about how young children learn to lie (Stouthamer-Loeber, 1986). This is particularly surprising, considering that lying is viewed as a serious problem behavior as early as the preschool years (Alston, 1980; Sack & Sack, 1974).

Developmental theorists, such as Kohlberg (1976), Flavell (1968), and Lickona (1976), building on Piaget's (1932/1965) work, have described children younger than age 7 as largely egocentric, with limited skills for understanding and taking into account another person's perspective, and lacking a differentiated set of moral and social rules. Such children would be incapable of intentional deception. Piaget (1932/1965, p. 160) stressed the concept of "pseudo-lies" of young children—untrue statements made without attempting to deceive or even being conscious of what one is doing—which he sees as different from later lying and therefore of little consequence to the development of this later behavior. Piagetian theories, however, have been based primarily on children's ability to make verbal distinctions on cognitive tests and have described cognitive–verbal, rather than behavioral, development. Evidence shows that, when more appropriate tests are used, preschoolers are capable of far more than they had been given credit for by cognitive theorists. Many of these capabilities seem to be related to children's ability to *anticipate and act on* the knowledge of another person's feelings and probable reactions. Examples of these capabilities are role taking, empathy, and altruism; other behaviors have to do with moral judgment and making a distinction between conventional and moral rules, as well as with the understanding of the concept of lying (Borke, 1971; Eisenberg-Berg & Roth, 1980; Hoffman, 1976; Light, 1980; Shantz, 1975; Turiel, 1977; Weston & Turiel, 1980; Wimmer, Gruber, & Perner, 1984; Zahn-Waxler & Radke-Yarrow, 1982). With such an array of capabilities, it seems most likely that children much younger than 7 are able to tell an intentional untruth.

The notion that young children may be capable of intentional deception clearly does not imply that all verbal misrepresentations of reality by young children are lies. Children may unintentionally tell untruths, because they do not know the proper use of certain words, or because they confuse reality and fantasy. Further, they may not be able to always distinguish between whether something really happened or whether they only thought or heard about it, or, perhaps, saw it happen to someone else (Flavell, Flavell, & Green 1983; Johnson & Foley, 1984). In short, their limited cognitive development may make them less than accurate reporters. In addition, a child's moral development may not have progressed to the point where she or he consistently values veracity; one story may seem to the child as good as another. Whether young children's untruths are unintentional mistakes or lies therefore is not always clear. Examples of statements that may or may not be expressed by young children with the intent to deceive are blaming someone else, excuses, talking about imaginary things as if they were true, exaggerations, denial of having done something, and telling about something happening that, in fact, did not happen. Therefore, the study of lying in young children is inextricably linked to the study of verbal misrepresentations of reality in general.

A fundamental problem in the study of verbal misrepresentations of reality in children is the question of how to collect data. Should we set up laboratory experiments, attempt naturalistic observations, or rely on reports of adults in the child's environment? If we are interested in children's behavior in the natural environment, laboratory experiments often provide only limited answers because of the problems of the generalizability of the findings to other settings (Eron, Walder, Huesmann, & Lefkowitz, 1978; Hartshorne & May, 1928). Additionally, ethical problems are attached to experiments that might induce children to lie. Independent observations would be ideal with regard to the accuracy of reporting and the standardization of definitions; however, the low base rate of the behaviors under study make it uneconomical to undertake naturalistic observations. Additionally, a judgment as to the truthfulness or untruthfulness of a statement often requires knowledge of events that may have occurred before the observation time frame. Therefore, in most studies that address the issue of children's lying, adults have been used as reporters of children's behavior (see for a review Stouthamer-Loeber, 1986). In the study reported following, this approach was also adopted. The experiments by Hartshorne and May (1928) and by Lewis, Stanger, and Sullivan (1989) are some exceptions to this general approach. It should be clearly kept in mind that, throughout this chapter, I am considering *adults' perceptions* of children's behaviors and intentions.

In this chapter, I will address certain basic questions about young children's verbal misrepresentations of reality, such as: At what age are children judged capable of lying, and what is the prevalence of lying and of verbal misrepresentations in general? In addition, I will explore the relationship of lying and verbal misrepresentations of reality to parenting behaviors and to other child behaviors. This exploration will lead to questions such as: How do adults react to these behaviors, what do adults' see as reasons for children's misrepresentations of reality, how does lying relate to other child behaviors, and which parenting behaviors are related to lying?

The review of the literature will be complemented by data from a study in which mothers and day-care and preschool teachers of 80 four-year-olds were interviewed about children's misrepresentations of reality. The combination of literature review and discussion of findings from a research study has been chosen purposefully, because it seemed the most efficient way of addressing the questions posed.

Subjects

In Stage 1 of the study, respondents were 80 mothers and 21 teachers of 80 four-year-old boys and girls from 11 day-care centers or preschools in an urban area. Only children with English-speaking parents were selected. The method of subject acquisition depended on each facility's guidelines for release of information about attending children. In five centers or schools, parents of eligible children were contacted directly by letter, followed by a phone call. In the remaining six centers or schools, letters were left for the mothers, who would then contact me if they were interested. As expected, the direct-contact method yielded a higher participation rate than the indirect contact method (83% v. 36%). Because selective participation may affect the results of a study, the information on child behaviors from mothers who were contacted directly ($N = 47$) was compared with that from the remaining mothers ($N = 33$). No significant differences were found; therefore, the two groups were combined. The combined sample consisted of 40 boys and 40 girls, of whom 75% were white and 25%, minorities. The average age was 4 years and 5 months. Using Hollingshead's Index of Socioeconomic Status (Hollingshead, 1975), 73% of the whites and 79% of the minorities fell into the top two strata (major business and professional, and medium business, minor professional, or technical). Stage 1 of this study will be referred to in this chapter as the preschool study.

When mothers consented to participate in stage 1, they were asked whether they were also interested in participating in a 12-week diary study (stage 2) in which mothers were trained as observers and instructed to keep a diary of their children's verbal misrepresentations of reality. Seventy-two percent of the mothers expressed interest, of which 20 mothers were randomly selected to be trained. When three mothers could not finish the 12-week period, another three mothers were added. The 23 mothers yielded detailed structured reports on about 1,200 instances of their 4-year-olds' misrepresentations.

The demographic characteristics of this subsample resemble closely those of the main sample. Of the 23 subjects, 78% were white, 61% came from the top two strata of Hollingshead's Index of Socioeconomic Status (Hollingshead, 1975), and 52% of the target children were boys. Stage 2 of this study will be referred to as the diary study.

Measures and Procedures

Preschool Study

The children's mothers and their teachers were the respondents in interviews lasting about 2 hr per respondent. Certain answers required coding after all interviews had been conducted. The average percentage of agreement for two coders for individual questions was 93%, ranging from 85% to 98%, calculated on 40 mother interviews and all 21 teacher interviews. The questions used in this report, and their temporal stability, calculated over 10 subjects with a 1-month interval (unless otherwise stated), are listed following. For questions with more than one category, the overall reliability, rather than the reliability for each code, is given, because the sample size of 10 was not large enough to provide sufficient data on each individual code. The questions follow:

1. At what age are children able to tell a deliberate lie (90% test–retest agreement using 12-month age ranges)?

2. What is the frequency of the following verbal misrepresentations; (a) having a make-believe friend, animal, or toy; (b) talking about imaginary things as if they were real; (c) playing a joke by saying something that is not true; (d) talking about something happening as if it were true when respondent knows it is not; (e) exaggeration; (f) boasting; (g) saying she or he has complied with a request or command when it is not the case; (h) denying something she or he has done; (i) blaming someone else; and (j) making up excuses? The questions were rated on a 5-point scale from never to very often (test–retest r [88] = .78), except for the question on make-believe friends, which had a yes–no answer format (100% test–retest agreement).

3. The previous 10 questions on verbal misrepresentations of reality were all followed by a question asking the respondent to describe her

reaction to these behaviors. Up to three reactions were recorded. The reactions were subsequently coded into 20 categories (test–retest agreement 79%). *Positive categories* were: comfort, play along, help, and reinforce. *Neutral categories* were discuss, explain, explain reality, no attention, listen, and ask question. *Negative categories* were angry, berate, confront, correct, show disappointment, discourage, negative consequences, punish, make finish, and threaten.

4. Whether the adult had explained to the target child what a lie is and what had been said. Answers were coded in the following categories: (a) incorrect story; (b) story that is made up; (c) story told for a particular reason; and (d) story that child knows is not true (100% and 90% test–retest agreement, respectively).

5. The respondent's perception of 4-year-olds' reasons for not telling the truth. Up to three responses were recorded. The following categories were used to code the answers: fear of punishment, didn't know any better, getting one's way, play or fantasy, protect self-image, tries to please, joking, to cause trouble, and to protect someone (test–retest agreement 78%).

6. Behavior problems. Mothers filled in the Preschool Behavior Questionnaire (Behar & Stringfield, 1974). Two subscales of this 30-item checklist are considered here: hostile–aggressive and anxious–fearful. Satisfactory interrater and test–retest reliability have been reported (Behar, 1977). The hostile–aggressive scale contains two items concerned with truthfulness, which were not include in the present hostile–aggressive score.

7. Interpersonal relationships and parenting. The child's relationship with the mother was measured by an 18-item questionnaire assessing the mother's feelings toward the child. Internal reliability of the scale, measured with Cronbach's alpha was .87. Test–retest correlation, calculated on 19 subjects with an interval of 1 week, was .86. Getting along with other adults and getting along with children were both measured in the interview, with one question each. Test–retest correlations were .87 and .72, respectively. In addition, the mothers had been administered the Child Rearing Practices Report (Block, 1965), a Q-sort method designed to assess parenting methods and attitudes. For the present study, only the subscales, mother enjoyment of child, supervision, inconsistent parenting, guilt induction, and suppression of aggression were used. For scale construction, reliability, and validity of the Q-sort, see Block (1965) and Roberts, Block, and Block (1984).

8. Mothers' honesty. Mothers' general attitude toward honesty was measured with a 30-item scale assessing how good or bad mothers rated various lies on a 7-point scale. Cronbach's alpha was .71; test–retest correlation, calculated over 19 subjects, with a 1-week interval, was .71. Mothers' lying to their children was measured by four questions in the mother interview. Cronbach's alpha was .65, and the test–retest correlation .75.

Diary Study

Diary Training

An adaptation of Radke-Yarrow and Zahn-Waxler's training manual (1973) was used to train mothers to observe their children's verbal misrepresentations of reality and keep systematic daily diaries. The training was spread over three sessions of 2 hr each. At each session, mothers were tested by filling out diary sheets on vignettes containing relevant and irrelevant material. At the end of the training period, all mothers were able to fill out the test diary sheets correctly. During the data collection period, retraining sessions were held once every 3 weeks. Once a week, mothers were contacted by telephone to make sure that no problems had arisen. There telephone calls were also meant to serve as a reminder of the mothers' role in the study. Mothers were paid $15/week for observing, keeping a daily diary, and attending meetings.

Diary Data Collection

Although diary data have been successfully used by a number of researchers (Goodenough, 1931; Radke-Yarrow & Zahn-Waxler, 1973; Yarrow & Waxler, 1977; Zahn-Waxler, Radke-Yarrow, & King, 1979), the very need for this method precludes the possibility of independently establishing the accuracy and completeness of the data thus collected. In the present study, an effort was made to evaluate the reliability of the diary method, realizing the imposed limitations of this effort. Ideally, two aspects of the mothers' performance require verification. The first aspect concerns the accurateness of the mothers' description of events. Because only the mothers could provide the information on the overall accuracy of diary stories, they were asked at each of the three retraining sessions, to estimate the percentage of times they might have softened or changed the stories in their diaries somewhat in the telling. The average was 2%, with a range of 0% to 10%.

The second aspect concerns the completeness of recording of all events. Again, at retraining sessions, mothers estimated what percentage of all events they had recorded, which averaged 85%, with a range of 50% to 100%. Mothers felt that missed events were mainly due to their not always being able to make a note immediately after the event occurred so that they would remember it later. Additionally, a comparison was made of the number of events reported in the diaries on days that mothers had been telephoned ($n = 202$) with the number of events reported on the remainder of the days ($n = 1492$). It was expected that if mothers were lax in their reporting, the telephone calls might act as a reminder; therefore, call days might show a higher proportion of reported events than noncall days. The average number of events per day on call days was .67, compared with .64 on noncall days, a 5% difference (paired t test [22] = 1.02, n.s.).

The average number of events that mothers reported in the diaries was 4.9 per week, yielding a total of 1,171 events. Trained coders coded the information on the diary sheets. Intercoder reliabilities were 74% agreement on child behavior, 81% agreement on antecedents, and 82% agreement on mothers' perception of why the child made the statement.

Issues and Results

Depending on the availability of data, I will sometimes present data on verbal misrepresentations of reality, referring to inaccurate statements that may, or may not, be intentionally, untruthful. At other times I will present data on lying, for which the untruth is assumed to be intentional.

AGE AT WHICH CHILDREN ARE ABLE TO TELL A LIE

Adult care givers of young children frequently must decide whether what a child said was a deliberate untruth or whether the child did not know any better. These are important decisions, because the adult's reaction to the child's statement most likely depends on how the adult judged the statement. When the child makes an inaccurate statement resulting from lack of knowledge, explanation may be the reaction of choice, whereas, if the adult judges the inaccurate statement to have been made on purpose, the reaction may be more negative. As mentioned earlier, in the Piagetian school of thought (Piaget, 1932/1965), children were seen as not fully capable of telling deliberate lies until they were about 7 years of age. In the preschool study, most parents and teachers considered children capable of lying at a much earlier age. Table 3.1 shows that 29% of the adults considered a child capable of deliberately lying by age 3. More than three quarters of the adults believed that a 4-year-old can lie deliberately. Only 10% of the mothers and 5% of the teachers considered a 5-year-old too young to be lying deliberately, and all adults thought 6-year-olds could lie on purpose. Thus, adults, in daily contact with young children, considered them capable of intertional deceit at an earlier age than generally has been accepted (e.g., Piaget, 1932/1965). Mothers' and teachers' judgments of children's capability of lying largely had a similar distribution over various ages, although the teachers' range was somewhat narrower than that of the mothers.

TABLE 3.1. Percentage of adults who judge children capable of telling a deliberate lie.

Adults	Age of child (years)										
	1	1.5	2	2.5	3	3.5	4	4.5	5	5.5	6
Mothers ($n = 80$)	1	1	9	11	29	37	77	78	90	92	100
Teachers ($n = 21$)	0	0	0	5	29	33	76	76	95	100	100

The fact that mothers and teachers see young children as capable of lying does not mean necessarily that they are good at it, in the sense that they are successful in deceiving others. Hyman (1989), in discussing the literature on children's ability to deceive, suggests that successful deception takes a few years of practice, and only around age 10 to 12 do children become reasonably skilled in this. Nevertheless, even at an earlier age, lies such as, "I did not do it" can often create sufficient uncertainty in the parent's mind to prevent the consequences that would have followed an outright admission.

PREVALENCE OF VERBAL MISREPRESENTATIONS OF REALITY AS REPORTED BY MOTHERS AND TEACHERS

To what extent do young children engage in verbal misrepresentations of reality? Only a few studies (e.g., Achenbach & Edelbrock, 1981; Behar, 1977; MacFarlane, Allen, & Honzik, 1962) have reported prevalence data on different forms of verbal misrepresentations of reality among 4-year-olds. I will first discuss the data on lying, which usually are based on only one or two questions. Achenbach and Edelbrock (1981) found that, for 4- to 5-year-olds, parents reported "lying and cheating" for 21% of the girls and 23% of the boys in a non clinic sample. The question about lying, however, was asked within the context of problem behaviors; therefore, these figures may not reflect the number of children who lie but, rather, the number of children whose parents consider their children's lying a problem. It is interesting to note that Achenbach and Edelbrock (1981) did not find any age differences in their data for children aged 4 to 16. According to the parents in Achenbach and Edelbrock's (1981) study, 4-year-olds were as likely to lie as 16-year-olds. In the MacFarlane et al. study (1962), two questions about lying were asked within the framework of normal child development, which may account for the higher percentages of 49% for girls and 33% for boys. In the preschool study, the Preschool Behavior Questionnaire (Behar, 1977) contained a question about "telling lies," and 57% of the 4-year-olds were reported by their mothers as telling lies sometimes and 3% as lying frequently. The comparable figures for teachers were 31% and 5%, respectively. Thus, although basic descriptive data on lying in young children are still relatively scarce and based on few questions, findings indicate that adults judge that a sizable proportion of young children engage in lying.

In the preschool study, mothers and teachers were asked to report on the frequency of 10 different forms of verbal misrepresentation of reality, regardless of how they judged children's intent. The first question about verbal misrepresentations of reality concerned having a make-believe friend. Slightly more than half the mothers reported that their children had never had a make-believe friend (53%), while the remaining reported that their children did have a make-believe friend (29%) or had had one

TABLE 3.2. Adults' perceptions of frequency of verbal misrepresentations of reality in 4-year-olds.

	Never		Seldom		Sometimes		Often		Very often	
	M	T	M	T	M	T	M	T	M	T
Talks about imaginary things as if true	21.3	38.8	32.5	31.3	25.0	20.0	18.8	5.0	2.5	5.0
Plays a joke by telling untruth	16.3	22.5	36.3	28.8	36.3	35.0	8.8	12.5	2.5	1.3
Tells about something happening that is not true	25.0	42.5	41.3	41.3	30.0	12.5	2.5	3.8	1.3	0.0
Exaggerates	13.8	23.8	36.3	28.8	38.8	38.8	11.3	3.8	0.0	5.5
Boasts	25.0	28.8	20.0	18.8	36.3	33.8	16.3	15.0	2.5	3.8
Says she or he has done something she or he has not done	13.8	26.3	25.0	47.5	35.0	16.3	21.3	5.0	5.0	5.0
Denies something she or he has done	11.3	31.3	30.0	31.3	43.8	23.8	13.8	13.8	1.3	0.0
Blames someone else	10.0	21.3	27.5	23.8	43.8	33.8	15.0	15.0	3.8	6.3
Makes up excuses	8.8	12.5	10.0	20.0	45.0	41.3	31.3	22.5	5.0	3.8

M, mother; T, teacher.

in the past (19%). Teachers could report only over the period that they had known a child, and thus, far fewer children were reported as having had a make-believe friend (5%). The remaining questions about verbal misrepresentations of reality are listed in Table 3.2. According to both mothers and teachers, very few children engaged in any of the behaviors very often (range 0% to 6%). When the categories "sometimes," "often," and "very often" were combined, however, the percentages of children engaging in these behaviors ranged from 16% (teacher report) and 34% (mother report) for telling about something happening that is not true, to 68% (teacher report) and 81% (mother report) for excuses. Averaged across the nine behaviors, 55% of the children according to the mothers and 42% according to the teachers fell within the combined categories of "sometimes," "often," and "very often," showing a general tendency for the mothers to report the behaviors with higher frequencies than the teachers.

To test for sex, vocabulary skills, socioeconomic status, and racial differences with regard to the frequency of the verbal misrepresentations of reality, multivariate analyses of variance (MANOVAS), were performed on the mother and teacher data separately. The only significant result was for race on the mother report (Hotelling's T square 22.38, $F[10, 69] = 1.98$, $p < .05$). This significant MANOVA was mainly due to a higher prevalence of mothers of white children reporting their child as saying she or he had done something she or he had not done ($t[1, 78] = 2.77$, $p < .01$). Because this was only one of 10 behaviors tested in the MANOVA, I consider the evidence not strong enough to suggest a racial difference in the frequency of children's verbal misrepresentations of reality.

ADULTS' REACTIONS TO VERBAL MISREPRESENTATIONS OF REALITY

As young children expand their verbal skills, their messages may become more accurate. Adults may teach children to express themselves more accurately in several ways. First, adults, through approval and disapproval, instruct children as to which verbal statements reflect reality and which do not. Second, adults can verbally define or explain behaviors to children, thereby increasing children's ability to differentiate between truth and untruth. Both methods convey the desirability or undesirability of particular verbal statements and may influence the child's actual behavior.

Table 3.3 shows that mothers reported reacting differentially to various verbal misrepresentations of reality. Mothers' reactions to make-believe friends, talking about imaginary things as if they were true, and joking were to a large extent positive (comfort, play along, help, reward) or neutral (discuss, explain, explain reality, no attention, listen, ask questions), ranging from 86% to 100% for the combined neutral and positive categories. This is also reflected in the individual categories most used

TABLE 3.3. Mothers' reactions to verbal misrepresentations of reality.

	Children (n)	Responses (n)	Negative[a] (%)	Neutral[a] (%)	Positive[a] (%)	Most frequent consequences (> 30%)[b]
Make-believe friend	38	49	2	49	49	Play along (61)
Talks about imaginary things as if true	63	92	0	62	38	Explain reality (37) / Play along (33)
Plays a joke by telling untruth	67	74	15	26	60	Play along (63)
Tells about something happening that is not true	60	91	26	65	9	Question (30)
Exaggerates	69	89	22	61	17	
Boasts	60	83	14	76	10	No attention (53)
Says she or he has done something she or he has not done	69	109	77	17	6	Make finish (55)
Denies something she or he has done	79	122	49	49	2	Confront (35) / Question (30)
Blames someone else	77	107	45	53	2	Confront (35) / Question (35)
Makes up excuses	76	102	49	51	0	Discourage (41)

[a] Percentage given is percentage of total number of responses.
[b] Number in parentheses is percentage of mothers using consequence.

by mothers, which were play along and explain reality. The next three behavious in Table 3.3, telling about something happening that is not true, exaggerations, and boasting, were mainly followed by neutral consequences (ranging from 61% to 76%). The individual category most used was no attention, although 30% of the mothers reported questioning the child when she or he talked about something happening that was not true. For the last four behavious, says she or he has done something that she or he has not, denials, blaming, and excuses, mothers reported negative consequences (angry, berate, confront, correct, show disappointment, discourage, negative consequences, physical punishment, make finish, threaten) to a greater extent than any of the previous behaviors. The percentage of negative consequences for these behaviors ranged from 45% to 77%. For denials, blaming, and excuses, an almost equal percentage of consequences was neutral. Mothers very rarely applied positive consequences to these behaviors.

Table 3.4 shows the responses of teachers to children's verbal misrepresentations of reality. Only four children were reported by their teachers to have make-believe friends; therefore, there was insufficient information on how teachers react to this behavior. Talking about imaginary things and joking had, again, the highest proportion of positive consequences in the table. The next three behaviors, talking about something happening that is not true, exaggerations, and boasting, were predominantly followed by neutral teacher consequences. Saying she or he has done something she or he has not done, denials, blaming, and excuses were followed, to a large extent, by negative consequences, ranging from 43% to 70%, with very few positive consequences, ranging from 0% to 9%. There were certain specific consequences that both mothers and teachers frequently used for the first six child behaviors and hardly ever (less than 10%) for the last four behaviors, such as explain reality, no attention, play along, and listen. On the other hand, confront, discourage, and make finish were categories that adults frequently used for the last four behaviors but seldom for the first six. Thus, teachers' and mothers' reactions to these child behaviors are remarkably similar.

Adults' different reactions teach children not only about the incorrectness of their statements but also about the relative valence of the statements and the urgency for change. The reaction of adults also may include defining the child's behavior for him or her so that it becomes clearer for the child what not to do. Do adults explain what a lie is, and, if so, how do they explain it? In the preschool study, mothers and teachers of 4-year-olds were asked whether they had explained to the children what a lie is and what they had said. More than three quarters (79%) of the mothers had explained what a lie was, although five of them could not remember specifically what they had said. Out of the 58 codable answers, 48 mothers (83%) had explained a lie as something that was not true, without mentioning any qualifiers. Only one mother (2%) specified in her definition the

TABLE 3.4. Teachers' reactions to verbal misrepresentations of reality.

	Children (n)	Responses (n)	Negative[a] (%)	Neutral[a] (%)	Positive[a] (%)	Most frequent consequences (>30%)[b]
Make-believe friend	4	4	0	100	0	Listen (100)
Talks about imaginary things as if true	49	87	5	67	29	Listen (57)
Plays a joke by telling untruth	62	114	23	35	42	Play along (74)
Tells about something happening that is not true	46	89	24	71	6	Question (59)
Exaggerates	61	94	17	71	12	Explain reality (36) Question (34)
Boasts	57	91	16	70	13	Listen (46)
Says she or he has done something she or he has not done	59	86	70	27	3	Make finish (51) Confront (49)
Denies something she or he has done	80	110	43	48	9	Confront (49)
Blames someone else	75	98	54	46	0	Confront (57)
Makes up excuses	77	121	57	43	0	Discourage (53)

[a] Percentage given is percentage of total number of responses.
[b] Number in parentheses is percentage of children receiving consequence.

knowledge that what is being said is not true. Two mothers (3%) implied some motive, such as getting attention or avoiding punishment, whereas seven mothers (12%) defined lying as simply making up a story.

Only seven of the 21 teachers reported to have explained to the children in the study what a lie is. Five of these seven teachers had defined lying as not telling the truth (71%), whereas the other two teachers specified in their definitions knowledge about the untruth of what was said. Thus, based on the reports of both mothers and teachers, explanations to 4-year-olds of what a lie is frequently were incomplete and rendered a lie indistinguishable from a verbal mistake. This often incomplete explanation may contribute to the finding that young children find it difficult to *verbally* explain the difference between a lie and a mistake (Piaget, 1932/1965), although they may be able to show their appreciation for the concepts involved (Wimmer et al., 1984).

WHY DO CHILDREN LIE?

Given that young children are capable of intentionally deceiving, why do they do it? This is a crucial question if we want to prevent the development of lying or to change the frequency of its occurrence. A variety of motivations may cause children to intentionally hide the truth. DePaulo and Jordan (1982) speculated that the main motivation for lying in young children is to escape punishment. This is supported by Vasek (1984), who asked young children for reasons why a child would lie. Avoiding punishment was the main reason young children mentioned. Schadler and Ayers-Nachamkin (1983) suggested that, at least in the case of fabricated excuses, protection of self-esteem is the main motivation.

In the preschool study, by far the most frequent reason for the child's behavior as judged by adults was fear of punishment (44.2% of the reasons given by mothers and 42.0% for teachers), which, together with getting one's way (obtaining something or avoiding doing something by not telling

TABLE 3.5. Reasons why 4-year-olds may not tell the truth, as judged by mothers and teachers.

	Percentage of answers by mothers	Percentage of answers by teachers
Fear of punishment	44.2	42.0
Did not know any better	14.9	8.0
Getting one's way	14.3	16.0
Play or fantasy	7.1	2.0
Protect self-image	5.8	12.0
Tries to please	5.8	6.0
Joking	2.6	10.0
To cause trouble	2.6	0.0
To protect someone	.7	4.0
Unclear	2.0	0.0

the truth) made up nearly 60% of all the reasons given by both mothers and teachers (Table 3.5). Despite many similarities between the reasons given by mothers and teachers, there were small differences in the frequency with which some reasons were mentioned. A larger percentage of the mothers' answers implied that they thought that the child did not know any better (15% vs. 8% for teachers) and that the child was playing or making up a fantasy (7% vs. 2% for teachers). Teachers more frequently mentioned protection of the child's self-image (12% vs. 6% for mothers) and joking (10% vs. 3% for mothers). However, the similarities between mothers' and teachers' judgment of motivation for children's lying outweighed the differences.

Mothers' diary data yielded similar results; mothers attributed half of the behaviors such as blaming and denial to fear of consequences, whereas they attributed two thirds of the behaviors such as excuses and saying she or he has done something she or he has not done to the child wanting to get his or her way.

Another way of looking at why children lie is by examining the immediate antecedents of the child's verbal misrepresentation of reality. In the diary study, almost 80% of the antecedents of the child's saying she or he has done something she or he has not done, denial and blame were negative events, such as breaking a rule, taking or damaging something, or hurting someone. This is in contrast with, for example, excuses, for which almost 75% of the antecedents were neutral events.

RELATIONSHIP OF LYING TO OTHER PROBLEM BEHAVIORS

If mothers and teachers feel that the major reason for 4-year-olds' not telling the truth is to avoid punishment, these children must be doing things that may warrant punishment. What other evidence is there for a relationship between lying and other problem behaviors? Starting out with a very global measure, one would expect that lying would be more prevalent in clinic-referred children than in groups of normal children. Reviewing studies that have measured lying in clinical and normal samples of children, clinical samples were found to have about $2\frac{1}{2}$ times the prevalence of lying compared with normal samples (see Stouthamer-Loeber, 1986). This finding also held when only the youngest children were considered. Achenbach and Edelbrock (1981) found a prevalence of 21% and 23% for nonreferred 4- and 5-year-old boys and girls, respectively, compared with 50% and 60% for their referred counterparts. In another study with 3- to 6-year-olds, Behar (1977) compared normal and referred children and found that referred children were seen by their teachers as lying significantly more often than the nonreferred children. Although the majority of referrals is for conduct problems rather than for the more internalizing problems, these studies cannot answer the question of whether lying is related more to conduct problems or is related more generally to any kind of problem behavior in children. Data addressing this queation in young children are scarce. In older children, however, several studies have found lying to be more strongly related to conduct problems than to neurotic or internalizing problems (Rutter, Tizard, & Whitmore, 1970; Stewart & DeBlois, 1984). Some evidence indicates that older the children are, the stronger the relationship between lying and other conduct problems (Stouthamer-Loeber & Loeber, 1986).

To return to the younger children, is there any evidence that this relationship between lying and other problem behaviors is also found at an age at which lying has only just begun to develop? To examine this, the kinds of verbal misrepresentations of reality were restricted so as to exclude those untruths resulting largely from children's lack of cognitive development (e.g., did not know any better or untruths occurring in the course of make-believe play). On the basis of the diary material, behavior categories were included only if, in less than 10% of the incidents, mothers gave as reasons lack of cognitive development, playing, joking. Mothers saw the remaining categories (blame, excuse, denial, misleading confirmation) as overwhelmingly intentional and these were combined to form a lying score. The data previously mentioned show that each of these behavior categories combined in the lying score (except excuses) generally was preceded by negative antecedents in the diary data. The lying score also correlated, .34 (df 78, $p < .001$), with the hostile–aggressive scale score of the Preschool Behavior Questionnaire (Behar, 1977) but not with the anxious–fearful scale (.14, df 78, n.s.), thus showing that, even at age 4, lying is perceived as part of a cluster of conduct problem behaviors.

Given the foregoing, it is not surprising that mothers get along less well with those children they see as lying more frequently. Table 3.6 shows that lying was negatively correlated with children's relationships with mothers and other adults but not with their peers.

It is possible, however, that the negative correlation of lying with relationships with adults was mainly due to the association of lying with con-

TABLE 3.6. Correlations of children's lying and conduct problems with children's social relations.

	Lying		Conduct problems	
	r	Partial r^a	r	Partial r^b
Getting along with children	−.15 n.s.	−.08 n.s.	−.22*	−.22*
Getting along with adults	−.31**	−.25*	−.24*	−.15 n.s.
Mother–child relationship	−.30**	−.17 n.s.	−.46***	−.42***
Mother enjoyment of child	−.21*	−.18*	−.13 n.s.	−.07 n.s.

n.s., nonsignificant.
* $p = < .05$.
** $p = < .01$.
*** $p = < .001$.
[a] Controlled for conduct problems.
[b] Controlled for lying.

duct problems. As can be seen from Table 3.6, conduct problems had a particularly strong negative correlation with mother–child relationship ($r = -.46$, df 78), as reported by the mothers. Therefore, partial correlations were calculated between lying and relationship variables, controlling for the level of conduct problems. Although all partial correlations are somewhat lower than the simple correlations, the correlation of lying with mother–child relationship is most affected and becomes nonsignificant. The child's getting along with other adults continues to be significantly correlated with lying when controlled for the level of conduct problems. When lying was partialled out in Table 3.6, conduct problems still showed a strong correlation with how well the child gets along with the mother and, to a lesser extent, with other children; the correlation with getting along with other adults becomes nonsignificant.

PARENTING AND LYING

A final question addresses whether particular parenting behaviors are related to children's lying. Various researchers have concentrated on different aspects of parents' behavior or attitudes as they relate to children's lying, such as parental affect (Burton, 1976), inconsistent discipline (Lewis, 1931), and parental dishonesty (Hartshorne & May, 1928; Kraut & Price, 1976; Lewis, 1931).

Table 3.6 shows that mothers of children who lie frequently do not have a warm relationship with their children, and the children are not perceived as getting along well with other adults. Additionally, in another study with 4th-, 7th- and 10th- grade boys, mothers' rejection had an average correlation of .40 (dfs ranging from 45 to 68) with lying (Stouthamer-Loeber & Loeber, 1986). The lack of a warm relationship, however, can be construed as a cause just as well as a result of the child's behavior, particularly considering that lying often co-occurs with other problem behaviors. Curiously, the only parenting behaviors relating to those verbal misrepresentations that were seen by mothers as being primarily due to a lack of cognitive development, were measures of mothers' affect, that is, mother–child relations ($r[78] = -.22$) and mother's enjoyment of the child ($r[78] = -.25$).

In the study of the 4th-, 7th-, and 10th-grade boys (Stouthamer-Loeber & Loeber, 1986), poor parental supervision seemed to be particularly related to lying (average $r = .49$, dfs ranging from 36 to 55) and, to a lesser extent, poor discipline (average $r = .39$, dfs ranging from 14 to 17). For the 4-year-olds, supervision, as measured with the Childrearing Practices Report (Block, 1965), did not seem to be related to lying ($r = .04$, df 78, n.s.). Significant correlations were found, however, for inconsistent parenting ($r = .35$, df 78, $p < .001$) and guilt induction ($r = .29$, df 78, $p < .01$). Negative correlations were found with suppression of aggression ($r = -.29$, df 78, $p < .01$).

Studies that have investigated the relationship between parental honesty and the honesty of their offspring have used measures of general honesty or lying rather than measuring the parents' dishonesty toward their children. Both forms of dishonesty provide opportunities for children to imitate the behavior; however, we would expect that parents lying to children would be a more powerful example than general dishonesty. In our study with 4-year-olds we measured both forms of mothers' dishonesty and found that mothers' lying to their children correlated significantly with their children's own lying ($r[78] = .29, p < .01$). Mothers' more global attitude toward dishonesty was only marginally related to children's lying ($r[78] = .18, p < .10$).

In general, less than optimal parenting strategies and affect seemed to go hand in hand with lying, even at the early age of 4. Except for lack of supervision, the findings for the younger children are in concordance with what was found in the literature for older children (e.g., Stouthamer-Loeber, 1986).

Summary and Discussion

Since Piaget (1932/1965), little research has been done on children's truthfulness. Recently, however, interest in this topic has been revived. This revived interest may have been fuelled on the one hand by the studies from the last few decades of children's moral development (e.g., Damon, 1988; Kohlberg, 1976). On the other hand, concern about children's capabilities as witnesses in court has spurred on research in the areas of deception and the detection of deceit (e.g., DePaulo & Jordan, 1982; Ekman, Roper, & Hager, 1980). Several recent publications have been devoted to reviewing what we know about lying in children (e.g., Chagoya & Schkolne, 1986; Ekman, 1989; Stouthamer-Loeber, 1986). The present chapter has attempted to bring together information primarily on preschoolers. As is evident from the data presented here, knowledge is still relatively sketchy. This is to some extent a result of our relatively recent "rediscovery" of lying in young children as an area of inquiry. It also has to do with the methodological problems mentioned at the beginning of this chapter. The preponderance of the evidence presented here was garnered from adults' interpretations of children's behaviors. This approach falls short of yielding rigorously objective evidence. Although the imperfections of this method are obvious, alternatives for improvements in collecting information on this kind of low base rate events in the natural environment are not so obvious, and until children are old enough to report on their own intentions, the decision to call something a child said a lie or simply a mistake is always a matter of inference.

Keeping these caveats in mind, the studies brought together in this chapter have shed light, albeit still imperfect, on young children's misrepresentations of reality. The data demonstrate that 76% of those adults who are in daily contact with children considered them capable of telling a deliberate lie by age 4, and almost all the adults considered this behavior possible by age 5. This is also reflected in the reasons mothers and teachers gave for children not telling the truth, with only a small percentage of all reasons attributed to confusion between reality and fantasy, or confusion between what is true and what is not true. Thus, the bulk of the reasons assumed intent and primarily concerned fear of punishment. This is in accordance with the suggestion made by DePaulo and Jordan (1982). Whether this fear of consequences is occasioned by the strictness of the adults or by the child's frequent problem behavior, which "sets the occasion" for lying, remains to be seen.

Clearly many 4-year-olds tell untruths fairly frequently. On the average, about half of the children were reported to engage in the various categories of verbal misrepresentation at least sometimes. What proportion of each of these verbal misrepresentations was considered by adults as having been committed purposely is a matter for future research. Several child behaviors, however, such as saying she or he has done something she or he has not done, denials, blaming, and excuses, which were reported to be followed by two to three times as large a proportion of negative consequences as the remaining verbal misrepresentations of reality. The reason for the negative consequences may be that adults see these behaviors as clearer instances of *intentional deceit* meriting a more negative reaction, as opposed to behaviors that are seen as having been caused by confusion or mistakes. Another possibility is that adults consider these behaviors more reprehensible because of their *consequences*, for example, causing harm to others. A third possibility is that part of the negative reaction to these behaviors is triggered by *accompanying undesirable behavior*. The consequence pattern alone, therefore, may not provide sufficient information for classifying the verbal misrepresentations in terms of intent to deceive. These alternative explanations are at present only speculations that need to be addressed in future research.

Children only slowly acquire the ability to articulate what a lie is. Piaget (1932/1965) defined young children's thinking about lying as moral realism; that is, behavior is morally judged by its outcome rather than by its intention. For instance, even though children may know the difference between a mistake and an intentional untruth, both are considered bad, and both are defined as a lie. Wimmer et al. (1984) have pointed out that the moral realism of the young child is to be found on a verbal level only and is not reflected in the child's actions. This duality becomes more understandable in the light of our finding that mothers and teachers, in their explanation of what a lie is, generally did not comment on intentionality but simply pointed out the incorrectness of the statement. The verbal moral realism of the child (Piaget, 1932/1965) seems to be shared by the adults when they talk to young children. It is likely, however, that children learn the difference between an intentional and unintentional untruth by the differential consequences applied by adults, rather than by how adults explain the behavior.

Lying, at any age during childhood, was found to be associated with getting along less well with adults and with conduct problems, but not with the more internalizing problems such as anxiety. One of the reasons for the stability of the relationship of lying with conduct problems across ages may be the finding that a considerable amount of lying is *temporally* related to conduct problems in that conduct problems often precede the lying, and lying is directly related to the covering up of this problem behavior. In the diary study, two thirds of the lies were perceived as preceded by negative antecedents. Not all these negative antecedents may have merited punishment; however, one third of the lies were perceived as motivated by fear of consequences. Thus, it seems that a considerable proportion of 4-year-olds' lies are *reactive*, that is, in response to a situation created by their own behavior (or lack of it). DePaulo and Jordan (1982) suggested that children's skills in generating lies for obtaining illicit rewards in the absence of any obvious eliciting cue develops later than the reactive lies to escape punishment or other negative consequences. The lack of planning inherent in reactive lies may add to the ineptness of young children's attempts at deceit. Both kinds of lies, however, are largely in the service of other problem behaviors.

Thus, very few children lie frequently without showing other problem behaviors. The high rate of negative antecedents of lying may have some implications for the treatment of lying. Often, in discipline confrontations, the misdeed, rather than the lie about the misdeed, takes prominence, and lying may be in danger of being ignored as a problem. In those cases, youngsters have nothing to lose, and everything to gain by telling lies. Parents should make it clear to children that not telling the truth is an *additional* undesirable behavior that warrants its own negative consequences, whereas spontaneous confessions, regardless of what is being confessed, merit encouragement. On the other hand, only focusing on lying as a problem without tackling the concomitant problems that cause the child to lie, may also be fruitless.

Parental rejection, inconsistent parenting, parental dishonesty, and in older children, lack of supervision all have been found to be related to children's lying. It should be pointed out that these parenting deficits are not unique to lying; a similar pattern may be found for other conduct problems, including delinquency in older children (see, e.g., Loeber & Stouthamer-Loeber, 1986). In addition, because all studies reviewed here were correlational and most were cross-sectional, inferences about causality should be made with extreme caution. Nevertheless, until more research has been done, correlational findings such as these can yield *hypotheses* about what may work in treatment.

References

Achenbach, T.M., & Edelbrock, C.S. (1981). Behavioral problems and competencies reported by parents of normal and disturbed children aged four through sixteen. *Monographs of the Society for Research in Child Development*, *46*, 1–82.

Alston, L. (1980). Defining misconducts: Parents vs. teachers in Head Start centers. *Child Care Quarterly*, *9*, 203–205.

Behar, L. (1977). The Preschool Behavior Questionnaire. *Jouranl of Abnormal Child Psychology*, *5*, 265–275.

Behar, L., & Stringfield, S. (1974). *Manual for the preschool behavior questionnaire*. Durham, NC: Dr. Lenore Behar.

Block, J.H. (1965). *The childrearing practices report*. Berkeley, CA: Institute of Human Development, University of California.

Bok, S. (1978). *Lying: Moral choice in public and private life*. New York: Pantheon Books.

Borke, H. (1971). Correspondence between behavioral and doll-play measures of conscience. *Developmental Psychology*, *5*, 320–332.

Burton, R.V. (1976). Honesty and dishonesty. In T. Lickona (Ed.), *Moral development and behavior* (pp. 173–197). New York: Holt, Rinehart & Winston.

Chagoya, L., & Schkolne, T. (1986). Children who lie. *Canadian Journal of Psychiatry*, *31*, 665–669.

Damon, W. (1988). *The moral child; nurturing children's natural moral growth*. New York: Free Press.

DePaulo, B., & Jordan, A. (1982). Age changes in deceiving and detecting deceit. In R.S. Feldman (Ed.), *Development of nonverbal behavior in children* (pp. 180). New York: Springer Verlag.

Eisenberg-Berg, N., & Roth, K. (1980). Development of young children's prosocial moral judgement: A longitudinal follow-up. *Developmental Psychology*, *16*, 375–376.

Ekman, P. (1989). *Why kids lie*. New York: Charles Scribner's Sons.

Ekman, P., Roper, G., & Hager, J.C. (1980). Deliberate facial movement. *Child Development*, *51*, 866–891.

Eron, L.D., Walder, L.O., Huesmann, L.R., & Lefkowitz, M.M. (1978). The convergence of laboratory and field studies of the development of aggression. In W.W. Hartup & J. De Wit (Eds.), *Origins of aggression* (pp. 213–246). The Hague, The Netherlands: Mouton.

Flavell, J.H. (1968). *The development of role-taking and communication skills in children*. New York: John Wiley & Sons.

Flavell, J.H., Flavell, E.R., & Green, F.L. (1983). Development of the appearance-reality distinction. *Cognitive Psychology*, *15*, 95–120.

Goodenough, F.L. (1931). *Anger in young children*. Minneapolis, MN: University of Minneapolis Press.

Hartshorne, H., & May, M. (1928). *Studies in the nature of character: Vol I. Studies in deceit*. New York: Macmillan.

Hoffman, M.L. (1976). Empathy, role-taking, guilt, and development of altruistic motives. In T. Lickona (Ed.), *Moral development and behavior* (pp. 124–143). New York: Holt, Rinehart & Winston.

Hollingshead, A.B. (1975). *Four factor index of social status*. Unpublished manuscript.

Hyman, R. (1989). The psychology of deception. *Annual Review of Psychology*, *40*, 133–154.

Johnson, M.K. & Foley, M.A. (1984). Differentiating fact from fantasy: The reliability of children's memory. *Journal of Social Issues*, *40*, 33–50.

Kohlberg, L. (1976). Moral stages and moralization. In T. Lickona (Ed.), *Moral development and behavior* (pp. 31–53). New York: Holt, Rinehart & Winston.

Kraut, R.E., & Price, J.D. (1976). Machiavellianism in parents and their children. *Journal of Personality and Social Psychology*, *33*, 782–786.

Lewis, M. (1931). How parental attitudes affect the problem of lying in children. *Smith College Studies in Social Work*, *1*, 403–404.

Lewis, M., Stanger, C., & Sullivan, M. (1989). Deception in three year olds. *Developmental Psychology*, *25*, 439–443.

Lickona, T. (1976). Research on Piaget's theory of moral development. In T. Lickona (Ed.), *Moral development and behavior* (pp. 219–232). New York: Holt, Rinehart & Winston.

Light, P. (1980). The social concomitants of role-taking. In M.V. Cox (Ed.), *Are young children egocentric?* (pp. 127–145). New York: St. Martin's Press.

Loeber, R., & Stouthamer-Loeber, M. (1986). Family factors as correlates and predictors of juvenile conduct problems and delinquency. In M. Tonry & M. Morris (Eds.), *Crime and justice and annual revue of research* (Vol. 7, pp. 29–150). Chicago: University of Chicago Press.

MacFarlane, J.W., Allen, L., & Honzik, M.P. (1962). *A developmental study of the behavior problems of normal children between twenty-one months and fourteen years*. Berkeley, CA: University of California Press.

Piaget, J. (1932/1965). *The moral judgment of the child*. Glencoe, IL: Free Press. (Original work published 1932)

Radke-Yarrow, M., & Zahn-Waxler, C. (1973). *Developmental studies of altruism*. Washington DC: NIMH Protocol 73–M–02.

Roberts, G.C., Block, J.H., & Block, J. (1984). Continuity and change in parents' childrearing practices. *Child Development*, *55*, 586–597.

Rutter, M. Tizard, J., & Whitmore, K. (1970). *Education, health, and behavior*. New York: Wiley.

Sack, T., & Sack, K. (1974). Attitudes of teachers and mental hygienists about behavior problems of children. *Psychology in the Schools*, *11*, 445–448.

Schadler, M., & Ayers-Nachamkin, B. (1983). The development of excuse-making. In C.R. Snyder, R.L. Higgins, & R.J. Stucky (Eds.), *Excuses, masquerades in search of grace* (pp. 159–189). New York: Wiley.

Shantz, C.U. (1975). The development of social cognition. In E.M. Hetherington (Ed.), *Handbook of child psychology* (4th ed., pp. 257–323). New York: Wiley.

Stewart, M.A., & DeBlois, C.S. (1984). *Diagnostic criteria for aggressive conduct disorder*. Unpublished manuscript.

Stouthamer-Loeber, M. (1986). Lying as a problem behavior in children: A review. *Clinical Psychology Review*, *6*, 267–289.

Stouthamer-Loeber, M., & Loeber, R. (1986). Boys who lie. *Journal of Abnormal Child Psychology*, *14*, 551–564.

Turiel, E. (1977). Distinct conceptual and developmental domains: Social convention and morality. In H.E. Howe, Jr. (Ed.), *Nebraska symposium on motivation* (Vol. 25, pp. 77–116). Lincoln, NE: University of Nebraska Press.

Vasek, M.E., (1984). *Lying: The development of children's understanding of deception*. Unpublished master's thesis, Clark University, Worcester, MA.

Weston, D.R., & Turiel, E. (1980). Act–rule relations: Children's concepts of social rules. *Developmental Psychology, 16*, 417–424.

Wimmer, H., Gruber, S., & Perner, J. (1984). Young children's conception of lying: Lexical realism–moral subjectivism. *Journal of Experimental Child Psychology, 37*, 1–30.

Yarrow, M.R., & Waxler, C. (1977). Emergence and functions of prosocial behavior in young children. In R.D. Parke & E.M. Hetherington (Eds.), *Child psychology: Contemporary readings*. New York: McGraw-Hill.

Zahn-Waxler, C., & Radke-Yarrow, M. (1982). The development of altruism: Alternative research strategies. In N. Eisenberg (Ed.), *The development of prosocial behavior* (pp. 109–137). New York: Academic Press.

Zahn-Waxler, C., Radke-Yarrow, M., & King, R.A. (1979). Childrearing and children's prosocial imitations toward victims of distress. *Child Development, 50*, 319–330.

4
Children's Cue Use and Strategies for Detecting Deception

KEN J. ROTENBERG

There has been a growing effort by researchers to understand adults' and children's detection of deception (see Chapter 6). Four major questions have been addressed: (1) What are the actual cues that distinguish between lying and telling the truth. (Ekman, Friesen, & O'Sullivan, 1988)? (2) What cues do individuals perceive or believe distinguish between lying and telling the truth (Zuckerman, Koestner, & Driver, 1981[1])? (3) What is the relation between the preceding "actual" cues and the "perceived" cues (Zuckerman, Driver, & Koestner, 1982)? (4) Are individuals able to differentiate between lying and telling the truth (DePaulo & Rosenthal, 1979)?

The present chapter, and study, will address the second of those questions—the "believed cue" question. The goals are to identify the types of cues that children believe reveal whether others are lying rather than telling the truth (regarded as deception in the present chapter) and the strategies that children use to detect deception. This converges with the primary purpose of this book, because children's interpersonal trust is by definition (see Chapter 1) affected by children's judgments that others are lying or telling the truth and, correspondingly, the cues and strategies that children use to arrive at those judgments.

This "believed cue" question was addressed following a consideration of the existing research. It has been found that adults and children are very poor at discriminating between lying and telling the truth simply from hearing and observing others (see DePaulo, Stone, & Lassiter, (1985).[2]

---

[1] Zuckerman et al. (1981) distinguished between perceived and believed cues for deception. I did not make the distinction in this chapter, because the two phenomena are stongly related and the difference between them is largely methodological. Perceived cues are those that individuals report using when attempting to determine whether a given person was deceptive. Believed cues are those that individuals espouse regarding the types of cues they believe to generally reveal deception. Not surprisingly, Zuckerman et al. (1981) found a strong correlation between perceived and believed cues. The methodology employed in the present study represents an integration of both types of methods.

Also, the research indicates that there are many discrepancies between actual and perceived cues for deception (Zuckerman et al., 1981). Such findings have led researchers, such as DePaulo et al., 1985), to propose that the *appearance* of telling the truth plays a very important role in determining whether a communication is regarded as truthful. These researchers argue "that in order to be perceived as sincere, it may not always be sufficient simply to tell the truth. If a completely innocent truth teller happens to engage in behaviors that others perceive as signs of deception (even though they are not), a person risks being labeled as a liar" (DePaulo et al., 1985, p. 343). Consistent with this argument, researchers have found evidence for a "demeanor bias," in which some individuals appear to be lying even when telling the truth, whereas some individuals appear to be telling the truth even when they are lying (Bond, Kahler, & Paolicelli, 1985). This line of reasoning leads to the conclusion that a comprehensive understanding of children's judgment of lying or telling the truth requires an understanding of what they regard as the appearance of lying or telling the truth and, correspondingly, what cues the children believe reveal it.

Understanding Deception

Children's identification of cues for lying or telling the truth requires that they have a fundamental understanding of deception. Researchers now propose that, in order to achieve that understanding, children need to have formed theories of the mind; mental representations of their own and other's beliefs, desires, and feelings (see Olson, Astington, & Harris, 1988). According to this approach, children need to acquire two concepts to achieve an understanding of deception. First, they need to understand the difference between real and apparent events to distinguish between what a speaker actually believes, feels, etc., and what he or she expresses (see Harris, Donnelly, Guz, & Pitt-Watson, 1986). This requires a mental representation of the mental–emotion functioning of others, as distinct from observed action. Second, children need to have a mental representation of others having false beliefs in order to understand that others can be, or are deceived (see Chapter 9). In the context of emotional deception, children need to understand that an individual will control the expression of an emotion by concealing it or feigning another emotion in order to cause others to hold a false belief about the actual emotional state.

---

[2] It is interesting to note that Wilson and Carroll (see Chapter 7) have found that children can identify classmates who provide untrustworthy communications. Presumably, the children have had the opportunity to determine whether their classmates' communications are correct or accurate.

There is considerable dispute over the age at which children understand deception. Chandler describes (see Chapter 9) the early-onset versus later-onset account of the development of children's understanding of deception. The early-onset account advanced by Chandler and his colleagues posits that $2\frac{1}{2}$-year-old children have a rudimentary understanding of deception, whereas the later-onset account advanced by authors such as Wimmer and Perner (1983) posits that children understand deception by 5 to 6 years of age. (See Chapter 9 for a complete description of this issue.)

Evidence for children's understanding of deception is provided by research on the phenomena known as children's understanding of display rules (Gnepp & Hess, 1986; Harris et al., 1986; Saarni, 1979). These studies were designed to assess whether children understand how and when persons misinform others about their emotional states either by concealing them or feigning other emotions. In this line of research, these are all acts of deception but ones that are presumed to be socially approved (e.g., a child saying that he or she liked a gift, even when he or she did not, to protect the giver's feelings). Investigation of this phenomena has shown that even 4-year-old children demonstrate a fundamental understanding of the hiding or concealing of an emotion (Harris et al., 1986). The studies show, though, that there are increases across the 4- through 9-year age span in children's understanding of the various situations and communication channels in which the expression of emotion is inhibited or feigned (Gnepp & Hess, 1986; Saarni, 1979).

Cue Use and Strategies

Some evidence that children encounter extensive opportunities for identifying cues for deception during the course of childhood is provided by the anecdotal observations of DePaulo, et al. (1985). They noted that "probably every major category of play—for example, card games, board games, party games, and sports—includes numerous games for deceit" (p. 359–360). The authors argue that by playing such games, children learn about deception and develop extensive strategies (correct or incorrect) for detecting it. From my observations, I believe that it is quite common for children to be involved in heterosexual "games" in which they conceal or feign their liking or disliking for peers. Because the importance of heterosexual games increases with age, there should be increases with age in children's experiences with that form of deception and in their acquisition of an extensive array of cues and strategies for its detection.

The extensive research on adults' actual and perceived cues for deception provides some insight into the types of cues that children may believe reveal deception. In fact, children should acquire those perceived cues simply because they eventually attain adulthood. Four domains of "adult" cues have been identified (see DePaulo et al., 1985): verbal cues, vocal–

paralinguistic cues, visual cues (comprising visual–facial and visual–body cues), and miscellaneous cues. Based on an extensive review and analysis of existing research, DePaulo et al. (1985) concluded that individuals are able to control the visual–facial channel more than they are other channels of communication, and as a consequence, visual–facial cues are the most misleading to others when individuals attempt to deceive. The cues that adults primarily believe to reveal deception are (a) the vocal–paralinguistic cues of speech hesitations, pitch, speech errors, latency, and speech rate; (b) visual cues of gaze, postural shifts,and smiling; and (c) the discrepancy between between facial and vocal cues (Zuckerman et al., 1982).

Some of the cues that adults believe to reveal deception have a realistic basis. A growing body of research indicates that, during the act of deception, individuals' *leak* their true beliefs or feelings through physiological or overt behavioral cues (see Ekman & Friesen, 1969; Ekman et al., 1988; Feldman, 1976). Adults appear to adopt this notion in their consideration of the discrepancy between verbal and nonverbal communication (see Blanck & Rosenthal, 1982). Consideration of discrepancy cues depends, in large part, on the belief that an emotion inhibited for expression in one channel of communication will be displayed in another that the individual had failed to control. In order to master the leaking concept and use of discrepancy cues, children need to acquire a corresponding "emotional control–multichannel" principle. This entails believing that, when an individual inhibits the expression of an emotion in one channel of communication, then it becomes manifested in physiological or in overt behavioral cues (other channels) that the individual could not, or did not, control.

One related principle that underlies adults' beliefs about cues for deception, and may have *some* basis in reality, is found in the GSR and similar "lie detector" tests (see Lykken, 1974). This is that the act of deceiving is accompanied by anxiety that is shown in physiological or in overt behavioral cues, involuntarily. Adults show an appreciation of this principle by their beliefs that nervous behaviors (e.g., postural movements, pitch) reveal deception, even though a number of these may not be correct (see Kraut, 1978; Zuckerman et al. 1982). To achieve adult functioning, children would have to acquire such beliefs.

Researchers have attempted to examine whether children believe that discrepancy cues reveal lying or telling the truth (Blanck & Rosenthal, 1982; Bugental, Kaswan, & Love, 1970; Friedman, 1979; Rotenberg, Simourd, & Moore, 1989). Rotenberg et al. have examined this (1989) in the context of the verbal–nonverbal consistency principle. This prescribes that truth–sincerity is inferred from the consistency between the affect exhibited in verbal and nonverbal communication, whereas lying–insincerity is inferred from the inconsistency between those. Researchers have found that children's use of the verbal–nonverbal consistency principle increases with age from kindergarten through fourth grade and that it is evident in a sophisticated fashion in fourth-grade children (Rotenberg et al., 1989) and high school students (Blanck & Rosenthal, 1982; DePaulo, Stone, & Lassiter, 1985; Friedman, 1979). In addition, Rotenberg et al. (1989) found that facial cues played an important role in children's perceptions of lying or truth, with positive facial expressions being associated with telling the truth.

The present study was designed to investigate whether children believe that the various "adult" cues, including the verbal–nonverbal discrepancy cues, reveal lying or telling the truth. Children beginning at second grade were selected for investigation, because research indicates that children at that age have a fundamental understanding of deception (as previously cited) and lying (Chapter 2). Also, the study was designed to investigate the types of strategies that children use to detect deception. Although the term *strategy* has been used in the literature, the phenomena has been treated virtually the same as children's use of the various cues for deception. Strategy was conceptualized in the study as the *actions* that children would undertake to determine whether others were lying or telling the truth. In this context, the actions are a product of children's *intended* or *planned* means of revealing deception. This was assessed in the present study by asking children how they would find out whether others were lying as opposed to telling the truth. This functioned as a measure of children's *reported* strategies for detecting deception. Because of the lack of existing knowledge, hypotheses were not advanced regarding children's strategies for detecting deception.[3]

Method

Subjects

The subjects were 16 children (8 males and 8 females) from each of second, fourth, and sixth grades of a public elementary school, located in Thunder Bay, Ontario. The mean ages of the children in the three grades were 7 years 7 months, 9 years 10 months, and 11 years 9 months, respectively. The children's participation was secured by parental letters and consent.

Stimuli

The verbal communication stimuli were composed of children's statements of their preferences for food they ate or for a blouse/shirt another child was wearing. In total, four verbal communications were employed, the result of two types of preferences (liking versus not liking) of two objects

---

[3] I thank Wanda Andraka for her assistance in the study.

(food vs. shirt/blouse). These were the following: (1) he/she liked the food he/she ate; (2) he/she did not like the food he/she ate; (3) he/she liked the shirt/blouse the other child was wearing; (4) he/she did not like the shirt/blouse the other child was wearing. Each subject was presented a pair of verbal communications that comprised either the first and fourth or the second and third of the preceding communications. They thereby received a liking preference for one object and not-liking preference for the other object. The two pairs were used with equal frequency for each grade, and the order of their presentation was counterbalanced. The verbal communications were presented with the speaker and the other child (when appropriate) as the same sex as the subject; boys for the male subjects and girls for female subjects.

Procedure

The subjects were tested individually, and the experimenter presented all the questions verbally. After a short introduction, the experimenter stated, "Let's say that a girl [or boy—same sex] said. . . . " and completed this by one of the two verbal communications. After the child had successfully repeated the statement on request, the experimenter asked the subject, "Tell me how you would know whether the girl [boy] was lying, rather than telling the truth about her or [his] feelings about the food [or blouse or shirt]." This served as the general question. The experimenter continued by posing three sets of specific questions. (a) "Would you look at her [his] face to tell? If so, what would you look at? (b) Would you look at her [his] body to tell? If so, what would you look at? (c) Would you listen hard to how she [he] had told you she [he] liked [not liked] the food [shirt/blouse]? These sets of questions were designed to assess reference to three broad domains of visual–facial, visual–body and vocal–paralinguistic cues, respectively.

The subject's strategy for detecting deception was assessed by asking the subject, "If you had a chance to talk to the girl [boy], what would you do to find out whether she [he] was lying, rather than telling the truth?" This was further probed by asking the subject, "Would you ask questions? If so, what questions would you ask?" Next, this entire procedure was followed for the second verbal communication.

Coding

The cue categories were adapted from the perceived and actual vocal–paralinguistic and visual sets of cues that were described by DePaulo et al. (1985). The verbal set of cues was excluded because the verbal communications were stated second hand, and therefore the corresponding cues were not viable. The visual set of cues was divided, into visual–facial and visual–body cues. Almost all of the vocal–paralinguistic and visual sets of cues listed by DePaulo et al. (1985) were used but a few were modified or eliminated and a few cues were added. The following changes were made: (a) Hand movements were included with the leg and foot movements to yield a broader category of nervous movements of the limbs. (b) Gestures, shrugs, and adaptors were not viable categories because of their infrequency. (c) Facial expressions, eyebrow movements, and giggling were included because subjects used them with some frequency. The grinning–smiling cue category applied to the subjects' reference to a mischievous grin (giggling was a vocal–paralinguistic cue for this).

For the general question *only*, the subjects' answers were coded according to whether they referred generally to visual–facial, visual–body, or paralinguistic–vocal cues. It should be pointed out that the subjects were given credit for an answer to a specific cue question only if they provided an answer concerning a very specific cue (e.g., he would be grinning) that could not be attributable to the information contained in the question itself.

In addition, two other sets of cue categories were employed, "discrepancies" and "internal states." The set of discrepancies cues was used to code the subjects' identification of lying as the inconsistency between the verbal communication and the speaker's: (a) nonverbal cues (nonverbal); or (b) later verbal communications (verbal); or (c) behavior (behavior). The former corresponds to the verbal–nonverbal discrepancy cue that has been examined in adults and children (i.e., Rotenberg et al., 1989). This included children's suggestions that the person would provide a nonverbal expression of emotion that was incompatible with his or her stated preference (e.g., he was smiling while he said he disliked the shirt). The latter two reflect the subjects' beliefs that lying is revealed when the speaker made statements or showed behavior that were inconsistent with his or her initially stated preference. As an example of verbal discrepancy, one subject stated that the person might state that he likes rather than dislikes a similar shirt at another time. As an example of behavior discrepancy, one subject stated that the person would ask for seconds of food he said he disliked. The set of "internal states" cues was the subjects' reference to internal states of the speaker, such as worried, guilty. Although this set of cues is worthwhile to note, the children's use of it was too infrequent to be considered in the results and data analyses.

Separate categories were generated to code the subjects' answers to the strategies for detecting deception questions. The categories were as follows: (a) direct inquiry—directly asking the speaker whether he or she likes or does not like the object; (b) reason inquiry—asking the speaker the reasons for his or her preferences to assess whether those were a product of genuine rationales; (c) truth inquiry—asking the speaker whether he or she is telling the truth or lying; (d) confidences—offering the speaker confidentiality of his or her feelings if revealed; (e) verbal testing—assessing whether the speakers' later verbal communications were consistent with his or her initial verbal communications; and (f) behavioral testing—assessing whether his or her behavior was consistent with his or her initial verbal communications.

Transcripts of the subjects' tape-recorded answers were made and scored. The answers to the questions were coded, first, in terms of utterances; defined as a single phrase or thought. Then two raters were employed, one scored all the answers, and the other served to establish and maintain reliability. The two raters scored the first quarter (0% to 25%) and second quarter (50% to 75%) of the answers from each grade. The average interrater agreement for the former was 87% (agreements— agreements and disagreements) and for the latter was 91%.

Results

Initial analyses indicated there were no differences between the answers to the liking and not-liking preference communications, and the data were collapsed across this variable. If a subject repeated reference to a given category when answering the same question for the same communication, then it was scored as a *single* reference to that category. This yielded the subject's use of a *type* of category.

Cue Use for the General Question

The frequencies of the cue categories to the general question are presented in Table 4.1. The frequencies were summed within each broad category (i.e., visual–facial, visual–body, and vocal–paralinguistic) to obtain sufficient sizes for analysis, and those were subjected to a 3(grade) × 2(sex) × 3(category) log-linear analysis. This yielded effects of grade, χ^2 (2, N = 48) = 17.26, p < .001 and of category, χ^2 (2, N = 48) = 22.71, p < .0001. The corresponding frequencies are shown in Table 4.2. The frequency of the categories increased with grade, with frequencies of 9, 17, and 35 for second, fourth, and sixth grades, respectively. The category of visual–facial (frequency = 35) was more frequent than visual–body (frequency = 20), which was more frequent than the vocal–paralinguistic (frequency = 6).

The frequencies of the discrepancies were subjected to a 3(grade) × 3(category) log-linear analysis; the data were collapsed across sex to provide sufficient frequencies for analysis. This yielded an effect of grade, χ^2 (2, N = 48) = 8.36, p < .025. There were increases with grade, with frequencies of 7, 15, and 19 for the second, fourth, and sixth grades, respectively. The analysis yielded an effect of category, χ^2 (2, N = 48) = 24.90, p < .001; the behavioral category (frequency = 25) was more

TABLE 4.1. Frequencies of cues categories as a function of type of question and grade.

| Cue category (type of question) | Grade | | | | | |
| | Second | | Fourth | | Sixth | |
	G	Sp	G	Sp	G	Sp
Vocal–paralinguistic						
Speech						
Speech–hesitations	0	0	0	2	0	4
Pitch	2	3	1	3	3	6
Speech rate	0	0	0	0	2	3
Response rate	0	0	0	3	0	0
Giggling	0	3	0	0	0	0
General	3	—	1	—	8	—
Visual–face						
Facial expressions	0	3	6	5	7	6
Grinning/smiling	1	9	2	5	2	2
Eyes						
Dilation	0	1	2	5	0	2
Blinking	0	1	0	1	0	1
Brows	0	4	0	2	0	4
Movements	1	1	0	1	0	2
Gaze	1	2	3	7	2	8
General	1	—	0	—	7	—
Visual–body						
Hand, foot, leg						
Movements	0	4	2	6	0	8
Postural						
Movements	0	3	0	2	1	3
Head movements	0	2	0	0	2	2
General	0	—	0	—	0	—
Discrepancies						
Nonverbal	0	3	0	6	2	5
Behavioral	4	8	12	7	9	5
Verbal	3	5	3	4	8	6

G, general question; Sp, specific question.

frequent than the verbal category (frequency = 14), which was more frequent than the nonverbal category (frequency = 2).

Cue Use for the Specific Questions

The frequencies of the cue categories to the specific questions are shown in Table 4.1. The summed frequencies within each broad category were subjected to a 3(grade) × 2(sex) × 3(category) log-linear analysis. This yielded a main effect of category, χ^2 (2, $N = 48$) = 27.36, $p < .0001$ and a two-way sex × grade interaction, χ^2 (2, $N = 48$) = 11.83, $p < .01$. These were qualified, however, by a three-way, grade × sex × category interaction, χ^2 (4, $N = 48$) = 16.34, $p < .01$. The frequencies for this inter-

TABLE 4.2. Frequencies of cue categories as a function of type of question, sex, and grade.

		Type of question					
		General			Specific		
Grade	Sex	V-P	V-F	V-B	V-P	V-F	V-B
Second	Boy	1	3	0	0	15	7
	Girl	4	1	0	6	6	2
	Across	5	4	0	6	21	9
Fourth	Boy	0	7	2	5	10	2
	Girl	2	6	0	5	16	6
	Across	2	13	2	10	26	8
Sixth	Boy	9	8	3	10	16	10
	Girl	4	10	1	3	9	3
	Across	13	18	4	13	25	13

V-P, vocal-paralinguistic category; V-F, visual-facial category; V-B, visual-body category.

action are shown in Table 4.2. To clarify this complex interaction, separate analyses were conducted for each sex. The analysis for boys yielded effects of grade, χ^2 (2, $N = 24$) = 7.52, $p < .025$, and of category, χ^2 (2, $N = 24$) = 14.81, $p < .001$. These were qualified by a two-way, grade $\times$ category interaction, χ^2 (4, $N = 24$) = 13.86, $p < .01$. The interaction was due to a lack of a difference between grades in the visual–facial cues and an increase in vocal–paralinguistic cues with grade. The analysis for girls yielded effects of grade, χ^2 (2. $N = 24$) = 6.40, $p < .05$, and of category, χ^2 (2, $N = 24$) = 14.20, $p < .001$. There was a curvilinear relation with grade, with the frequencies increasing from second to fourth grades (frequencies of 14 and 27, respectively) and a return to approximately the same frequency by sixth grade (frequency of 13). In sixth grade, the boys showed greater cue usage than did the girls (frequencies of 27 and 13, respectively), and this difference was evident for each of the three categories.

The frequencies of the discrepancies were subjected to a 3(grade) $\times$ 3(category) log-linear analysis; the data were collapsed across sex to provide sufficient frequencies for analysis. This did not yield significant effects. The frequencies across grades of the nonverbal, behavioral, and verbal discrepancies were, 14, 20, and 15, respectively.

Strategies for Detecting Deception

For the purpose of analysis, the verbal testing and behavioral testing were collapsed into a "testing" category, because they were strongly associated. Also, the facial, vocal, and body betrayals were collapsed into a physical betrayal category, because they were too infrequent as individual categories. In addition, the "confidences" category was not subjected to analysis because it was only evident in sixth grade (frequency = 6). The

TABLE 4.3. Frequencies of the search-strategy categories as a function of category and grade.

Grade	Testing	Direct inquiry	Reason inquiry	Truth inquiry	Cue betrayal
			Search strategy categories		
Second	15	6	3	9	5
Fourth	26	9	3	4	12
Sixth	8	18	9	6	4

frequencies of the five categories were subjected to a 3(grade) × 2(sex) × 5(category) log-linear analysis. This yielded an effect of category, χ^2 (4, 48) = 26.08, $p < .001$, that was qualified by a two-way, grade × category interaction, χ^2 (8, 48) = 24.85, $p < .001$. The frequencies for this interaction are shown in Table 4.3. To assess this interaction, the frequencies for each category were subjected to separate analyses. These yielded an effect of grade on the direct request category, χ^2 (2, $N = 48$) = 6.84, $p < .05$; there was an increase with grade in this category, with frequencies of 6, 9, and 18 for second, fourth, and sixth grades, respectively. Also, these analyses yielded an effect of grade on the testing category, χ^2 (2, $N = 48$) = 10.20, $p < .01$; the frequencies of this category decreased with grade, with frequencies of 15, 26, and 8 for second, fourth, and sixth grades, respectively. Testing was the most frequent strategy at second and fourth grades, whereas direct inquiry was the most frequent strategy at sixth grade.

Discussion

There were increases with age in the children's identification of the various cues for deception. Although comparison of the results from general and specific questions is problematic (e.g., they were in a fixed order), the age differences apparently were stronger in the former than the latter. Furthermore, this was due, in part, to the tendency for the younger children to show greater competence when answering the specific than general questions. Younger children may have had difficulty with the general questioning because (1) it is an abstract problem and/or (2) it required them to spontaneously identify the cues. For example, the broad cue domains included in the specific questions may have helped the children to imagine the physical activities and therefore generate the relevant cues. In the future, researchers may wish to examine the hypothesis that children younger than those tested in the present study will demonstrate substantial competence in identifying cues for deception when the questioning and task are made more concrete or cue evoking.

Still, the children showed the ability to identify a large number of cues for deception, particularly when posed the *specific* questions. They identified the range of cues comparable to those found by researchers in the investigation of adults' actual and believed cues for deception (with the exception of verbal cues that were not viable in the study). There were some similarities and differences between the cues that adults and those that children believed to reveal deception. Similar to adults, children frequently identified gaze, smiling, and pitch as cues for deception. Unlike adults, though, children frequently identified hand, foot, and leg movements rather than postural movements as visual–body cues for deception. Also, children identified the verbal–nonverbal discrepancy cues that have been found in children of approximately the same ages (Rotenberg et al., 1989) and in adults (Zuckerman et al., 1982). Additionally, the children identified other types of discrepancy cues that reflected the consistency between verbal behavior (the stated preference) and other verbal behavior or overt behavior.

The findings indicated that children most frequently identified visual–facial cues, than either visual–body or vocal–paralinguistic cues, as revealing deception. The dominance of visual–facial cues is consistent with the finding of Rotenberg et al. (1989) that facial cues play an important role in children's identification of lying or telling the truth. This may stem from the fact that, from early in development, facial cues are very salient social features for children (see Caron, Caron, Caldwell, & Weiss, 1973). Furthermore, facial cues are particularly salient cues for emotion, although their impact and role in defining emotions for children may change with age (see Hoffner & Badzinski, 1989). Regarding the present study, it is quite logical, then, for children to focus on the face when deciding how to detect whether a person was lying about an emotion. It is interesting to place these findings in the context of DePaulo et al.'s (1985) conclusions. If the visual–facial channel is the most controllable communication and results in optimal deception, then children's reliance on visual–facial cues places them at great risk for being deceived. A definitive conclusion, though, of children's relative use of visual–facial, visual–body, and vocal–paralinguistic cues must wait until researchers investigate this issue with methods that rely comparatively less on children's verbal comprehension and production.

There were some sex differences in the children's identification of cues for lying or telling the truth. For the specific questions, no appreciable age differences were demonstrated in boys' identification of visual–facial cues, although the identification of vocal–paralinguistic cues increased with age. By contrast, girls showed a curvilinear pattern in which the frequencies of cues increased from second to fourth grade and declined from fourth to sixth grade. One explanation of this surprising pattern is provided by Rosenthal and DePaulo (1979a, 1979b). These researchers found that females show superiority over males in decoding communication from very controllable channels (e.g., facial cues) but that female superiority decreased as the communication channels became less controllable (the body or tone of voice) and hence more likely to leak unintended or inconsistent communications. Rosenthal and DePaulo (1979a, 1979b) proposed that females refrain from identifying the less controllable and leaky cues for deception because they are socialized to be *polite*. The surprising tendency in the present study for the sixth-grade girls to return to a second-grade level of identifying cues for deception may reflect such a socialization process toward politeness. Some findings, however, decrease the attractiveness of this account. Notably, the sixth-grade girls identified fewer facial cues, as well as body and vocal cues, than did sixth-grade boys; the former are controllable channels, at least by adult standards. Also, no sex differences were found in the children's use of the more leaky discrepancy cues. Further research is necessary to assess the reliability of the observed sex differences and to explore the "politeness" hypothesis.

The assessment of children's reported strategies for detection of deception was revealing. The reference to the testing strategy decreased with age, and the reference to the direct-inquiry strategy increased with age. One account of these age differences is provided by the finding that only the oldest children referred to confidences as a strategy. It may be that, with age, children abandon the strategy of attempting to "trick" the person into revealing the truth and adopt the strategy of offering the person confidentiality of his or her disclosure. This may signal the emergence of children's consideration of establishing trust as a means of eliciting truth from others.

Until researchers undertake further investigation, it is not possible to confidently determine what concepts or notions underlie the children's cue identifications and their reported strategies for detecting deception. The findings, however, provide some tentative evidence for the following conclusions. First, the children appeared to understand that deception was accompanied by anxiety that was manifested involuntarily in physiological and overt behavioral cues. Children frequently identified as cues for deception, body movements, eye movements, and pitch that are common physiological signs of anxiety. Second, children identified various types of discrepancy cues for lying or telling the truth and therefore demonstrated some appreciation of "emotional control-multichannel" principle, whereby persons leak their emotion in other channels of communication (broadly defined). Children's appreciation of this principle was demonstrated further by their reference to the use of testing strategies to detect deception. These were attempts to construct situations that would trip up persons into revealing their true feelings through various channels of communication. Further research is necessary to explore these issues.

References

Blanck, P.D., & Rosenthal, R. (1982). Developing strategies for decoding "leaky" messages: On learning how and when to decode discrepant and consistent social communications. In Robert S. Feldman (Ed.), *Development of nonverbal behavior in children* (pp. 206–229). New York: Springer-Verlag.

Bond, C.F. Jr., Kahler, K.N., & Paolicelli, L.M. (1985). The miscommunication of deception: An adaptive perspective. *Journal of Experimental Social Psychology*, *21*, 331–345.

Bugental, D.E., Kaswan, J.W., & Love, L.R. (1970). Perception of contradictory meanings conveyed by verbal and nonverbal channels. *Journal of Personality and Social Psychology*, *16*, 647–655.

Caron, A.J., Caron, R.F., Caldwell, R.C., & Weiss, S.J. (1973). Infant perception of the structural properties of the face. *Developmental Psychology*, *9*, 385–399.

Chandler, M., Fritz, A.S., & Hala, S. (1989). Small-scale deceit: Deception as a marker of two-, three-, and four-year olds early theories of mind. *Child Development*, *60*, 1263–1277.

DePaulo, B.M., Jordan, A., Irvine, A., & Laser, P.S. (1982). Age changes in the detection of deception. *Child Development*, *53*, 701–709.

DePaulo, B.M., & Rosenthal, R. (1979). Telling lies. *Journal of Personality and Social Psychology*, *37*, 1713–1722.

DePaulo, B.M., Stone, J.I., & Lassiter, G.D. (1985). Deceiving and detecting deceit. In Barry R. Schlenker (Ed.), *The self and social life* (pp. 323–370). New York: McGraw-Hill.

Ekman, P., & Friesen, W.V. (1969). Nonverbal leakage and clues to deception. *Psychiatry*, *32*, 88–106.

Ekman, P., Friesen, W.V., & O'Sullivan, M. (1988). Smiles when lying. *Journal of Personality and Social Psychology*, *54*, 414–420.

Feldman, R.S. (1976). Nonverbal disclosure of deception and interpersonal affect. *Journal of Educational Psychology*, *68*, 807–816.

Friedman, H.S. (1979). The interactive effects of facial expressions of emotion and verbal messages on perceptions of affective meaning. *Journal of Experimental Social Psychology*, *15*, 453–469.

Gnepp, J., & Hess, D.L.R. (1986). Children's understanding of verbal and facial display rules. *Developmental Psychology*, *22*, 103–108.

Harris, P.L., Donnelly, K., Guz, G.R., & Pitt-Watson, R. (1986). Children's understanding of the distinction between real and apparent emotion. *Child Development*, *57*, 895–909.

Hoffner, C., & Badzinski, D.M. (1989). Children's integration of facial and situational cues for emotion. *Child Development*, *60*, 411–422.

Lykken, D.T. (1974). Psychology and the lie detector industry. *American Psychologist*, *29*, 725–739.

Olson, D., Astington, J.W., & Harris, P.L. (1988). Introduction. In Janet W. Astington, Paul L. Harris, & David R. Olson (Eds.), *Developing theories of mind* (pp. 1–15). Cambridge, UK: Cambridge University Press.

Rosenthal, R., & DePaulo, B.M. (1979a). Sex differences in eavesdropping on nonverbal cues. *Journal of Personality and Social Psychology*, *37*, 273–285.

Rosenthal, R., & DePaulo, B.M. (1979b). Sex differenes in nonverbal communication. In R. Rosenthal (Ed.), *Skill in nonverbal communication* (pp. 68–103). Cambridge, MA: Oelgeschlager, Gunn & Hain.

Rotenberg, K.J., Simourd, L., & Moore, D. (1989). Children's use of a verbal–nonverbal consistency principle to infer truth and lying. *Child Development*, *60*, 309–322.

Saarni, C. (1979). Children's understanding of display rules for expressive behavior. *Developmental Psychology*, *15*, 424–429.

Wimmer, H., & Perner, J. (1983). Beliefs about beliefs: Representation and constraining function of wrong beliefs in young children's understanding of deception. *Cognition*, *13*, 103–128.

Zuckerman, M., Driver, R., & Koestner, R. (1982). Discrepancy as a cue to actual and perceived deception. *Journal of Nonverbal Behavior*, *7*, 95–100.

Zuckerman, M., Koestner, R., & Driver, R. (1981). Beliefs about the cues associated with deception. *Journal of Nonverbal Behavior*, *6*, 105–114.

5
Children's Responses to Authentic Versus Polite Smiles

DAPHNE BLUNT BUGENTAL, HAL KOPEIKIN AND
LINDA LAZOWSKI

Interpersonal communication between adults consists of complex patterns of verbal and nonverbal behaviors that simultaneously reveal information about underlying states, dispositional characteristics, and social motives. In "polite" interactions, further complexities are introduced by the presence of cultural rules regarding acceptable and unacceptable expressive displays. The ultimate product may involve a web of minor deceptions in which unfelt positive affect is displayed and negative affect is inhibited or masked. Our interest here is in one critical behavior within such "polite" systems—the smile. Perhaps more than any other aspect of nonverbal behavior, the smile may be used in the service of intentional impression management. Therefore, it is important to understand how the developing child comes to understand the various meanings of the smile.

In this chapter, we have two central concerns. First of all, we are interested in the use of the smile by adults in interactions with children. In particular, we are concerned with the subtle distinctions in the properties of smiles that accompany a positive state or attitude ("authentic" smiles) versus those that do not ("polite"smiles). Second, we are interested in the differential response patterns shown by children to authentic versus polite smiles. To what extent do children demonstrate an understanding of this distinction? Are there developmental changes in the ability to make such distinctions? And are there individual differences in the course of this acquisition process?

Past research on developmental differences in the ability to interpret complex interpersonal messages has focused on the resolution of inconsistencies across communication channels (e.g., Bugental, Kaswan, & Love, 1970; DePaulo & Jordan, 1982; Rotenberg, Simourd, & Moore, 1989). In the present investigation, however, we were more concerned with individual and developmental differences in responses to the features

Research described here was supported by National Institute of Health Grant RO1 MH39095. The authors would like to express their appreciation to Paul Ekman for his helpful comments on this chapter.

of smiles that accompanying "polite" conversation (neutral or positive in tone). With the acquisition of cultural norms, children are likely to learn that it is socially appropriate to respond positively to the smiles of others in such settings. At the same time, however, they may also recognize distinctions between types of smiles. A smile whose features are discrepant from the norm may pose a stimulus that represents a source of ambiguity and confusion. For example, the polite but "unfelt" smile may appear exaggerated. The child may either respond to smiles as generic markers of positive intent, or he or she may respond to distinguishable stimulus features that offer cues to the discrepant stimulus features per se. Acquisition of cultural norms regarding expressive behavior is more likely to produce the first response. But wariness regarding adults may produce the second response.

Authentic Versus Polite Smiles

Theoretical Positions

Before we can meaningfully consider children's responses to the smiles of adults, it is important to consider theoretical positions and empirical evidence regarding the significance and typology of smiles. Popular lore as well as scientific evidence suggest that adults do not necessarily use smiles to communicate genuine positive affect, nor do they necessarily trust the smiles of others. We refer to the extent to which someone "smiles with their eyes" as a cue to the extent to which the smile can be believed. Some smiles may indicate positive affect or at least the motivation to engage in positive interactions with another person. Some may simply be used as conventional conversation markers in polite conversation. Other smiles may indicate deference and the effort to ward off potential social threat.

The various popular views of smiles are reflected in differing theoretical positions on the origins and significance of facial expression. Contemporary emotion theorists present the view that facial displays reflect "primary affect" programs that represent biologically based, involuntary indications of felt emotion. These behaviors may, however, come under intentional control and be deliberately managed in the service of individual impression management and social regulation (Buck, 1984; Izard & Malatesta, 1987) and/or cultural display rules (Ekman, 1971) and thus deviate from biological programs. Facial expressions may, then, reflect some combination of underlying affective states along with the symbolic or intentional use of facial actions. The smile may be manifested as an indicator of genuine amusement or happiness; it may be used as an indicator or responsiveness in conversation regulation; or it may be used to give a desired impression (Ekman, Friesen, & O'Sullivan, 1988).

Still others have argued that facial actions are used exclusively for communicative functions rather than as reflections of underlying affective states (e.g., Dawkins & Krebs, 1978; Fridlund, in press). The focus within these approaches is on the social signal value of the smile. Smiles reflect the individual's intentions and signal probable future behavior. From a broad ethological standpoint, smiles (and homologous infrahuman primate displays) have been described in terms of their significance for receptivity or submission (van Hooff, 1972). From this point of view, smiles signal positive or nonthreatening intentions and are used as part of social regulation processes; but they do not serve the function of a positive "hedonic readout."

For the first position, the smile may be either an authentic reflection of underlying amusement, happiness, and the like, or it may be a deliberately controlled behavior acting in the service of personal motives or cultural rules. For the second position, the smile is a social signal with evolutionary origins. It occurs in the presence of others for socially adaptive reasons. The two positions differ in the extent to which the smile may reveal accurate affective state information but essentially agree on the potential management or deliberate control of the smile. It is, then, of general interest to determine how children acquire an understanding of the strategic use of the smile.

Encoding Studies

Ekman and Friesen and their colleagues (Ekman, Davidson, & Friesen, 1990; Ekman et al., 1988) have suggested that facial actions associated with positive affect can be distinguished from facial actions associated with deliberate or managed attempts to use a smile to conceal negative affect or to simulate happiness. Smiles may potentially involve two portions of the face. The corners of the mouth may be raised upward to the cheekbone (involving zygomatic major actions); and the cheeks may be lifted and the skin gathered around the eyes by the actions of the orbicularis oculi muscle. In honor of the pioneering work on the spontaneous smile by the French anatomist, Duchenne de Boulogne, Ekman and his colleagues use the term, "Duchenne smile," to refer to the spontaneous enjoyment smile. Ekman and Friesen (1982) found that unlike Duchenne smiles, other smiles (i.e., smiles not associated with positive affect) are more likely to involve zygomatic actions only; that is, they are less likely to be accompanied by cheek lifting and orbicularis oculi action. This is congruent with the popular stereotoype that genuinely happy people smile with their eyes as well as the mouth. In this paper, our use of the term "authentic smile" is synonymous with Ekman et al.'s "Duchenne smile," and our use of "polite smile" is encompassed within Ekman et al.'s "other smiles."

Ekman et al. (1988) followed this earlier investigation with an analysis of smiles that accompany honest interviews (describing feelings about watching a pleasant nature film) versus deceptive interviews (hiding feelings about watching a film about amputations and burns). In the latter investigation, they were concerned with "masking smiles," that is, smiles that are used to conceal negative affect. They observed that smiles occurring during deceptive interviews were more likely than smiles occurring during honest interviews to be accompanied by facial action units associated with negative affect.

Ekman and Friesen (1982) also have noted patterning and sequential features of smiles that may have implications for their "sincerity." For example, smiles while lying are more likely to be asymmetrical. They have also suggested that "overlong" or very brief smiles also may have implications for the significance of smiles. In support of this notion, Weiss and Blum (1987) observed that smiles associated with attempts to simulate positive affect were likely to have unusually long onset times.

Unfortunately, the majority of research that has dealt with the manifestation of smiling behavior under different circumstances has not been concerned with type of smile. For example, Ickes, Patterson, Rajecki, and Tanford (1982) noted that adult subjects were somewhat more likely to smile during social interactions in which they had been given the advance expecations of an *unfriendly* rather than a friendly encounter. One wonders whether the smiles shown in the two situations might have varied in their qualitative properties. Research by Bugental, Love, and Gianetto (1971) documented gender differences in use of the smile among parents but was uninformative with regard to type of smile. Smiling behavior among fathers was more likely to be associated with positive verbal content than was the smiling behavior of mothers; but we have no information on differences in the types of smiles shown.

Decoding Studies

As is true for encoding studies, the majority of research concerned with the decoding of smiles has been mute with regard to the nature of those smiles, leaving us to wonder what differences there may have been as a function of type of smile depicted. On the one hand, cross-cultural research by Ekman and Friesen and their colleagues (e.g., Ekman, Sorensen, & Friesen, 1969) has made use of stimuli that include a Duchenne smile, that is, a smile whose characteristics tend to be associated with displays shown during positive experiences. With the use of this type of smile, reliable interpretations were made concerning the presence of happy affect.

In other research, however, such may not have been the case. For example, Keating et al. (1981), in their cross-cultural study of the affective and dominance implications of facial displays, made of use of stimuli that included a "slight smile." Although these "slight" smiles typically were seen as "happy," there were a surprising number of exceptions. That is, a substantial number of observers from some cultures identified few of the smiling faces as happy. Conceivably, this may have been due to the introduction of some smiles that lacked eye involvement, that is, the use of smiles that could be identified as potentially insincere.

Adult judges show relatively low discriminative ability when asked to rate the happiness of individuals manifesting authentic or felt smiles as opposed to polite or unfelt smiles (Ekman et al., 1988). We do not, however, know the extent to which they show differential *behavioral* responses to the two patterns of smiles during actual interaction. We argue that it is important to determine actual response patterns to smiles as well as judgments of smiles. Affective displays may easily be conceptualized as elicting preconscious or unaware response patterns (e.g., Epstein, 1984) that are less likely to be reflected in judgment processes but may influence behavior.

Authentic Versus Polite Smiles to Children

A program of research initiated by Bugental and her colleagues (Bugental, 1986; Bugental, 1989; Bugental, Blue & Lewis, 1990; Bugental, Caporael, & Shennum, 1980; Bugental & Shennum, 1984) has concerned the differential reaction of women to "difficult" (unresponsive, uncooperative) and "easy" (responsive, cooperative) children. This research provided the opportunity to observe the features of smiles shown to difficult children versus easy children. It was expected that features believed to be associated with *authentic* smiles would be more common during interactions with easy children and that features believed to be associated with *polite* smiles would be more common during interactions with difficult children. Additionally, it was anticipated that women with more adaptive caregiving beliefs (high perceived control) would show more authentic smiles, whereas women with less adaptive care-giving beliefs (low perceived control) would show relatively more polite smiles.

In one such study, the timing features of adult smiles shown to difficult children were compared with the timing features of adult smiles shown to easy children (Bugental, 1986). The children with whom adults interacted were either trained or selected to act in a socially responsive (difficult) or unresponsive (easy) fashion. Smiles directed to difficult children were found to be characterized by unusual offset properties, that is, smiles were likely to end quite abruptly. Additionally, women with low perceived control as care givers were likely to show unusual smiling onset properties, that is, their smiles showed rather abrupt onsets. It is likely that these unusual timing features were a side effect of the *strategic* production of polite smiles (as opposed to the production of smiles in response to felt pleasure). In a reciprocal feedback pattern, children were observed to become increasingly unresponsive when interacting with women whose smiles manifested these relatively unusual timing features.

More recently, Bugental and her colleagues (Bugental, 1989; Bugental, Blue, & Lewis, 1990) have been concerned with affect directed to children from distressed or abusive family backgrounds. We videotaped children from families in counseling at a child abuse agency interacting with their mothers. Some of the mothers in counseling had abused their children and some had not. The only expressive behavior that distinguished abusive from nonabusive mothers was their use of the authentic smile. The authentic smile was defined as a smile that was accompanied by cheek lifting and orbicularis oculi action and that was *not* accompanied by facial action units (AUs) suggesting other meanings. Abusive mothers showed a markedly depressed use of such smiles, producing authentic (Duchenne) smiles at a rate of 1.3/min in contrast with the rate of 2.5/min shown by nonabusive mothers. Depressed levels of authentic smiles appear to be associated with the dysphoria more commonly found in abusive families.

We went on to observe the interactions between children from families in counseling and strangers (unrelated mothers) (Bugental, 1989; Bugental, Blue, & Cruzcosa, 1989; Bugental, Blue, & Lewis, 1990). We observed the interaction of these women with two children drawn from distressed families—one of whom was more likely to be seen as difficult at home (and more likely to be abused) and one of whom was more likely to be seen as easy (and less likely to be abused). Measures were taken of the frequency of occurrence of happy and sad affect in both vocal intonation and facial behavior. Unrelated mothers were found to show selective differences in their responses to these two groupings of children. Specifically, they directed more dysphoric nonverbal affect to difficult children than to easy children. *Authentic smiles* were produced at a rate of 3.1/min in interaction with difficult children and 3.3/min in interaction with easy children (although this difference did not reach significance, it was consistent with the overall difference found in affect directed to difficult and easy children).

We also measured the use of *polite smiles* by unrelated women during their interactions with difficult and easy children. Polite smiles included a number of deviations from the previously described pattern of authentic smiles: (a) smiles that were not accompanied by cheek lifting and orbicularis oculi action, (b) smiles that were accompanied by facial actions associated with negative affect (e.g., a "worried brow"), and (c) smiles that were accompanied by raised eyebrows (typically used in conversation regulation). Women with low perceived control—in particular, those who attributed high negative control to children—produced an unusually high frequency of polite smiles during interactions with difficult children. These women produced polite smiles at the rate of 1.26/min with difficult children but only .39/min with easy children. In contrast, women with higher levels of perceived control produced polite smiles at a rate of .50/min with difficult children and .68/min with easy children.

This line of research gave general support for our expectations. In particular, smile features associated with polite smiles were found to be more common for women with lower levels of perceived control during interactions with difficult children.

Children's Understanding of Complex Affective Messages

Given the fact that meaningful distinctions can be made between adult *use* of authentic versus polite smiles, it is important to determine the extent to which children actually do respond to these distinctions. Although we know little about developmental or individual differences in response to smiles per se, a substantial literature discusses children's affective decoding abilities and acquisition of cultrual rules for affective displays.

Developmental Shifts in Processing Complex Affective Messages

By middle childhood, children manifest an increased level of sophistication in processing conflicted or deceptive emotional information as a combined function of specific learning and increased ability to make inferences regarding the inner states of others. By this age, they have come to understand that expressed and experienced affect need not be correspondent (e.g., Gnepp, 1983; Saarni, 1984). Research that has concerned children's resolution of complex affective messages has focused on (a) their changing ability to resolve conflicting affective cues, and/or (b) their increasing understanding of deception. Early research by Bugental et al. (1970) suggested that cues to negative affect receive greater weight than cues to positive affect in the processing of inconsistent messages by young children. A developmental shift has been found in middle childhood in the ability to recognize deception and to understand the cues that might be used as indicators of deception (Blanck & Rosenthal, 1982; DePaulo & Jordan, 1982). Rotenberg et al. (1989) have suggested that children may respond to inconsistency itself as a cue to the presence of deception; use of inconsistency information is, however, more frequently used with increasing age (see Chapter 4 for a more complete discussion of relevant developmental issues in inconsistency resolution). Additionally, some evidence indicates that children may place increasing reliance on visual (as opposed to auditory) information with increased age (Zuckerman, Blanck, DePaulo & Rosenthal, 1980).

Other investigators have directed their attention to children's developing understanding of display rules. Saarni's program of research has documented the developmental shifts in children's understanding and use of cultural display rules (a concept introduced by Ekman and Friesen, 1969)—rules that necessarily involve deception (Saarni, 1979, 1984). Children come to understand that certain affects should be hidden or masked, either in the service of protecting the feelings of others or in the service of avoiding negative reactions from others. Saarni's initial resarch (1979) demonstrated that across middle childhood, children become increasingly aware of the "rules" regarding such polite deceptions. Subsequently, Gnepp and Hess (1986) have confirmed that children's knowledge concerning the appropriate use of emotional displays shows a clear increase at this stage of development.

Although a great deal of attention has been given to children's responses to facial affect as a whole (including the smile), we have little evidence with regard to children's ability to distinguish between authentic versus polite smiles. Saarni's research (1984) has produced some suggestive leads in this connection, however. She found that among older children, receipt of a disappointing gift (in comparison with a suitable gift) led to a decline in broader smiles but an increase in "*slight smiles*" (presumably, smiles lacking eye involvement and thus categorizable as polite smiles). Apparently, during middle childhood, children increasingly make use of polite smiles in their management of their own expressive behavior. Still unanswered, however, is the question concerning developmental changes in their ability to distinguish such subtleties in the facial behaviors of others.

Individual Differences in Processing Complex Affective Messages

Developmental shifts in response to complex affective messages can be understood as reflecting an interplay between the child's emerging cognitive abilities and their specific learning experiences. Very reasonably, then, it can be anticipated that differences in socialization history will influence their processing of affective information.

GENDER DIFFERENCES

The greatest concern with individual differences in children's response to affective messages has been with gender effects. Girls typically receive more extensive socialization regarding polite or considerate expressive deception—for example, hiding negative reactions that might hurt someone else's feelings or displaying polite positive behavior to make someone else feel good (e.g., Block, 1973). Consistent with this expectation, girls have been found to be able to manage their expressive displays at younger ages than are boys (e.g., Saarni, 1984). Additionally, Shennum and Bugental (1982) found distinctions in the types of encoding skills acquired by boys and girls; during middle childhood, boys became more adept in concealing negative affect (hiding negative affect with a neutral expression), whereas girls became more adept in dissimulation (e.g., using a smile to cover negative affect).

Rosenthal and DePaulo (1979) have suggested that females, beginning in childhood, are more nonverbally accommodating than are males. That is, they follow "politeness norms" in their decoding of messages and interpret the expressive displays of others in ways that are intended by those individuals. This accommodation involves increased attention to facial expressions (intentional displays) and reduced attention to vocal cues (less controlled and more revealing of hidden affect). Although this same pattern is found for boys, it emerges at a younger age for girls (Blanck, Rosenthal, Snodgrass, DePaulo, & Zuckerman, 1981).

DISTRESSED FAMILY BACKGROUND

Even though the increased cognitive skills of middle childhood bring the possibility of improved inference capacities in understanding the inner states of others, a suitable social environment is needed before such skills can be developed. Children who have experienced emotionally distressed socialization may not have had opportunities for acquiring the knowledge structures and social inference competencies necessary for skilled interpretation of the expressive behavior of others. In some cases, dysfunctional family systems may act to foster the retention of immature patterns of emotional interpetation. For example, Reilly, Muzekari, and Goldman (1979) found that emotionally disturbed children, regardless of age, manifested a decoding pattern more typical of younger children. Specifically, they were more likely to rely on verbal content in the interpretation of ambiguous expressive behavior.

In general, parents who show deficiencies in their own emotional expression have been found to have children who have poorly developed expressive and decoding skills (e.g., Daly, Abramovtich, & Pilner, 1980). Recently, particular attention has been directed to the emotional environment of physically abused children. Research has concerned both typical affective patterns shown in these families and the expressive and decoding accuracy of family members. Both abusive parents and their children have been found to display high levels of negative affect and low levels of positive affect in their interpersonal behavior (George & Main, 1979; Lyons-Ruth, Connell, Zoll, & Stahl, 1987; Main & George, 1985; Trickett & Kuczynski, 1986). Camras and her colleagues (Camras, Grow, & Ribordy, 1983; Camras, Ribordy, Hill, Martino, Spaccarelli, & Stefani, 1988) also found that both abusive mothers and their children are deficient posers and processors of expressive information. Rieder and Cicchetti (1989) have shown that maltreated children are particularly likely to show discrepant response patterns compared with nonmaltreated children in their response to aggressive cues.

Deficiencies in the production and processing of expressive cues by children from abusive families (or other emotionally conflicted families) are likely to have had multiple causation. Most directly, abused children have had poor role models in their parents. Abusive parents show poorly developed social skills (Spinetta & Rigler, 1972), a pattern that is mirrored in the hostile, unskilled social behaviors of their children (George & Main, 1979). Additionally, the level of negative affect and arousal that characterizes their home life can be expected to lead to a narrowed and inefficient social information-processing system (e.g., Isen, 1984). Wolfe (1985), in his review of the literature on child abuse, noted that abusive parents appear to be highly reactive to a variety of types of life stressors. Life events are more readily interpreted as posing a source of threat. It is likely that abused children themselves experience elevated levels of reactivity to potential sources of threat or stress. Just as the aggressive children studied by Dodge and his colleagues (e.g., Dodge, Murphy, & Buchsbaum, 1984) have been shown to interpret ambiguous events in a hostile fashion (and thus, court confirming hostile responses from others), abused children can be expected to have a hostile explanatory bias in response to ambiguous social encounters.

Study of Children's Responses to Authentic Versus Polite Smiles

Up to this point, we have reviewed information regarding the differential production of smiles by adults, and some of the potential differences that one might expect in children's reponses to smiles. Adults who experience difficulty in interacting with a child show an elevated level of polite smiles and a decreased level of authentic smiles. In middle childhood, well-functioning children show an increased capacity to make inferences about the expressive behavior of others, including more complex affective displays; they have improved information-processing skills, and they have been specifically socialized with regard to culturally normative affective displays, including the use and understanding of polite deceptions. Children from abusive backgrounds, however, may lack both social information-processing skills and relevant socialization. This impairment may lead them to a very general wariness in response to complex or ambiguous social cues. It was anticipated that greater avoidance would be manifested by young children in response to polite rather than authentic smiles; but this pattern was expected to be present at all ages among children from abusive backgrounds.

Visual responsiveness (maintenance or breaking of gaze) was selected as a variable that may yield information about wariness in response to social cues. Beginning in infancy, gaze acts to maximize visual information and represents an indicator of social interest; conversely, gaze aversion acts to terminate social interaction and limits levels of arousal. By the third quarter of the first year of life, gaze aversion can be regularly observed as a response to fear-inducing situations (Waters, Matas, & Sroufe, 1975). Although gaze maintenance has the potential for increased information acquisition, it may also act to increase risk in potentially agonistic social interactions. Ethologists have noted that many species of animals have been found to manifest eye aversion as a way of cutting off social interaction and thus warding off potential attack (Chance, 1962). This strategy appears to be more common among submissive animals (Hall & DeVore, 1965). In our past research, we observed a relationship between abuse history and visual unresponsiveness (Bugental, Blue, & Lewis, 1990). In the present investigation, the goal was to test the extent to which the polite smile may act to elicit this behavior.

Subjects

ABUSED AND NONABUSED CHILDREN

Bugental, et al. (Bugental, Blue, & Cruzcosa, 1990; Bugental, et al., 1989) recruited forty families undergoing counseling at a local child-abuse agency for participation. As described elsewhere, half of the families seen had a recent history of physical abuse; mothers in the other half of the families were concerned about their potential to be abusive but had not actually abused any of their children. The examiners assessed abuse by a combination of maternal report on the Conflict Tactics Scale (Straus, Gelles, & Steinmetz, 1980) and counselor report. The Conflict Tactics Scale identifies the following behaviors as abusive: kicking, biting, hitting, beating up, and threatening with or use of weapon. Within each family, ratings (Conflict Tactics Scale) were obtained on all children between the ages of 3 and 13. Although the examiners observed two children within each family (for other purposes), the sample employed here was limited to one child from each family. Nineteen children were drawn from families with a history of abuse, and 18 children were drawn from families without such a history (3 cases were lost because of the absence of any instances of polite smiles). Children were selected for balanced distribution across age groupings. Age groups were 3 to 6 years ($N = 11$), 7 to 9 years ($N = 12$), and 10 to 13 years ($N = 14$). The sample included 24 boys and 13 girls.

UNRELATED MOTHERS

Forty women (mothers of children between the ages of 3 and 13) were recruited from the community by the use of publicly placed ads. Their mean age was 38.6 ($SD = 7.1$), and their mean education was 15.3 years ($SD = 2.0$).

Procedure

PARENT ATTRIBUTION TEST

In advance of observational procedures, all adult subjects were given the Parent Attribution Test (PAT). The PAT (described in Bugental, Blue, & Cruzcosa, 1989) assesses causal attributions for care-giving success and failure. In our past research, dysfunctional interactions have been found to be associated with low perceived "balance of control" over care-giving failure. That is, care givers who respond to more difficult children with more negative affect and coercive care giving are likely to attribute low control to self and high control to children over care-giving failure.

MEASUREMENT OF FACIAL EXPRESSION

The investigators videotaped interactions between adults and children at the agency where families were seen in counseling. The observation area was set up as a waiting room with a mirror on one wall. Chairs were placed in preset positions for comfortable conversation. Two cameras behind the mirror were focused to give a close-up view of the adult's face and the child's face, respectively. The investigators instructed subjects to "just talk to each other for a few minutes while we get the game set up" (a second part of the study, which is not relevant for the present investigation). For all dyads, 4 min of videotaped interaction was obtained (images were fed through a special effects generator to give a split-screen image of the two interactants). A time code was placed on all tapes during this initial recording.

For each adult–child dyad, the interaction was analyzed by means of Ekman and Friesen's Facial Action Coding System (FACS) (Ekman & Friesen, 1978). The FACS coder was blind to descriptive information on the adults being rated. She was trained on FACS (Ekman & Friesen, 1978) and had a reliability of .76 on standard messages provided within the FACS training system. All affects were coded on the basis of Ekman and Friesen's Emotion Dictionary. Authentic smiles were defined as those that also included lifted cheeks and orbicularis oculi action (AU 6) but did not include action units associated with other competing affects. Polite smiles included (a) smiles that were not accompanied by AU 6 (43% of polite smiles); (b) smiles accompanied by action units associated with negative affects (e.g., AU 4, AU 10, AU 1 + 4) (26% of polite smiles); and (c) smiles that included action units associated with conversation regulation, e.g., AU 1 + 2 (brow flash) (31% of polite smiles).

To establish the independence and affective meaning of authentic and polite smiles, we obtained correlations between frequencies of these two patterns and facial sadness. Authentic smiles were not significantly related to polite smiles ($r = -.10$). Authentic smiles were negatively and sig-

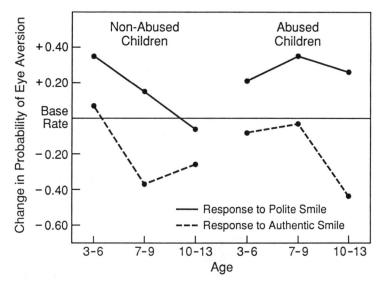

FIGURE 5.1. Eye aversion shown by abused and nonabused children in response to polite versus authentic smiles of unrelated adults.

nificantly correlated with sad facial effect ($r = -.31$), whereas polite smiles were *positively* correlated with sad facial affect ($r = .32$).

We also conducted a preliminary analysis of the verbal content associated with authentic versus polite smiles to establish that any effects of smiles were not simply artifacts of associated content. Four judges (mothers of school-aged children) made independent judgments of all messages produced by adult subjects; ratings were made on 7-point scales that ranged from +3 (pleasant, friendly) to −3 (unpleasant, unfriendly). An analysis of variance estimate of interjudge reliability (Winer, 1962) yielded a coefficient of .73. The average rating given to messages associated with polite smiles (smiles that occurred during messages or within 1 s following messages) was 1.05 ($SD = .41$). The average rating given to messages associated with authentic smiles was 1.03 ($SD = .36$). The difference between these means yielded a nonsignificant t of .20.

Results and Discussion

Child eye aversion was assessed during the time period immediately following different types of adult smiles. We calculated conditional probability indices for eye aversion during the 5 s following adults' polite smiles, authentic smiles, and eight randomly selected times (no significant relationships or trends were found between base-rate eye aversion levels shown during random times and individual difference variables, that is, age, gender, and abuse history of child).

OVERALL CHILD DIFFERENCE IN RESPONSE TO POLITE VERSUS AUTHENTIC SMILES OF ADULTS

In the first analysis, child eye aversion measures were compared in a repeated measures analysis of variance. A comparison was made of child eye aversion following three stimulus conditions: authentic smiles by adults, polite smiles by adults, and random times. The main effect for stimulus condition was significant; $F(2, 62) = 30.17, p < .001$. Eye aversion was significantly greater following polite smiles by adults than following random times; and eye aversion was significantly lower following authentic smiles by adults than following random times (post-hoc Tukey tests were found to be significant, at better than the .01 level of confidence). In other words, the results showed a significant difference in the way children (across age and history) responded to polite versus authentic smiles. Authentic smiles were very likely to elicit levels of sustained gaze (low eye aversion) that exceeded base rates, whereas polite smiles were more likely to elicit eye aversion. Thus, the two types of smiles appear to have quite different stimulus value.

DIFFERENTIAL RESPONSE PATTERNS OF CHILDREN FROM ABUSIVE VERSUS NONABUSIVE FAMILIES

A significant interaction was found between age and family abuse history, $F(4, 62) = 2.62, p = .043$. The pattern of age-related change for children from abused versus nonabused families is shown in Figure 5.1. Eye aversion is shown as the change from base rates, that is, increased or decreased levels of child eye aversion following adults' smiles in comparison with base rates of child eye aversion shown during random time periods. Below the age of 7, children from nonabusive families showed elevated eye aversion in response to the polite smiles of strangers, but by age 10, they showed no significant deviation from base rates. Follow-up analyses were conducted in which separate comparisons were made for (a) increased eye aversion in response to *polite* smiles (i.e., difference in eye aversion to polite smiles versus base-rate times) and (b) decreased eye aversion (gaze maintenance) in response to *authentic* smiles. For elevated eye aversion to *polite* smiles, a trend was found for the interaction between age and abuse history, $F(2, 31) = 2.58, p = .092$. A post-hoc t test comparing the predicted difference between the oldest and the youngest age groups for nonabusive families was significant at the .01 level of confidence ($t = 2.73$).

No significant effects were found for visual responses to *authentic* smiles. A trend, however, was found for age, $F(2, 31) = 2.68, p = .084$. Children (in both groups) showed an increase in gaze maintenance to polite smiles with age.

To check on the possibility that children's response patterns were limited to interactions with strangers, a limited analysis was conducted on visual response patterns to smiles produced by their own mothers. Although too few *related* mothers (N = 15) manifested polite smiles for a full analysis of interactions in related dyads, clearly children showed the same pattern of elevated eye aversion to polite smiles with their own mothers as they did with unrelated women. The effect of eliciting conditions was significant, F (2, 26) = 3.81, p = .035; the highest levels of eye aversion by children were shown in response to polite smiles of their own mothers (in comparison with random times or authentic smiles). Thus, the observed eye aversion appears to occur in response to the stimulus properties of the expression rather than simply to "strange behavior by a stranger."

In *nonabusive families*, a regular course of development appears to occur in visual approach and avoidance in response to smiles. Even though younger children showed that they could distinguish authentic and polite smiles (they continued gazing at base-rate levels with the former and showed elevated eye aversion for the latter), they did not as yet show a "mature" response pattern. They responded to the polite smiles with visual withdrawal, that is, as if this facial behavior had threat value as a cue. At this younger age, children do not yet understand the complex cultural rules that dictate polite behavior; thus, the polite smile may have had significance only as a discrepant stimulus. Eye aversion in this case may be understood as reflecting emotion regulation, behavior that serves the function of avoiding excess levels of negative affect or arousal (Campos, Campos, & Barrett, 1989; Campos & Stenberg, 1978).

By 10 years of age, nonabused children did not show significant visual approach or avoidance to the polite smiles of strangers (i.e., their visual behavior continued at base-rate levels). Polite smiles could now be thought of as being "disregarded." By this age, children know and understand that expressed and experienced affect do not necessarily match and that many occasions are defined as calling for a "polite smile"; that is, the expression of a smile may come to be understood as (a) not necessarily reflecting a correspondent inner state of the other person and (b) being motivated by social display rules. Thus, the polite smile is no longer a cue to potential threat.

Children who had a family history of *abuse*, on the other hand, failed to show any developmental change in their response to polite smiles. They showed the usual level of eye aversion at younger ages, but no change in this pattern was found across middle childhood. These children continued to respond to polite smiles with withdrawal responses, suggesting that they had not learned cultural rules regarding the implications of such expressive patterns. Their pattern of withdrawal suggests that they continued to react to these discrepant displays as if they posed a threat. Although such a response appears to be quite normative for younger children, it may be relatively unusual and maladaptive for older children. Eye aversion serves the short-term goal of reducing excess negative stimulation or arousal but ultimately fosters dysfunctional relationships. Eye aversion in response to strangers not only may increase the discomfort of those adults, it also decreases the opportunity the child might have for learning about relatively complex communication patterns.

An example from an interaction between an abused boy (age 13) and an unrelated mother (whose attributional style reflected low perceived control over negative events by self but high perceived control by children) illustrates the process of interest.

The unrelated mother directs the initial conversation with a series of questions about school and comparisons with the boy's brother with whom she had just interacted. She appears friendly and smiles broadly, and regularly raises her eyebrows in inquiry. The boy initially gives a returning smile and returns her gaze. Within a short period of time, he increasingly looks away as her rapid dialogue, and questioning continues.

(Adult) "What do you like to do?" [brief pause] "Do you like to play soccer? Or . . . "

(Child) "Softball" [interrupting her and looking away]

(Adult) "Football!" [She exclaims as she nods and strains the already unnaturally broad smile on her face, which she has maintained since the beginning of the interaction. Her eyes are squinting, lips are stretched tightly back showing her teeth; her teeth remain parted even during the brief pauses when she is not talking.]

(Adult) "'Cause your brother likes soccer, he was telling me, and volleyball." [She nods.] "So, do you play on a team?"

(Child) [The boy briefly glances at her, no longer smiling, and a somewhat anxious expression appears on his face.] "No." [He quietly responds.]

(Adult) [She shakes her head and giggles through her strained smile.] "No? You just play with the neighborhood boys?"

(Child) [The boy nods, while looking behind him at the ceiling.]

From this point on, the stage is set for the remainder of the interaction. The boy occasionally glances at the mother (usually when she briefly looks away from him), and then averts his eyes and fidgets while she continues with her rapid pace series of questions. The only variations in her exaggerated grin is an occasional lip licking. Her eyes are either opened wide or in a tight squint. She consistently leans forward, steadfastly maintaining her gaze on the boy's face.

(Adult) "Do you guys have bikes?"

[He looks down quickly and mumbles his reply.] "No."

(Adult) "No?" [She giggles and tilts her head to one side, her smile continuing.]

(Adult) "What's your best friend's name?

(Child) "None."

(Adult) [Laughs] "You have lots of friends, huh?"

(The boy drops his head and nods very slightly.)

(Adult) [Nods and continues on] "Good, what's your favorite subject in school?"

GENDER DIFFERENCES IN RESPONSE TO SMILES

We conducted an analysis to test the interactive effects of gender and age on eye aversion. The interaction between gender, age, and eliciting condition approached significance, $F(4, 62) = 2.47$, $p = .054$. (Sample limitations did not allow a fully crossed analysis of abuse history, gender, and

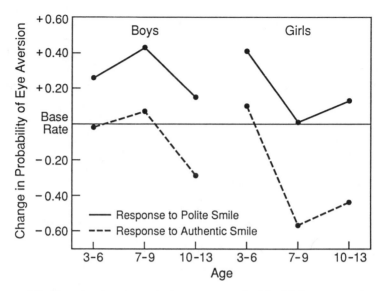

FIGURE 5.2. Eye aversion shown by boys compared with girls in response to polite versus authentic smiles of unrelated adults.

age; in an independent analysis that included abuse history and sex as grouping variables and eliciting condition as a repeated measure, we found no significant effects as function of the interaction between gender and abuse history.) The pattern (shown in Figure 5.2) should only be taken as taken as suggestive. Girls showed a trend toward a more "mature" visual response pattern at a somewhat younger age than did boys. That is, they showed a decline in eye aversion to polite smiles and an increase in gaze to authentic smiles at a younger age than did boys.

This slight advantage for girls in age at which more "polite" decoding occurs is consistent with typical gender-related findings. The differences found may reflect the same process of "nonverbal accommodation" observed by Blanck et al. (1981) to emerge at a younger age for girls than boys. Although there is no reason to believe that there are any differences in social inference abilities between boys and girls during middle childhood, there is reason to believe that they are the differential recipients of socialization concerning facial display rules.

Summary and Conclusions

We have shown preliminary support in this chapter for differential development in the acquisition of culturally "appropriate" response patterns to the polite deceptions of strangers in ordinary interactions. We have focused our attention on the polite smile as an extremely common deception tactic in human interaction. Among children less than 7 years of age, we found that children seemed to be captured by the perceptual salience of this type of display, possibly because of the discrepancy it poses from more usual facial displays observed with familiar adults. At this younger age, children typically responded with eye aversion. In contrast, they responded to authentic smiles with continuation of base-rate levels of visual behavior. By age 10, however, most children showed a change in their pattern of response to polite versus authentic smiles. They now disregarded polite smiles (i.e., they continued with base-rate levels of visual behavior) but showed somewhat elevated levels of sustained gaze in response to authentic smiles. This new pattern may reflect an increased understanding of the significance of these two types of smiles. The polite smile may now be understood as a minor deception commonly used in many situations, rather than as a discrepant stimulus that elicits social withdrawal. The authentic smile, on the other hand, appears to be accepted as a positive overture and receives the culturally appropriate response of sustained visual atention.

The exceptions we found to this developmental course suggest the importance of differential socialization experiences. For example, girls appeared to acquire an understanding of the subtleties of these facial displays at a somewhat younger age than do boys. This is not unexpected in view of the somewhat greater emphasis given to social courtesies and consideration in the socialization experiences of girls.

Perhaps our most important finding concerns the differential developmental course shown by children from abusive versus nonabusive families in response to polite smiles. The only significant developmental shifts were found for children from nonabusive families. These children showed changes that suggest increased sophistication in their understanding of the subtle implications of facial displays. Children from abusive families, on the other hand, showed little change. At all ages, they showed strong eye aversion to the polite smiles of strangers. Our findings are, of course, based on a relatively small sample—requiring appropriate caution in conclusions that can be drawn. The observed pattern is, however, consistent with previous findings of others, in particular with the findings of Camras and her colleagues (Camras et al., 1983), who observed that abused children are deficient in their ability to process affective information.

Our findings add to past research in that they suggest that children from dysfunctional families show an avoidance pattern that acts to maintain their social disadvantage. Visual withdrawal acts to reduce their immediate distress but ultimately acts both to foster negative reactions from others and to limit information-processing. Thus, the social deficits of these children may perpetuate social wariness and continued social interaction problems.

References

Barden, R.C., Zelko, F.A., Duncan, S.W., & Masters, J.C. (1980). Children's consensual knowledge about the experiential determinants of emotion. *Journal of Personality and Social Psychology, 39,* 968–976.

Blanck. P.D., & Rosenthal, R. (1982). Developing strategies for decoding "leaky" messages: On learning how and when to decode discrepant and consistent social communications. In R.S. Feldman (Ed.), *Development of nonverbal behavior in children* (pp. 203–229). New York: Springer-Verlag.

Blanck, P.D., Rosenthal, R., Snodgrass, S.E., DePaulo, B.M., & Zuckerman, M. (1981). Sex differences in eavesdropping on nonverbal cues: Developmental change. *Journal of Personality and Social Psychology, 41,* 391–398.

Block, J.H. (1973). Conceptions of sex role: Some cross-cultural and longitudinal perspectives. *American Psychologist, 28,* 512–526.

Buck, R. (1984). *The communication of emotion.* New York: Guilford Press.

Bugental, D.B. (1986). Unmasking the "polite smile": Situational and personal determinants of managed affect in adult–child interaction. *Personality and Social Psychology Bulletin, 12,* 7–16.

Bugental, D.B. (April, 1989). *A social developmental view of child abuse.* Paper presented at the meeting of the Society for Research in Child Development, Kansas City.

Bugental, D.B., Blue, J., & Cruzcosa, M. (1989). Perceived control over caregiving outcomes: Implications for child abuse. *Developmental Psychology, 25,* 532–539.

Bugental, D.B., Blue, J., & Lewis, J. (1990). Caregiver cognitions as moderators of affective reactions to "difficult" children. *Developmental Psychology, 26,* 631–638.

Bugental, D.B., Caporael, L., & Shennum, W.A. (1980). Experimentally-produced child uncontrollability: Effects on the potency of adult communication patterns. *Child Development, 51,* 520–528.

Bugental, D.E., Kaswan, J., & Love, L. (1970). Perception of contradictory meanings conveyed by verbal and nonverbal channels. *Journal of Personality and Social Psychology, 16,* 647–655.

Bugental, D.E., Love, L.R., & Gianetto, R.M. (1971). Perfidious feminine faces. *Journal of Personality and Social Psychology, 17,* 314–318.

Bugental, D.B., & Shennum, W.A. (1984). "Difficult" children as elicitors and targets of adult communication patterns: An attributional-behavioral transactional analysis. *Monographs of the Society for Research in Child Development, 49*(Serial No. 205, 1).

Campos, J.J., Campos, R.G., & Barrett, K.C. (1989). Emergent themes in the study of emotional development and emotion regulation. *Developmental Psychology, 25,* 395–402.

Campos, J.J., & Stenberg, C. (1978). Perception, appraisal and emotion: The onset of social referencing. In M.E. Lamb, & L.R. Sherrod (Eds.), *Infant social cognition* (pp. 273–314). Hillsdale, NJ: Lawrence Erlbaum.

Camras, L.A., Grow, J.G., & Ribordy, S.C. (1983). Recognition of facial expression by abused children. *Journal of Clinical Child Psychology, 12,* 325–328.

Camras, L.A., Ribordy, S., Hill, J., Martino, S., Spaccarelli, S., & Stefani, R. (1988). Recognition and posing or emotional expressions by abused children and their mothers. *Developmental Psychology, 24,* 776–781.

Chance, M.R.A. (1962). The interpretation of some agonistic postures: the role of "cut-off" acts and postures. *Symposium of the Zoological Society of London, 8,* 71–89.

Daly, E., Abramovitch, R., & Pilner, P. (1980). The relationship between mothers' encoding and their children's decoding of facial expressions of emotion. *Merrill-Palmer Quarterly, 26,* 25–37.

Dawkins, R., & Krebs, J.R. (1978). Animal signals: Information or manipulation? In J.R. Krebs, & N.B. Davies (Ed.), *Behavioural ecology,* (pp. 282–309). Sunderland, MA: Sinauer.

DePaulo, B.M., & Jordan, A. (1982) Age changes in deceiving and detecting deceit. In R.S. Feldman (Ed.), *Development of nonverbal behavior in children* (pp. 151–180). New York: Springer-Verlag.

Dodge, K.A., Murphy, R.R., & Buchsbaum, K. (1984). The assessment of intention-cue detection skills in children: Implications for developmental psychopathology. *Child Development, 55,* 163–173.

Ekman, P. (1971). Universal and cultural differences in facial expressions of emotion. In J. Cole (Eds.), *Nebraska symposium on motivation* (pp. 207–283). Lincoln: University of Nebraska Press.

Ekman, P., Davidson, R., & Friesen, W.V. (1990). The Duchenne smile: Emotional expression and brain physiology II. *Journal of Personality and Social Psychology, 58,* 342–353.

Ekman, P., & Friesen, W.V. (1978). *Manual for the facial affect coding system.* Palo Alto, CA: Consulting Psychologists Press.

Ekman, P., & Friesen, W.V. (1982). Felt, false, and miserable smiles. *Journal of Nonverbal Behavior, 6,* 238–252.

Ekman, P., Friesen, W.V., & O'Sullivan, M. (1988). Smiles while lying. *Journal of Personality and Social Psychology, 54,* 414–420.

Ekman, P., Sorenson, E.R., & Friesen, W.V. (1969). Pancultural elements in facial displays of emotion. *Science, 164,* 86–88.

Epstein, S. (1984). Controversial issues in emotion theory. In P. Shaver (Ed.), *Review of Personality and Social Psychology* (pp. 64–88). Beverly Hills, CA: Sage.

Fridlund, A.J. (In press). *Sociality of solitary smiling: Potentiation by an implicit audience. Journal of Personality and Social Psychology.*

George, C., & Main, M. (1979). Social interactions of young abused children: Approach, avoidance, and aggression. *Child Development, 50,* 306–318.

Gnepp, J. (1983). Children's social sensitivity: Inferring emotions from conflicting cues. *Developmental Psychology, 19,* 805–814.

Gnepp, J., & Hess, D.L.R. (1986). Children's understanding of verbal and facial display rules. *Development Psychology, 22,* 103–108.

Hall, K.R.L., & De Vore, I. (1965). Baboon social behavior. In I. De Vore (Ed.), *Primate Behavior* (pp. 241–270). New York: Holt.

Ickes, W., Patterson, M.L., Rajecki, D.W., & Tanford, S. (1982). Behavioral and cognitive consequences of reciprocal versus compensatory responses to pre-interaction expectancies. *Social Cognition, 1,* 160–190.

Isen, A.M. (1984). Toward understanding the role of affect in cognition. In R.S. Wyer, Jr., & T.K. Srull (Eds.), *Handbook of social cognition* (Vol, 3, pp. 179–236). Hillsdale, NJ: Lawrence Erlbaum.

Izard, C.E., & Malatesta, C.Z. (1987). Perspectives on emotional development: I. Differential emotions theory of early emotional development. In J. Osofsky (Eds.), *Handbook of infant development* (pp. 494–554). New York: Wiley-Interscience.

Keating, C.F., Mazur, A., Segall, M.H., Cysneiros, P.G., Divale, W.T., Kilbride, J.E., Komin, S., Leahy, P., Thurman, B., & Wirsing, R. (1981). Culture and the perception of social dominance from facial expression. *Journal of Personality and Social Psychology, 40*, 615–626.

Lyons-Ruth, K., Connell, D.B., Zoll, D., & Stahl, J. (1987). Infants at social risk: Relations among infant maltreatment, maternal behavior, and infant attachment behavior. *Developmental Psychology, 23*, 223–232.

Main, M., & George, C. (1985). Responses of abused and disadvantaged toddlers to distress in agemates: A study in the day care setting. *Development Psychology, 21*, 407–412.

Reilly, S.S., & Muzekari, L.H. & Goldman, A.R. (1979). Responses of normal and disturbed adults and children to mixed messages. *Journal of Abnormal Psychology, 88*, 203–208.

Rieder, C., & Cicchetti, D. (1989). Organizational perspectives on cognitive control functioning and cognitive-affective balance in maltreated children. *Developmental Psychology, 25*, 382–393.

Rosenthal, R., & De Paulo, B.M. (1979). Sex differences in eavesdropping on nonverbal cues. *Journal of Personality and Social Psychology, 37*, 273–285.

Rotenberg, K.J., Simourd, L., & Moore, D. (1989). Children's use of a verbal–nonverbal consistency principle to infer truth from lying. *Child Development, 60*, 309–322.

Saarni, C. (1979). Children's understanding of display rules for expressive behavior. *Developmental Psychology, 15*, 424–429.

Saarni, C. (1984). An observational study of children's attempts to monitor their expressive behavior. *Child Development, 15*, 424–429.

Shennum, W.A., & Bugental, D.B. (1982). The development of control over affective expression in nonverbal behavior. In R.S. Feldman (Ed.), *Development of nonverbal behavior in children* (pp. 101–121). New York: Springer.

Spinetta, J.J., & Rigler, D. (1972). The child-abusing parent: A psychological review. *Psychological Bulletin, 77*, 296–304.

Strauss, M.A. Gelles, R.J., & Steinmetz, S.K. (1980). *Behind closed doors: Violence in the American family.* New York: Anchor Press.

Trickett, P.K., & Kuczynski, L. (1986). Children's misbehaviors and parental discipline strategies in abusive and nonabusive families. *Developmental Psychology, 21*, 115–123.

van Hooff, J.A.R.A.M. (1972). A comparative approach to the phylogeny of laughter and smiling. In R.A. Hinde (Ed.), *Non-verbal communication* (pp. 209–237). Cambridge, England: Cambridge University Press.

Waters, E., Matas, L., & Sroufe, L.A. (1975). Infants' reactions to an approaching stranger: Description, validation and functional significance of wariness. *Child Development, 46*, 348–505.

Weiss, B., & Blum, G. (1987). Anatomically based measurement of facial expressions in simulated versus hypnotically induced affect. *Motivation and Emotion*, *11*, 67–81.

Winer, B.J. (1962). *Statistical principles in experimental design*. New York: McGraw-Hill.

Wolfe, D.A. (1985). Child-abusing parents: An empirical review and analysis. *Psychological Review*, *97*, 462–482.

Zuckerman, M., Blanck, P.D., DePaulo, B.M., & Rosenthal, R. (1980). Developmental changes in decoding discrepant and nondiscrepant nonverbal cues. *Developmental Psychology*, *16*, 220–228.

6
Children's Deception Skills and Social Competence

ROBERT S. FELDMAN AND PIERRE PHILIPPOT

An observer of U.S. history over the last few decades might well be for-given for concluding that lying and deception are an everyday part of official Washington. Indeed, both the Watergate and Iran-Contra scandals provide notable examples that bald-faced lying is not all that exceptional, even at the highest levels of government. Not only do governmental leaders lie to one another and to those whom they serve, but they raise moral justifications after being caught in the act.

Yet most of us view such deception as an aberration, something that happens only rarely and that goes against the grain of our most deeply held values. In fact, when we discuss deception and lying with our children, one of our first lessons we teach is that lying is inappropriate and that it is only under the most exceptional and limited circumstances that deception represents a reasonable behavioral choice.

At the same time, however, it turns out that—just as deception on a governmental level is more commonplace than we might wish—deception and lying are not as infrequent on an interpersonal level as we might at first expect. Despite the assumption that a basic goal of society is to teach children that lying is morally reprehensible and to be avoided, in fact, we spend an inordinate amount of time teaching children the benefits of deception and how to more effectively control their nonverbal behavior that might give such deception away.

Consider, for example, what happens when a teenage boy, expecting a particularly hard-to-get compact disc, is presented instead with a pair of socks, painstakingly (and inexpertly) knitted by his girlfriend. Although he might wish to frown, laugh, or roll his eyes, good etiquette—taught to him by his parents and teachers and perhaps even his peers—requires instead that he adapt a demeanor of pleasure over the gift. And what of the gift-giver? She likely will be carefully scrutinizing her boyfriend,

Note. Some of the research reported in this paper was supported by grants from the U.S. National Institute of Disabilities and Rehabilitation Research and from the Marks Meadow Research Council at the University of Massachusetts, Amherst.

plumbing his surface reactions for signs of his actual emotional response and attempting to ferret out any signs of deception.

Clearly, the adroitness with which all this psychological activity is carried out will have a profound impact on the success of the immediate social interaction, as well as on the long-term relationship between the two parties involved. And this type of social situation is hardly unique; we are constantly struggling to present ourselves effectively and appropriately and to understand the underlying meaning of others demeanor and nonverbal behavior.

In this chapter, we focus on deception and nonverbal behavior in children, particularly in terms of skill in the detection of nonverbal behavior and how it relates more generally to overall social competence. We begin broadly, considering the literature on the detection of deception from nonverbal behavior and its development in children. We then discuss the relation between general social competence and nonverbal behavioral skills. Finally, we speculate on the ways in which abilities related to the detection of deception and successful communication might be related to overall social competence.

Deception and Nonverbal Behavior

He speaks nonsense, rubs the great toe along the ground, and shivers; his face is discolored; he rubs the roots of his hairs with his fingers.

This quotation from a 900 B.C. papyrus manuscript provides us with one of the first recorded descriptions of the nonverbal behavior of someone who is being verbally deceptive (cited in Trovillo, 1939). It testifies that at least since the time of the ancient Egyptians, people have believed that nonverbal behavioral cues could be used to infer whether an individual was dissembling.

Not until the eras of Darwin and Freud, however, did the idea that nonverbal behavior could reveal when an individual was being verbally deceptive enter the realm of scientific theorizing and investigation (e.g., Darwin, 1872/1965; Freud, 1959), and today, literally dozens of empirical scientific studies have established the validity of the notion. For instance, Ekman and Friesen (1974) showed adult subjects both a pleasant and a stressful film, followed by the subjects participating in an interview by an experimenter. Subjects were told to inform the interviewer that the pleasant film was pleasant (honest condition) but that the stressful film was also pleasant (dishonest condition). Naive observers were able to distinguish, for the most part, which film (pleasant or stressful) the subjects had actually seen on the basis of subjects' facial expressions and body movements. Similar work by Feldman (1976) and Mehrabian (1971) also showed that dissembling individuals tend to disclose that they are being deceptive through nonverbal behavior.

Which specific nonverbal cues are associated with deception? In a meta-analysis, Zuckerman, DePaulo and Rosenthal (1981) demonstrated that pupil dilatation, blinking, shrugs, and gestural adaptors (gestures consisting in touching oneself or an object) were significantly associated with deception. Deceivers also tended to smile less. In the same vein, Riggio and collaborators (Riggio & Friedman, 1983; Riggio, Tucker, & Widaman, 1987) found that a decrease in eye and body contact, smiling, and laughing discriminates between truthfulness and deception. In a fine-grained analysis of facial expression, Ekman, Friesen, and O'Sullivan (1988) provided evidence that subtle forms of smiling distinguished when subjects were truthful and when they lied about experiencing a pleasant feeling. Specifically, people who were truchful tended to demonstrate muscular activity around the eyes in addition to smiling lips.

Perhaps the most consistent finding is that the face offers fewer cues to deception than the nonverbal cues originating from the rest of the body. Indeed, several studies have demonstrated that accuracy of lie detectors was greater when they were presented with shots of the body rather than with shots of the face of deceptive persons (Ekman & Friesen, 1974; Littlepage & Pineault, 1979; Riggio & Friedman, 1983; Zuckerman, DePaulo, & Rosenthal, 1982).

Such findings support the idea that people trying to hide their verbal deception are more effective at controlling their facial expression than the rest of their body. Similarly, the pitch of the voice and the rhythm of speech have proven to be far better cues of deception than facial expression (Noller, 1985; Zuckerman, Amidon, Bishop, & Pomerantz, 1982).

In sum, a fair amount of research has consistently established that nonverbal behaviors are accurate indicators of deception and that people may use such cues while attempting to detect deception in others. Dissembling thus is closely related to nonverbal mastery skills. An effective liar must be able to exercise control of several nonverbal channels, including not just facial expressions but voice pitch and body and gestural movements. Conversely, it seems reasonable that a good lie detector would be highly sensitive to an array of nonverbal cues.

Why should nonverbal behavior reveal when a person is being deceptive? Several alternative explanations for the phenomenon can be posed (for a detailed review, see Zuckerman, DePaulo, & Rosenthal, 1981; Zuckerman & Driver, 1985). One hypothesis holds that deceivers' attempts to control their verbal presentation and demeanor may result in behaviors that appear planned and unspontaneous (see, e.g., Knapp, Hart, & Dennis, 1974). Alternatively, because of people's limitation in controlling all their communication channels simultaneously and equally well, discrepancies may develop with true feelings leaking by some channels while deceptive message would be emitted by others (Zuckerman, Driver, & Koestner, 1982). Furthermore, attempts at controlling behaviors might also require increased cognitive processing, which then is reflected in nonverbal cues such as pupil dilatation (Kahneman, 1973).

Another hypothesis proposes that deceivers experience arousal, guilt, or anxiety while they are lying because of fear of punishment if they are caught or because of their prior learning history. The expression of such emotions, then, could be used as cues from which to infer deception (Kraut, 1980).

We still do not know which of these explanations provides the most valid account of why nonverbal behavior reveals when a person is being verbally deceptive. In fact, it is probably some combination of explanations that will ultimately prove most accurate. What is clear, though, is that an array of nonverbal cues relating to verbal deception are available to people who are motivated to detect deception in others. We turn now to some of the developmental issues related to this fact.

General Trends in the Development of Nonverbal Capabilities

The notion that dissembling is closely related to nonverbal behavior suggests that as children's nonverbal abilities develop, their deception and liedetection capacities should improve. Before examining the research related to this hypothesis, it might be useful to briefly present how nonverbal capacities generally develop during childhood.

Since the 1970s, numerous studies have examined the ontogeny of nonverbal behavior (Ekman & Oster, 1982; Feldman, 1982; Feldman & Rimé, 1991). Results have consistently shown that by the end of the first year, spontaneous expression of emotion is well established and undergoes relatively few changes subsequently (Izard, Huebner, Risser, McGinnes, & Dougherty, 1980; Field, Woodson, Greenberg, & Cohen, 1982 Hiatt Campos, & Emde, 1983). The voluntary control of emotion expression, however, which is critical for successful dissembling, is only mastered later. Even though preschoolers can already imitate recognizable facial expressions, convincing nonverbal displays rarely are produced before the 10th year (Odom & Lemond, 1972; Ekman, Roper, & Hager, 1980). Indeed, even adults have problems in voluntarily producing certain components of common facial expression. At all ages, though, expressions of positive emotions are easier to pose or imitate than expressions of negative emotions.

Conversely, the capability of identifying facial displays is also established slowly, parallel to the development of voluntary nonverbal expression. Indeed, although it seems that 6-month-old infants can discriminate among some very specific facial expression (e.g., Schwartz, Izard, & Ansul, 1985), preschoolers still have great difficulties in matching or identifying facial expressions by labeling them or telling a story about them (Field & Walden, 1982). Children's performance increases continuously up to the 10th year and levels off thereafter (Odom & Lemond, 1972). A consistent finding is that happiness is the first expression to be correctly discriminated and, throughout the life span, is the easiest display to recognize.

Another domain of research on nonverbal expression also carries important implications for the study of dissembling and its detection—that of display rules. Display rules are the norms prescribing the appropriateness of specific facial expression in a given context. They determine who can show which emotion to whom, when, where, and how. Display rules may originate from sociocultural and/or personal norms.

Ekman (1984) has listed four categories of expression regulation by which display rules operate. Individuals can either (1) minimize or (2) exaggerate their spontaneous expression; they can (3) neutralize it by keeping a "poker face"; or finally, they can (4) substitute a nonverbal display for another. In each of these instances, display rules constitute a form of dissembling. It also should be noted that the same rules that determine the editing of "true" spontaneous expression can be used by a suspicious "lie detector" to identify information that is being censored.

Some researchers have investigated at what age children learn these display rules. In a naturalistic study, Saarni (1984) observed 6- to 10-year-old children's reactions when receiving a disappointing gift. Younger children were more likely to show negative faces (their true reaction) than older children, who attempted to manipulate the impression that they were communicating. The results of this experiment have been replicated and extended by Cole (1985), who had the examiner remain present with the child in some cases and not in others. Significantly more smiling occurred when the examiner remained present compared with when he left.

Finally, Gnepp and Hess (1986) studied the different developmental patterns of verbal and facial display rules in 6- to 15-year-olds. The subjects were presented with eight stories of social interaction and were asked to predict what the protagonist might say and what their face would look like. The children's knowledge of how and when to control emotional display increased up to 10 years of age and leveled off thereafter. It is interesting to note that this trend closely parallels the development of the voluntary control of nonverbal expression. The children also manifested a control of verbal display rules at an earlier age than the nonverbal expression display rules.

In sum, children's performance in recognizing as well as in producing nonverbal expression apparently increases consistently and progressively up to 10 years of age and stabilizes thereafter. Not surprisingly, the control of spontaneous expression, according to social norms, presents the same pattern.

Nonverbal Behavior and Children's Deception

It seems reasonable that children's ability to dissemble or detect deception would follow the same developmental trends as those of general nonverbal capabilities. Indeed, because the control of nonverbal behavior has been shown to be an important factor in successful deceit in adults, we might expect that children would be unlikely to be effective liars before they fully master their skills at controlling their nonverbal behavior.

Using parallel reasoning, we would expect the story to be similar in terms of the detection of deception. Because the ability to detect specific nonverbal cues and discrepancies between verbal and nonverbal channels is required for accurate lie detection, it seems reasonable that children would become proficient detectors only when their sensitivity in decoding the meaning of nonverbal cues would be sufficiently developed. Because our brief overview of the literature shows that such nonverbal skills generally are not acquired before 10 years of age, we might well assume that children are unlikely to be effective in dissembling and detection abilities before this age.

To test whether this hypothesis is plausible, Feldman and co-workers conducted several studies investigating the development of the use and control of nonverbal behavior in children who were verbally dissembling. In a first experiment (Feldman, Devin-Sheehan, & Allen, 1978), the goal was simply to demonstrate that children's nonverbal behavior would indeed reflect when they were being deceptive. The study used a tutoring situation in which grade-school-aged children acted as teacher to a confederate who was playing the role of student. The subjects (teachers) were instructed always to praise the responses of the students (confederates), regardless of whether or not the answers were correct. The confederate students always answered most items correctly in one condition and incorrectly in another. Thus, the subjects' responses were veridical when the confederates performed well and falsehoods when the students performed poorly. A group of naive judges reviewed silent videotaped samples of the subjects to rate how pleased the subjects actually were with their students.

Results showed that subjects appeared significantly happier when their praise was veridical than when it was nonveridical. Moreover, an objective analysis of subject's nonverbal behavior demonstrated that dissembling subjects smiled less, showed less pleasant mouth expressions, and had greater nervous hand movements as well as pauses in speech.

Still, these results did not reveal any age differences in the development in skill in successful deception. To investigate this question directly, Feldman, Jenkins, & Popoola (1979) carried out an experiment using three widely divergent age groups: first graders, seventh graders, and college students, with modal ages, respectively, of 6, 13, and 19 years. Subjects were asked to sample two drinks. One was a sweetened grape beverage, and the other was prepared without sugar and tasted really bitter. Subjects were instructed to persuade an interviewer that both tasted good, regardless of the actual taste. According to the cover story, the purpose of the study was to determine how much ability people had in deceiving an observer, as actors in television commercials do.

In addition, subjects were randomly assigned to be interviewed in either a public or a private situation. Those interviewed publicly were asked questions about the drinks in the presence of an interviewer and therefore realized that their facial expressions and body movements could be observed. Subjects who were interviewed privately received directions and questions from an audiotape recorder. In both groups, a hidden videotape camera was used to record a frontal view of subjects' head and shoulders during the interview.

Results clearly showed that the age of the subject influenced observers' accuracy in detecting deception on the basis of facial expression. Indeed, naive observers could readily discern from facial expressions when first graders were being deceptive. In contrast, the seventh graders and college students were successful in avoiding detection of deception. Analysis of the videotapes, however, indicated that the seventh graders and college students used different strategies to avoid detection. While the seventh graders appeared equally pleased by both drinks, the college students tended to exaggerate their nonverbal behavior so that they appeared to enjoy the unpleasant drink more than the pleasant one.

Finally, the data also showed that, at all three age levels, subjects appeared to be more pleased in the public interview than in the private situation. This indicates that even the first graders had some degree of control over their nonverbal behavior. The inability of these children to avoid detection, however, suggests that they may lack more subtle types of nonverbal skills.

Although the results of this study indicate that children become more proficient in their ability to act deceptively with increasing age, this conclusion is based solely on consideration of the subjects' facial expressions. Research from the adult literature, however, suggests that deception is revealed more by body movements than by facial expressions.

According to Ekman and Friesen (1974), the face is the predominant and primary channel of communication: It can transmit a considerable amount of information that others readily perceive. Therefore, one tends to be very aware of the expression reflected in one's face, and the face tends to be attended more in attempting to control one's own nonverbal behavior. From a developmental perspective, this implies that young children, who are relatively insensitive to the need to control their nonverbal behavior and who lack the skills to do so, should be more revealing in their facial nonverbal behavior than in their bodily nonverbal behavior. Furthermore, as their age increases, children's deception might be decreasingly revealed by their face—which they are learning to control—and increasingly revealed by nonverbal behaviors originating from their body.

To test this hypothesis, Feldman and White (1980) replicated the study of Feldman et al. (1979) with a sample of children ranging in age from 5 through 12. This time, however, two cameras simultaneously recorded each child. One was focused on the subject's face, while the other provided a view of the child's body from the neck down. Again, naive judges rated silent, videotaped samples of the children, indicating the degree to which the children appeared deceptive.

The results of the study revealed distinctly differing developmental trends for boys and girls, depending on whether the face or body was being rated. The hypothesis of a decrease with age in how much the face revealed was fully confirmed in the girls' data. Unexpectedly, however, ratings of their body disclosure tended to increase with age. Thus, the girls showed a decrease in their facial revelation and an increase in their body revelation with age.

Also surprising was the fact that the boys' data presented a pattern that was the opposite of that of the girls. Boys' facial disclosure of deception significantly increased with age, while their body disclosure tended (although nonsignificantly) to decrease with age. Although Feldman and White (1980) do not have a definitive explanation for the discrepancy between boys' and girls' ratings, a possible explanation rests on the differential socialization accorded to boys and girls. For instance, Buck (1984) suggests that girls may be rewarded for being more emotional and thus may have greater opportuinties to learn and become proficient in their nonverbal displays of emotion. In contrast, boys, who may be less encouraged to display or to control their nonverbal behavior may become less adept at its manipulation. Such an argument is highly speculative, however, and until the finding of increasing male facial revelation is replicated, these results should be regarded as tentative.

Taken as a whole, the findings of these three studies (Feldman et al., 1978, 1979; Feldman & White, 1980) nicely fit our proposition that the ability to be nonverbally deceptive increases parallel to the development of the control of nonverbal behavior and levels off after around 10 years of age. But is it also the case for the ability to *detect* deception?

Unfortunately, the literature on this topic is insufficiently extensive to answer the question definitively. In one study, DePaulo and her collaborators (DePaulo, Jordan, Irvine, & Laser, 1982) tested subjects from five different age groups (6th, 8th, 10th, 12th, graders, and college students) on their ability to detect deception from nonverbal behavior. They found a linear increase with age in lie-detection accuracy. The younger subjects, however, were better than the older ones at identifying the true affect that the stimulus person was trying to hide. In other words, if older subjects were better lie detectors, younger ones were better at detecting the leakage cues of the true affect.

A study by Rotenberg, Simond, and Moore (1989) used younger age children (kindergartners and second and fourth graders). Subjects had to judge the truthfulness of a stimulus person expressing one of the nine combinations of a message that was either positive, negative, or neutral, in either the verbal or nonverbal channel. The results showed that the use of a verbal–nonverbal consistency principle to infer truth or lying increased monotonically with age. Indeed, for the oldest subjects, telling the truth was implied by a consistency of the affective value between the verbal and nonverbal channels. In contrast, the younger subjects tended to identify telling the truth with expressing a positive message. Thus, in support of the hypothesis that skill in detecting deception increases with age, the results of this study indicate that the use of individual channels of nonverbal behavior and of discrepancies between communication channels to detect deception increases between 5 and 9 years of age.

In sum, the evidence that we have reviewed indicates that success in acting deceptive increases with age and—although the research is less extensive—that skill in detecting deception in others also improves with age. People become better at acting deceptive, and at detecting the lies of others, as they become older.

Children's Social Competence, Nonverbal Behavior, and Deception

The research that we have just reviewed is clear in suggesting that nonverbal behavioral skill, and in particular proficiency in acting and detecting deception, improves with age. Unfortunately, though, a good deal of the research supportive of this conclusion is largely atheoretical and descriptive, focusing relatively little on the underlying explanatory mechanisms.

One useful theoretical approach to understanding the developmental aspects of deception comes from the notion of social competence. In this part of the chapter, we make use of the notion of social competence to provide an explanatory framework for understanding the development of children's abilities to detect deception in others.

Development of Social Competence

Psychologists have given the concept of "social competence" many denotations, evolving from widely divergent perspectives, and approaches have ranged from the molar (as in the study of general peer relations) to the molecular (maintenance of a specific impression; e.g., Parker & Asher, 1987). Furthermore, studies of social competence have ranged from work on communicative and emotional competence to examination of cognitive competencies assumed to underlie social competence. Much of the use of the term *social competence*, then, has suffered from a lack of precision.

We consider social competence as a hypothetical construct relating to evaluative judgments of the adequacy of a persons' social performance (e.g., Gresham, 1981). These evaluations may be based on normative data; judgments by knowledgeable observers (parents, teachers, or peers); or by performance in relation to some specific criterion.

Furthermore, we assume that social competence comprises a set of specific behaviors or cognitions relating to social performance (Gresham, 1981). Thus, using this approack, social competence encompasses a multi-dimensional domain that includes (but is not limited to) verbal and nonverbal skills.

Consideration of social competence as a hypothetical construct that encompasses individual and discrete social skills permits several theoretical and practical advantages. For one thing, this approach emphasizes that social competence is not a univariate dimension but a set of related skills of a behavioral, cognitive, and emotional nature. Furthermore, it allows us to investigate the skills independently and to examine the degree of interrelatedness of particular skills.

Using this perspective, it is possible to consider the effective use of nonverbal behavior during social interaction as a critical social skill, one that is related to the maintenance and facilitation of social interaction. In particular, this approach suggests that nonverbal encoding and decoding skills both can be viewed as manifestations of social competence. Effective decoding of nonverbal behavior facilitates the understanding of the emotional and cognitive state of others and thereby permits a more accurate understanding of the social situation as a whole. Ultimately, such understanding leads to at least the potential for more effective social interaction.

In the same vein, effective nonverbal encoding—which occurs in situations in which people display nonverbal behavior that either accurately reflects an internal state that they intend to convey or creates an intended impression—can be seen as a critical social skill. If nonverbal encoding can be appropriately decoded by others, we would expect it to facilitate social interaction, because other interactants would be better able to understand others' actual or intended communication.

Of course, it is important to keep in mind that "appropriate" or "intended" decoding and encoding are not (necessarily) isomorphic with "accurate" decoding and encoding. For example, some studies show that in certain cases effective decoding is manifested by a motivated disregard of certain unintended portions of nonverbal messages communicated by an interactant (e.g., Rosenthal & DePaulo, 1979). In such cases, socially competent use of nonverbal behavioral cues is demonstrated by an apparent (but not necessarily actual) lack of decoding accuracy. The distinctions between decoding and encoding of intended versus unintended messages, of course, becomes particularly crucial when discussing the nonverbal aspects of deception.

The conception that nonverbal behavioral encoding and decoding abilities represent social skills is supported by several converging theoretical and empirical threads. For one thing, nonverbal behavior—because of its role in providing information about emotional states and attitudes—is a primary medium for the communication of affect, empathic processes, and affective binding (e.g., Buck, 1984; Bretherton et al., 1986). By understanding the affect being experienced by others, as well as by communicating their own affect accurately, the effectiveness of individuals' social interaction ought to be increased, thereby leading to greater general social competence.

In addition, regulation of social interaction and communication occurs via nonverbal behavior. For example, gestures that accompany speech both augment and modify the meaning of speech in significant ways (Ricci Bitti & Poggi, 1991). The degree to which social discourse is enhanced through use of nonverbal behavior cues suggests that abilities in the nonverbal behavioral realm would be related to overall social competence.

Finally, nonverbal behavioral display rules determine the appropriateness of a particular response given the social context and relationship of interactants in a particular situation (e.g., Saarni, 1988). People who fail to comply with display rules face social sanctions and may be considered deviants by members of their own cultural group. On the other hand, individuals who follow display rules successfully would be expected to show considerably more skill in deciphering the nonverbal messages of people with whom they are interacting.

In general, then, several reasons suggest that nonverbal behavioral skill would be associated with general social competence. Furthermore, a body of empirical literature supports this view and is discussed next.

Social Competence and the Decoding of Nonverbal Behavior

Several studies support the notion that ability in the decoding of nonverbal behavior represents a component of social skill. For example, Edwards, Manstead, and MacDonald (1984) used a self-report scale in which groups of 8- to 11-year-olds were asked how friendly they were with each of their classmates. Those subjects scoring highest and lowest on this measure were then assigned to one of two experimental groups. The subjects viewed a series of photographs of adults or children demonstrating facial expression of one of six emotions (anger, disgust, fear, happiness, sadness, and surprise), and subjects were asked to choose the emotion in the photo. The results found that sociometric status had a significant effect on identification ability, with more popular subjects performing better than the less popular ones.

Similarly, Spence (1987) asked a group of children in kindergarten to identify three classmates with whom they would most and least like to carry out a series of activities. Each of these classmates then viewed a group of photos depicting adults and children experiencing the emotions of anger, disgust, fear, happiness, sadness, or surprise. A strong positive correlation was found between the classmates' popularity and their skill at identifying the appropriate emotion.

Another study examined preschoolers' and third graders' abilities to identify several emotions portrayed in a series of slides (Reichenbach & Masters, 1983). The results showed a significant positive correlation between family stability and subjects' decoding abilities. Furthermore, they found that children from families that were relatively "disrupted" were less likely to misapply the emotion of happiness but were more likely to misjudge a given expression as anger.

Such findings are congruent with research showing differences in decoding ability in children from homes that differ in their characteristic amount of family expressivity. For instance, children from homes in which expression of emotion is relatively high are more popular, less aggressive, and more prosocial than children coming from less expressive homes (Halberstadt, 1991). Furthermore, research suggests that children with accurately expressive mothers are better decoders than children of less accurately expressive mothers (e.g., Daly, Abramovitch, & Pliner, 1980). (Interestingly, though, the correlation between family expressiveness and decoding ability appears to become negative by the time individuals reach adulthood. Apparently, people from less expressive homes, who lack appropriate or accurate expressive models, are more motivated to become proficient in decoding, and by the time they reach adulthood, they are more skilled at decoding than individuals who are raised in highly expressive family environments, where accurate decoding is relatively simple [Halberstadt, 1984].)

Research from our own laboratories also supports the notion that social competence is related to nonverbal behavioral decoding skill. In one study (Philippot & Feldman, 1990), we used a group of 3- and 5-year-olds from middle-class families who were either high or low in general social competence, as determined by their score on the Social Competence scale of the Achenbach Child Behavior Checklist (Achenbach & Edelbrock, 1982). This scale, completed by the subjects' parents, assesses a child's performance in peer and family relations, participation in organized groups, and recreational activities. The scale does not measure any aspects of nonverbal behavioral skills, and it constitutes a well-standardized, reliable measure of social competence within normal populations. Moreover, it has the advantage of being uncorrelated with intelligence, a possible confounding factor. We showed the children in the study a series of nine 10- to 20-s videotaped, silent scenarios. Each scenario consisted of an adult character participating in a setting that typically evoked the emotion of happiness, sadness, or fear and that was readily understandable to preschoolers. In each of the scenes, the protagonist's face was blacked out electronically. After training in the procedure, subjects were asked to choose a face appropriate to the scenario from among three photos of an adult model who was displaying the emotion of happiness, sadness, or fear.

As expected, the results showed that the subjects in the higher social competence group were more successful decoders of facial expression than the subjects in the low social competence group. The analysis of the data also revealed that the impact of social competence on nonverbal decoding was not modified by the age or sex of the subjects or by the type of emotion they had to decode. This study demonstrates, then, that even in a normal population of children from middle-class families, decoding of fundamental emotions may be impaired in children who are less socially competent, and this occurs even before the acquisition of social display rules, which begin to be learned around 3 years of age.

A second study, using older children, also found support for a relationship between social competence and nonverbal skills (Custrini & Feldman, 1989). In the study, children 9 to 12 years of age who were either high or low in social competence (as determined by the social competence scale of the Achenbach Child Behavior Checklist) were assessed in both the decoding and production of facial expressions relating to the emotions of anger, disgust, fear or surprise, happiness, or sadness.

Congruent with the hypothesis, the results showed that the children in the high social competence group showed greater overall accuracy than those in the less socially competent group, for both encoding and decoding. The effect, however, was due largely to the girls; the difference between high and low socially competent boys, was small and not significant, while the difference for girls was significant. Despite this sex difference, the results did provide strong evidence for the importance of facial expressions as a means of obtaining information from others and that the decoding of emotions from others' nonverbal behavior is related to the level of social competence in children.

In sum, a considerable amount of evidence supports the notion that nonverbal decoding abilities make up a specific social skill that is related to overall social competence. Children who are most generally socially competent also appear to be most proficient at accurately decoding the emotional meaning of others' nonverbal behavior.

Social Competence and Deception

Our analysis of social competence and nonverbal decoding skills so far has focused on how skill in the identification of emotion is related to overall social competence. Logically, however, it seems reasonable that skill in the decoding of deception might be construed in a similar vein. Specifically, we suggest that the ability to detect deception is a social skill that ought to be related to general social competence.

Unfortunately, the data to support such an assertion are relatively sparse, and those that do exist are indirect. But an approach to the detection of deception that views it as social skill raises several critical issues, including questions about how our knowledge of display rules changes as we develop and what are the components of nonverbal behavioral deception skill.

Two indirect (and unrelated) lines of evidence suggest that it is reasonable to consider the decoding of deception as a social skill, one that develops with increasing age and, theoretically, at least, may be related to social competence. The first comes from research on the development of display rules pertaining to deception and the second from work at improving the abilities of observers to decode successfully.

Development of Display Rules Regarding Deception

Carolyn Saarni has written extensively on the development of display rules in children (e.g., Saarni, 1982, 1985) and most recently on the way in which children develop their *understanding* of how and under what conditions deception occurs (Saarni, 1988). Examining children in grades 2, 5, and 8, Saarni found age and sex differences in subjects' predictions about others' deceptive nonverbal behavior in various sorts of situations.

For example, Saarni (1988) asked subjects to predict a person's nonverbal reaction to such situations as receiving an unwanted gift from his or her aunt or being bullied. Taken as a whole, the results indicated that children in middle childhood develop a subtle understanding of the rules that regulate the nature of appropriate emotional display, and they develop the capacity to comprehend under what circumstances actual, experienced emotion should be suppressed or dissembled.

It seems reasonable, then, to contend that such skill in the understanding of when deception is or is not appropriate would be related to overall social competence. In fact, Saarni (1988) found some direct evidence for such a contention: the majority of her subjects stated that children who "almost always showed [their] real feelings" and rarely controlled their nonverbal behavioral cues to emotion would be rejected by their peers. Similarly, children who were described to subjects as almost never showing their true emotions were most often perceived as dislikable, emotionally maladjusted, or difficult to get to know. Although these are only subjects' perceptions, their reactions suggest that ability to act deceptively effectively and to understand when others are deceptive may be a critical social skill.

Training of Nonverbal Behavioral Skill

A second area of research relevant to the notion that nonverbal behavioral deceptive abilities may be related to general social competence is work on training individuals to be more accurate in their identification of particular emotional states, including the identification of deception, in others. If it is in fact possible to train people to be more accurate decoders, support is provided for the conceptualization that nonverbal behavioral abilities are specific skills that may be improved with particular kinds of environmental experience and that such abilities might well be related to other social skills and overall general social competence.

Only one study has directly examined the possibility of training adults to be more accurate in their detection of deception, and it employed adults as subjects (Zuckerman, Koestner, & Alton, 1984). In the study, subjects viewed short videotaped clips of people who were either lying or telling the truth. Some of the subjects received feedback regarding the veracity of the person they had just seen (either before seeing the clip or following viewing it), while others, in a control condition, received no information regarding the individuals truthfulness. During a subsequent assessment stage of the study in which subjects were asked the judge the truthfulness of a set of new behavioral samples, subjects who had received feedback were more accurate in their choices regarding whether the same persons that they had seen earlier were being truthful or deceptive, although their increased ability did not generalize to judgments about other individuals. Overall, then, the experimenters were successful in enhancing the detection accuracy of the trained subjects.

Although no research has yet investigated the training of deception detection in *children*, other research has shown that children's nonverbal decoding abilities in other realms can be improved. One study, for example, focused on the decoding of one of three emotions: happiness, sadness, and fear (Beck & Feldman, 1990). In the study, a group of fifth- and sixth-grade children were shown videotaped samples of people who were experiencing one of the three target emotions. Following exposure to each clip, subjects were told which emotion was being experienced and shown the same segment a second time. A group of control subjects did not receive this information, although they did see the segment a second time. Results from a subsequent test showed that the subjects who received the feedback showed significantly higher decoding accuracy than a group of subjects who earlier had not received feedback.

In a follow-up study, Beck, Feldman, & Copes (1990) compared the efficacy of two different types of feedback in training emotional reactions and used both adults and children as subjects. In the study, subjects in one of the training conditions received feedback just after viewing a short clip of a person experiencing either happiness, sadness, or fear—as in the previous study (Beck & Feldman, 1990). In a second feedback condition, however, subjects received information about the emotion being experienced by the individual before viewing the sample clip. Beck et al. reasoned that knowing the emotion to be seen in a sample beforehand might encourage the development of anticipatory schemata that could be used to decode individuals more accurately in situations lacking feedback.

Results, however, showed no difference between the two types of training feedback: Both for the children and the adults, feedback—regardless of whether it was provided before or after a clip—produced equal amounts of decoding success, compared to subjects who had no training. Beck et al. (1990) also found an age effect, in which the adults were generally more proficient at decoding than the children.

Although the existing training studies thus indicate that it is possible to train nonverbal behavioral decoding abilities in adults and children, their implications for the present topic are somewhat limited. No study jointly considers children and their ability to be trained in the decoding of deception. And no study has yet investigated whether skill at detection of deception from nonverbal behavioral cues (or successfully acting deceptively, for that matter) is related to overall general competence.

What these studies do demonstrate, however, is that the potential exists for developing procedures that enhance children's skill at detecting and acting deceptively. Although quite speculative, it is possible that enhancing such skills might ultimately produce improvements in social competence.

Deception Skills and the Development of Social Competence: Some Caveats and Final Reflections

In this chapter, we have moved from concrete, well-substantiated evidence (showing that the detection of deception using nonverbal behavioral cues is a skill that improves with age) to more intemperate speculations on the relationship between skills in the detection and communication of deceptive messages and general social competence in children. Throughout the discussion, we have taken the implicit position that accuracy in the detection of deception is, by definition, appropriate and advantageous.

One may reasonably argue, however, that in certain instances, success at detecting deception in another brings with it certain risks. Consider, for example, a person who spends hours cooking what he thinks is just the right meal for a friend. If the friend maintains an outward appearance of pleasure, but is detected as actually feeling disappointed or—even worse—disgusted, it is hard to see how the social relationship will be advanced. In some cases, then, success in establishing that another individual is being deceptive may prove to be more of a liability than an asset (DePaulo, 1981).

The converse point holds true for the recipient of the meal. Clearly, good social graces call for someone who has been served a meal to appear as satisfied and grateful as possible when in the presence of the cook, no matter how great the true revulsion being experienced, to spare his feelings—a principle that is socialized in children at an early age. At the same time, one would not feel sanguine in teaching children to appear innocent when their teacher questions them about a transgression that they had actually committed; here, the lesson that society tries to impart to children is that honesty is the best policy.

In sum, children's socialization often encompasses contradictory information about when accurate detection of deception and transmission of deception is facilitative for social interaction. It is therefore quite possible that the correlation between deception skills (defined as the ability to accurately decode deceptive communications and to communicate deceptively) and overall social competence may not necessarily be strongly positive. Rather, it is probably necessary to separate the *skill* at controlling and reading others' nonverbal behavior from the *knowledge* of when and how that skill should be employed. Although virtually no research has attempted this task (Saarni's work on display rules being a notable exception), it seems theoretically crucial to take such an approach to gain an understanding of how people use nonverbal deception in the real world. Such understanding would allow us to take the next step: explicitly teaching children under what conditions deception is and is not permissible. Although such a task may seem overly ambitous, it is probably necessary to increase the level of interpersonal trust between individuals and to avoid the Watergates of the future.

References

Achenbach, T.M., & Edelbrock, C.S. (1982). *Manual for the Child Behavior Checklist and Child Behavior Profile*. Burlington, VT: Child Psychiatry, University of Vermont.

Beck, L., & Feldman, R.S. (1990). Enhancing children's decoding of nonverbal behavior. *Journal of Nonverbal Behavior, 13*, 269–277.

Beck, L., Feldman, R.S., & Copes, W. (1990). *Improving the decoding abilities of adults and children*. Unpublished manuscript, University of Massachusetts, Amherst.

Bretherton, I., Fritz, J., Zahn-Waxler, C., and Ridgeway, D. (1986). Learning to talk about emotions: A functionalist perspective. *Child Development, 57*, 529–548.

Buck, R. (1984). *The communication of emotion*. New York: Guilford.

Cole, P.M. (1985). Display rules and socialization of affective displays. In G. Zivin (Ed.), *The development of expressive behavior: Biology environment interactions* San Diego, CA: Academic Press.

Custrini, R.J., & Feldman, R.S. (1989). Children's social competence and nonverbal encoding and decoding of emotion. *Journal of Child Clinical Psychology, 18*, 336–342.

Darwin, C. (1965). *The expression of emotion in man and animals*. Chicago: The University of Chicago Press. (Original work published 1872).

Daly, E.M., Abramovitch, R., & Pliner, P. (1980). The relationship between mothers' encoding and their children's decoding of facial expressions of emotion. *Merrill-Palmer Ouarterly, 26*, 25–33.

DePaulo, B.M. (1981). Success at detecting deception: Liability or skill? *Annals of the New York Academy of Sciences, 364*, 245–255.

DePaulo, B.M., Jordan, A., Irvine, A., & Laser, P.S. (1982). Age changes in the detection of emotion. *Child Development, 53*, 701–707.

DePaulo, B.M., Lanier, K., & Davis, T (1983). Detecting the deceit of the motivated liar. *Journal of Personality and Social Psychology, 45*, 1096–1103.

Edwards, R., Manstead, A.S.R., & MacDonald, C.J. (1984). The relationship between children's sociometric status and ability to recognize facial expressions of emotion. *European Journal of Social Psychology, 14*, 235–238.

Ekman, P. (1984). Expression and the nature of emotion. In K. Scherer & P. Ekman (Eds.), *Approaches to emotion*. Hillsdale, NJ: Erlbaum.

Ekman, P., & Friesen, W.V. (1974). Detecting deception from the body or face. *Journal of Personality and Social Psychology, 29*, 288–298.

Ekman, P., Friesen, W.V., & O'Sullivan, M. (1988). Smiles when lying. *Journal of Personality and Social Psychology, 54*, 414–420.

Ekman, P., & Oster, H. (1982). Review of research, 1970–1980. In P. Ekman (Ed.), *Emotion in the human face*. Cambridge, UK: Cambridge University Press.

Ekman, P., Roper, G., & Hager, J.C. (1980). Deliberate facial movement. *Child Development, 51*, 886–891.

Feldman, R.S. (1976). Nonverbal disclosure of deception and interpersonal affect. *Journal of Educational Psychology, 68*, 807–816.

Feldman, R.S. (Ed.), (1982). *Development of nonverbal behavior in children*. New York: Springer-Verlag.

Feldman, R.S., & Rimé, B. (Eds.) (1991). *Fundamentals of nonverbal behavior*. Cambridge, UK: Cambridge University Press.

Feldman, R.S., & White, J.B. (1980). Detecting deception in children. *Journal of Communication, 30*, 121–128.

Feldman, R.S., Devin-Sheehan, L., & Allen, V.L. (1978). Nonverbal cues as indicators of verbal dissembling. *American Educational Research Journal, 15*, 217–231.

Feldman, R.S., Jenkins, L., & Popoola, L. (1979). Detection of deception in adults and children via facial expressions. *Child Development, 50*, 350–355.

Field, T.M., & Walden, T.A. (1982). Production and discrimination of facial expression by preschool children. *Child Development, 53*, 1299–1311.

Field, T.M., Woodson, R., Greenberg, R., & Cohen, D. (1982). Discrimination and imitation of facial expression by neonates. *Science, 218*, 179–181.

Freud, S. (1959). Fragment of an analysis of a case of hysteria. In *Collected papers* (Vol. 3). New York: Basic Books.

Fugita, S.S., Hogrebe, M.C., & Wexley, K.N. (1980). Perception of deception: Perceived expertise in detecting deception, successfulness of deception and nonverbal cues. *Personality and Social Psychology Bulletin, 6*, 637–643.

Gnepp, J., & Hess, D.L. (1986). Children's understanding of verbal and facial dispaly rules. *Developmental Psychology, 22*, 103–108.

Gresham, F.M. (1981). Assessment of social skills. *Journal of School Psychology, 19*, 120–133.

Halberstadt, A.G. (1984). Family expression of emotion. In C.Z. Malatesta, & C.E. Izard (Eds.), *Emotion in adult development* (pp. 235–252). Beverly Hills, CA: Sage.

Halberstadt, A.G. (1991). Socialization of expressiveness: Family influences in particular and a model in general. In R.S. Feldman, & B. Rimé (Eds.), *Fundamentals of nonverbal behavior*. New York: Cambridge University Press.

Hiatt, S.W., Campos, J.J., & Emde, R.N. (1983). Facial patterning and infant emotional expression: Happiness, surprise, and fear. *Child Development, 50*, 1020–1035.

Izard, C.E., Huebner, R.R., Risser, D., McGinnes, G.C., & Dougherty, L.M. (1980). The young infant's ability to produce discrete facial expression. *Developmental Psychology, 16*, 132–140.

Kahneman, D. (1973). *Attention and effort*. Englewood Cliffs, NJ: Prentice-Hall.

Knapp, M.L., Hart, R.P., & Dennis, H.S. (1974). An exploration of deception as a communication construct. *Human Communication Research, 1,* 15–29.

Kraut, R.E. (1980). Humans as lie detectors: some second thoughts. *Journal of Communication, 30,* 209–216.

Littlepage, G.E., & Pineault, M.A. (1979). Detection of deceptive factual statements from the body and the face. *Personality and Social Psychology Bulletin, 5,* 325–328.

Littlepage, G.E., Tang, D.W., & Pineault, M.A. (1986). Nonverbal and content factors in the detection of deception in planned and spontaneous communication. *Journal of Social Behavior and Personality, 1,* 439–450.

Mehrabian, A. (1971) Nonverbal betrayal of feeling. *Journal of Experimental Research in Personality, 5,* 64–73.

Noller, P. (1985). Video primacy: A further look. *Journal of Nonverbal Behavior, 9,* 28–47.

Odom, R., & Lemond, C. (1972). Developmental differences in the perception and production of facial expressions. *Child Development, 43,* 359–369.

Parker, J.G., & Asher, S.R. (1987). Peer relations and later personal adjustment: Are low-accepted children at risk? *Psychological Bulletin, 102,* 357–389.

Philippot, P., & Feldman, R.S. (1990). Age and social competence in preschoolers' decoding of facial expression. *British Journal of Social Psychology, 29,* 43–54.

Reichenbach, L., & Masters, J.C. (1983). Children's use of expressive and contextual cues in judgments of emotion. *Child Development, 54,* 993–1004.

Ricci Bitti, P., & Poggi, I. (1991). Symbolic behavior: Talking through gestures. In R.S. Feldman, & B. Rimé (Eds.), *Fundamentals of nonverbal behavior.* New York: Cambridge University Press.

Riggio, R.E., & Friedman, H.S. (1983). Individual differences and cues to deception. *Journal of Personality and Social Psychology, 45,* 899–915.

Riggio, R.E., Tucker, J., & Widaman, K.F. (1987). Verbal and nonverbal cues as mediators of deception ability. *Journal of Nonverbal Behavior, 11,* 126–145.

Rosenthal, R., & DePaulo, B.M. (1979). Sex differences in eavesdropping on nonverbal cues. *Journal of Personality and Social Psychology, 37,* 273–285.

Rotenberg, K.J., Simond, L., & Moore, D. (1989). Children's use of verbal-nonverbal consistency principle to infer truth and lying. *Child Development, 60,* 309–322.

Saarni, C. (1982). In R.S. Feldman (Ed.), *The development of nonverbal behavior in children.* (pp. 123–147). New York: Springer-Verlag.

Saarni, C. (1984). An observational study of children's attempts to monitor their expressive behavior. *Child Development, 55,* 1504–1513.

Saarni, C. (1985). Indirect processes in affect socialization. In M. Lewis & C. Saarni (Eds.), *The socialization of emotions* (pp. 187–209). New York: Plenum.

Saarni, C. (1988). Children's understanding of the interpersonal consequences of dissemblance of nonverbal emotional–expressive behavior. *Journal of Nonverbal Behavior, 12,* 275–294.

Schwartz, G.M., Izard, E.C., & Ansul, S.E. (1985). The five-month-old's ability to discriminate facial expression of emotion. *Infant Behavior and Development, 8,* 65–77.

Spence, S.H. (1987). The relationship between social-cognitive skills and peer sociometric status. *British Journal of Developmental Psychology, 5,* 347–356.

Trovillo, P.V. (1939). A history of lie detection. *Journal of Criminal Law and Criminology*, *29*, 848–881.

Zuckerman, M., & Driver, R.E. (1985). Telling lies: Verbal and nonverbalcorrelates of deception. In A.W. Siegman & S. Feldstein (Eds.), *Multichannel integration of nonverbal behavior* (pp. 129–148). Hillsdale, NJ: Erlbaum.

Zuckerman, M., Amidon, M.D., Bishop, S.E., & Pomerantz, S.D. (1982). Face and tone of voice in the communication of deception. *Journal of Personality and Social Psychology*, *43*, 414–420.

Zuckerman, M., DePaulo, B., & Rosenthal, R. (1981). Verbal and nonverbal communication of deception. *Advances in Experimental Social Psychology*, *14*, 1–59.

Zuckerman, M., DePaulo, B., & Rosenthal, R. (1982). Nonverbal strategies for decoding deception. *Journal of Nonverbal Behavior*, *6*, 171–187.

Zuckerman, M., Driver, R., & Koestner, R. (1982). Discrepancy as a cue to actual and perceived deception. *Journal of Nonverbal Behavior*, *7*, 95–100.

Zuckerman, M., Koestner, R., & Alton, A.O. (1984). Learning to detect deception. *Journal of Personality and Social Psychology*, *46*, 519–528.

Zuckerman, M., Koestner, R., & Colella, M.J. (1985). Learning to detect deception from three channels. *Journal of Nonverbal Behavior*, *9*, 347–357.

7
Children's Trustworthiness: Judgments by Teachers, Parents, and Peers

JOHN M. WILSON AND JAMES L. CARROLL

In developmental research and in clinical practice, lying has been identified consistently as an important indicator of current and future problems in social adjustment. It has been difficult, however, to define consistently what a lie is or, because successful lying is by definition a clandestine behavior, to collect reliable and valid data.

We review research on relationships between lying (variously defined) and indices of concurrent or future adjustment problems. We then define a typology of lies and describe how we used that typology in developing a way to assess a somewhat larger social–reputational variable, untrustworthy communication. Finally, we introduce a measure of trustworthy communication and provide data regarding the following issues: (a) consistency of judgments across peer, parent, and teacher perspectives; (b) distributions of attributions of trustworthiness and untrustworthiness from each perspective (and for each gender); and (c) social validity of trustworthiness ratings as indicated by patterns of relationships with measures of peer status.

Relationship of Lying to Other Problem Behaviors

Researchers and clinicians have been concerned with lying, because adults frequently regard it as a problem behavior in children and because of evidence of its relation to present and future adjustment problems. Parents, teachers, mental health professionals, and children rank lying among the most serious behavior problems (Stouthamer-Loeber, 1986), and research to date indicates that lying is related to serious behavior problems. Evidence of relations between lying and other serious behavior problems is present in data from studies using both clinical and empirical taxonomies of psychopathology (e.g., Achenbach & Edelbrock, 1981) and in studies of lying and predelinquent and delinquent behaviors (e.g., Mitchell & Rosa,

---

The basis for this study was the first author's master's thesis.

1981), peer acceptance and rejection (e.g., Carlson, Lahey, & Neeper, 1984), and overt and clandestine behavior problems (e.g., Loeber & Schmalling, 1985a). Also, prevalence rates for lying are much lower in normal than in clinical populations (Stouthamer-Loeber, 1986).

The relation between lying and other serious behavior problems is evident in research on childhood psychopathology. Clinically derived classification systems (e.g., *Diagnostic and Statistical Manual of Mental Disorders* [DSM-III-R], American Psychiatric Association, 1987; Group for the Advancement of Psychiatry [GAP], 1966 and International Classification of Disease [ICD-9], see Quay, 1979) typically include lying in descriptions of behavior patterns for antisocial, conduct disorder, and aggressive behavior problems. Other behaviors frequently included in those classifications are bullying, physical aggression, cruelty, stealing, defiance, destructiveness, disobedience, cheating, firesetting, forgery, truancy, and vandalism. Empirical classification systems are based on multivariate studies of teacher, parent, or other significant adult's ratings of children's behaviors. Factor-analytic studies show that lying items on behavior scales are significant contributors to factors labeled conduct disorder, socialized aggression, antisocial, and delinquent (Achenbach, 1966; Achenbach & Edelbrock, 1981; Behar & Stringfield, 1974; Conners, 1969, 1970; Gesten, 1976; Goyette, Conners, & Ulrich, 1978; Herbert, 1974; Kim, Anderson, & Bashaw, 1968; Kupfer, Detre, & Koral, 1974; Langner, Gersten, McCarthy, Greene, Herson, & Jameson, 1976; Miller, 1967; Pimm, Quay, & Werry, 1967; Quay & Peterson, 1983). In many of these factor-analytic studies, lying items rank high on a principal factor (Wilson, 1985).

Children's lying is also predictive of maladjustment (criminal, delinquent, and predelinquent behaviors) in adolescence and adulthood. In a study of the behavioral precursors of criminality conducted in England, Mitchell and Rosa (1981) followed up on children seen in a child guidance clinic. Thirty-four percent of children reported by parents and teachers as untrustworthy had committed one or more criminal offenses 15 years later. In comparison, only 5.4% of clinic subjects who were not viewed as untrustworthy had committed offenses. A study in Finland (Pulkkinen, 1983) also used criminal offenses as an outcome. Subjects who had committed serious criminal offenses at age 20 had received significantly higher scores on peer nomination and teacher ratings for lying and exaggeration at age 8 than subjects who committed less serious offenses or no offenses. Further, Loeber and Dishion (1983) reviewed delinquency-prediction studies and found that lying, stealing, and truancy ranked third as a predictor of delinquency, following parental management techniques and child problem behaviors (e.g., aggression). Lying, stealing, and truancy together ranked first as a predictor of recidivism. Robbins (1966) reported that 39% of children with the diagnosis of sociopath had problems with lying in childhood. Finally, Smith, Schwerin, Stubblefield, and

Fogg (1982) found that self-reported obedience, including truth telling, in grades 7 to 9 predicted lower rates of licit (cigarette) and illicit (cannabis) substance use 3 years later.

Children's lying also relates to peer rejection and acceptance (Carlson, Lahey, & Neeper, 1984; Dor & Asher, cited in Asher & Hymel, 1981). Structural equation modeling of data on 10-year-old boys provided strong evidence that antisocial behavior, including lying, is directly related to peer acceptance (Patterson, 1986). Conners (1970) reported that the item "problems keeping friends" was highly related to a lying item on a behavior scale. Patterson (1986) emphasized the importance of assessing both overt and clandestine forms of antisocial behavior when investigating the influence of child antisocial behavior on such important outcomes as peer acceptance, self-esteem, and academic achievement. Overt behaviors include such problems as noncompliance and fighting, whereas clandestine or covert behaviors include problems such as lying and stealing. Overt and aggressive behavior problems have received far more attention than lying and other clandestine behaviors.

Other recent investigations of overt and clandestine dimensions of antisocial behavior suggest that lying relates to both dimensions. Loeber and Schmalling (1985a) examined 28 factor- and cluster-analytic studies of child psychopathology to determine patterns of antisocial behavior. A multidimensional scaling analysis yielded one bipolar dimension. One pole consisted of overt or confrontive antisocial behaviors (e.g., arguing, temper tantrums, fighting), whereas the other pole consisted of covert or concealing behaviors (e.g., stealing, truancy, firesetting). Lying was located on the covert side of the dimension but toward the middle. These findings suggest that lying is related to both overt and covert behavior but is related most strongly to the covert dimension (Stouthamer-Loeber, 1986). The relationship between lying and both dimensions of antisocial behavior is stronger in older subjects (Stouthamer-Loeber & Loeber, 1986). At greatest risk are children who engage in both overt and clandestine antisocial behavior (Loeber & Schmalling, 1985b).

Edelbrock and Loeber (1985) reported the types of antisocial behaviors likely to precede and follow lying as behavior problems increase in seriousness. They analyzed parent ratings of conduct problems included on the Child Behavior Check List in the 1,300 referred children in Achenbach and Edelbrock's (1981) study and showed how combinations of these antisocial behaviors were related to each other. Children who were involved in the most serious antisocial behavior problems were likely to have progressed through four age-related stages of antisocial behavior (oppositional, offensive, aggressive, delinquent). Lying, in the offensive cluster, related to cruelty, disobedience at school, screaming, poor peer relationships, fighting, sulking, and swearing. The sequence began with highly overt behavior and progressed to covert behavior. In their study, children who lied were a subset of those who argued, bragged, demanded attention, disobeyed at home, teased, and were stubborn, loud, impulsive, and engaged in temper tantrums. Children who progressed to more serious antisocial behaviors (i.e., destroying, threatening, attacking people, interacting with bad friends, stealing at home, setting fires, stealing outside home, using alcohol or drugs, running away, and engaging in vandalism and truancy) had had problems with lying when younger and were likely to persist in lying.

Studies of prevalence rates of lying in children also strongly link lying with serious behavior problems. Higher proportions of children in clinical samples are rated as untruthful than children in normal samples. Rutter (1967) found that a lying item discriminated between antisocial, neurotic, and normal children of both sexes, aged 9 to 13. Achenbach and Edelbrock (1981) reported that one item, lying and cheating, accounted for 22% of the variance in clinical status between normal children and children referred for treatment. The prevalence of lying in normal males and females aged 4 to 16 ranged from 16% to 23%. In contrast, the prevalence among children the same age in the clinic-referred sample ranged from 50% to 85%.

Definition and Typology of Lies

Philosophers, authors, and researchers have been concerned with how to define and measure lying. Often, their definitions of lying include a person's use of intentional deception. In this chapter, we define lies as intentionally deceitful statements and distinguish such statements from other untruths (Bok, 1978; Freud, 1965; Jensen & Hughston, 1979; Piaget, 1932/1968). This definition excludes statements that are not intended to deceive, such as those made by children who fail to distinguish reality from fantasy (Freud, 1965; Piaget, 1932/1968) or statements that serve to maintain social convention. Children as well as adults can make these distinctions of intention and convention. For example, children think it is a minor moral transgression, if a transgression at all, to compliment someone even if the compliment does not reflect one's true feelings (Nucci, 1981; Turiel, 1977). Theorists and clinicians have described more specifically a number of types of lies and the purposes they serve (Bard, 1980; Blackham & Silberman, 1980; Burt, 1925; Freud, 1965; Healy, 1917; Piaget, 1932/1968; Wile, 1942).

We examined difinitions of lying in the literature to construct a typology of untrustworthy communications, and we developed a measure of untrustworthy communication based on that typology. A brief description of five types of lies follows:

The first type is the lie of self-preservation (Bard, 1980; Blackham & Silberman, 1980; Burt, 1925; Freud, 1965; Wile, 1942). This type takes two forms: avoiding blame, punishment, or disapproval by denying misdeeds, and avoiding embarrassment. A second type of lie is the lie of self-aggrandizement (Blackham & Silberman, 1980; Burt, 1925; Freud, 1965; Wile, 1942). This type is used to make individuals appear better than they really are. It consists of boasting or bragging about one's abilities, possessions, or accomplishments to receive attention, approval, or status. The lie of loyalty is a third type (Burt, 1925). It consists of lying about another individual's transgressions to protect that person. The lie of selfishness is a fourth type, and it serves to gain material advantage (Freud, 1965; Wile, 1942). The fifth type of lie is the antisocial or harmful lie, which is used to harm other individuals by falsely accusing them or belittling them (Burt, 1925; Wile, 1942).

Assessment of Lying

By any definition, lying is a low-frequency and clandestine behavior that is difficult to observe. In natural settings, low-frequency behaviors are generally difficult to observe, and, in the instance of lying, intent must be inferred.

Theoretically, there are several strategies for identifying children who lie. Ideally, one can select multiple methods for data collection (e.g., interviews, naturalistic and role-play observations, psychophysiological measurements, ratings, rankings, nominations) and then obtain information from multiple sources (e.g., self, peers, parents, teachers) (Nay, 1979). Clearly, some methods and sources are less useful than others. Naturalistic observation, self-report measures, psychophysiological measures, or experimental tasks are fraught with either technical, logistical, or ethical problems when applied to evaluating children's lying. Asking children to self-report on truth telling may yield unreliable data. If a child tends to lie, he or she is unlikely to speak honestly about his or her lying. Psychophysiological methods, used in lie-detector tests, are expensive, unreliable, and raise legal and ethical concerns. Also, the use of temptation or entrapment in experimental studies raises ethical and legal concerns.

Structured behavior ratings provide some of the most efficient and low-inference data on children's behavior problems. Rating methods, though subject to error from rater characteristics and the halo effect, are time- and cost-efficient, are easy to administer and score, and can be reliable and valid. Yet, lying has most often been represented by only one or two items in a larger set of items rated by teachers, parents, or peers. A review of 24 behavior problem rating scales and inventories revealed that 14 included one lying item, 4 included two items, 1 included three items, 1 included four items, and 3 included no lying item (Wilson, 1985). On many of these scales, the assessment of untrustworthy communication is broad (e.g., "lies"), but others assess one or few more specific untrustworthy communications (e.g., "accuses others falsely," "lies to protect friends," "denies wrongdoing"). Although a multifactor behavior problem scale is useful for screening, it samples a limited range of lying items. Therefore, it does not provide very specific information about lying.

The most difficult issue in assessing lying, however, is developing a reliable and valid sampling of the domain. Naturalistic observation is simply too intrusive, too inaccurate, and too expensive. We developed a rating scale to be completed by individuals who had observed the child with other children over a period of several months. Although this approach has the problems of any measure that allows a reputational effect, it has the advantages of (a) allowing specification of several types of lies and presentation of items for each type and (b) providing time for lying to be exposed.

To assess truth telling as well as lying, we developed positive as well as negative items for our rating scale, with items representing trustworthy communication as well as types of lies (untrustworthy communications). We wondered whether data gleaned from positive items would yield similar information to that provided by data on negative items. Did a low score on trustworthy items, that is, a relatively lower degree of trustworthiness, correspond to a high score on the untrustworthy items, that is, a relatively higher degree of untrustworthiness, and vice versa? Such a finding would seem to be intuitively logical. Further, if these scales are highly related, the use of only positive items in a trustworthy–untrustworthy scale could have the practical benefits of (a) not requiring adult judges to ascribe negative (untrustworthy) characteristics to children and (b) reducing the length of the scale. In contrast, we wondered whether inclusion of positive items would yield additional information not provided by data on negative items. Could children receive scores in the same direction on both positive and negative items (e.g., high trustworthiness, high untrustworthiness)? For example, could a child be highly trustworthy in peer interactions and highly untrustworthy in interactions with adults?

Trustworthy Communication Scale

The Trustworthy Communication Scale (TCS) is a three-part screening measure of trustworthy and untrustworthy communication (Wilson & Carroll, 1985, see Appendix 7.1). We wrote items to assess behaviors that were performed with an intent to deceive another individual (untrustworthy communication) or to communicate truthfully (trustworthy communication). Content of items included on the TCS reflects the typology of lies presented earlier. The types identify untrustworthy communications used to (a) avoid punishment, (b) avoid embarrassment, (c) boast or brag, (d) protect friends, (e) gain material advantage, and (f) belittle or harm others. In part 1, adult judgments of the degree to which statements are characteristic of a subject are obtained via ratings on a 4-point rating scale.

Response options range from not at all descriptive to very descriptive. In part 2, adults rate the frequency with which they have had to take some action in the past 10 days because of the subject's untrustworthy behavior. In part 3, adults rank order the types of lies a subject engages in from the most frequently observed to the least frequently observed.

Initial investigations of technical properties of the TCS are encouraging. Wilson and Carroll (1985) analyzed teacher ratings ($N = 15$) of untrustworthy items in part 1 of a sample of subjects ($N = 88$), ranging in age from 4 to 20. A Cronbach's alpha coefficient of .95 on 17 items suggested a highly homogenous set of items. A "total untrustworthy communication score," computed as the sum of ratings across all items, accounted for 68% of the variance in status between groups identified by teachers as untrustworthy or not. A factor analysis of teacher ratings of trustworthiness in a sample of fifth-grade students ($N = 126$) yielded a large bipolar factor, with each trustworthy (positive) item and untrustworthy (negative) item having the expected sign (Wilson, 1985). Internal consistency reliability was high for the set of positive items (alpha = .94), for the set of the negative items (alpha = .94), and for all items (alpha = .96). Coefficients of reliability for parent ratings ($N = 42$) were also high for the same sets of items (.95, .90, and .94).

A Study of Peer, Parent, and Teacher Judgments of Trustworthiness

Subjects

We collected data regarding trustworthy–untrustworthy communication from peer, parent, and teacher perspectives. Regular education teachers ($N = 7$), and male ($n = 64$) and female ($n = 62$) students from two suburban schools in the Southwest served as subjects. Students ranged in age from 10 years 1 month to 12 years 7 months ($M = 10$ years, 9 months, $SD = 6.6$ months). Parents of students were invited to participate in the study, and 51 (40%) returned completed rating scales. The parent-rated subsample consisted of 28 male and 23 female students who did not differ in age from the larger sample.

Procedures

Demographic data were collected for each student from school files. Teachers were given a procedure to select randomly 18 students from their classrooms and complete the TCS. Parents were requested in writing to rate their child's behavior on the TCS. We contacted parents who failed to respond to the first mailing by phone and sent them another set of scales.

We computed a trustworthy communication score (TC) and an untrust-worthy communication score (UTC) by summing ratings across trust-worthy and untrustworthy items in part 1, respectively. We standardized these scores within the classroom. Because TC and UTC scores were found to be highly correlated, a total trustworthy communication score (TTC) was computed using the formula [TC − UTC] + K, where K is a constant added to each score to avoid negative values. We added a dif-ferent constant to parent scores, because they remained on a raw score scale and had higher absolute values. Teacher and parent TTC scores therefore are not directly comparable by inspection.

We collected peer judgments via two traditional roster and rating socio-metric questionnaires (Roistacher, 1974), that is, "How much do you like to play with this person at school?" and "How much do you like to work with this person at school?" and a new sociometric questionnaire, that is, "How much do you trust this classmate to tell you the truth about some-thing important to you?" We prepared separate instruments for boys and girls to obtain same-sex ratings (Oden & Asher, 1977; Singleton & Asher, 1977). A 4-point rating scale ranging from 0 (not at all) to 3 (very much) appeared next to names of same-sex classmates. We computed the mean rating across peers for each sociometric item, yielding three indices of peer status (play, work, trust). Psychometric properties of rating sociometric measures are adequate for their use with elementary-school-aged children (Asher & Hymel, 1981; McConnell & Odom, 1986).

To collect sociometric data, examiners entered classrooms of participat-ing subjects, introduced themselves, and stated their purpose for collecting data. Examiners gave directions to students according to Singleton and Asher's (1977) procedures, explained the 4-point rating scale, and demon-strated how to complete the peer-rating questionnaires. The play ques-tionnaire was distributed to boys and girls. On completion of the play questionnaire, the examiner handed the subject a work questionnaire and took the play questionnaire. Examiners used the same procedure to com-plete the trust questionnaire. Examiners encouraged students to refrain from discussing responses with others. Finally, investigators thanked the students and teacher and left the classroom.

Results

GENDER DIFFERENCES

Table 7.1 presents mean peer sociometric ratings and parent and teacher ratings of trustworthy–untrustworthy communication by gender. Analyses of variance revealed that girls gave higher peer sociometric ratings to their female classmates than boys gave to their male classmates on the play sociometric index, $F(1, 123) = 9.69$, $p = .0023$; on the work sociometric index, $F(1, 123) = 7.82$, $p = .0060$; and on the trust sociometric index, $F(1, 123) = 6.70$, $p = .0108$.

TABLE 7.1. Means and standard deviations (in parentheses) of peer sociometric variables and trustworthy communication variables.

Variable	Boys ($n = 64$)	Girls ($n = 61$)
Play sociometric	1.73 (0.55)	2.00 (0.40)
Work sociometric	1.61 (0.57)	1.88 (0.48)
Trust sociometric	1.67 (0.59)	1.93 (0.51)

	Boys		Girls	
Variable	Teacher ratings ($n = 65$)	Parent ratings ($n = 28$)	Teacher ratings ($n = 61$)	Parent ratings ($n = 23$)
Total trustworthy communication	5.67 (1.98)	51.70 (1.04)	6.35 (1.72)	51.27 (1.10)
Trustworthy communication	34.05 (10.35)	34.05 (9.00)	37.20 (8.70)	26.70 (14.70)
Untrustworthy communication	8.48 (10.08)	9.28 (8.16)	5.12 (7.52)	8.16 (6.72)

We also found significant gender differences in both teacher and in parent ratings, but the pattern of gender differences was not consistent. Analysis of variance revealed that parents' trustworthy communication (PTC) ratings were higher for boys than girls, $F(1, 48) = 4.91, p = .0315$. Parents' untrustworthy communication (PUTC) and total trustworthy communication (PTTC) ratings were no different for girls than for boys. In contrast, analyses of variance revealed that teachers' trustworthy communication (TTC) ratings were higher for girls than for boys, $F(1, 124) = 3.70, p = .0568$; teachers' untrustworthy communication (TUTC) ratings were lower for girls than for boys, $F(1, 124) = 4.05, p = .0463$; and teachers' total trustworthy communication (TTTC) ratings were higher for girls than for boys, $F(1, 124) = 4.22, p = .0420$.

CONSISTENCY OF JUDGMENTS ACROSS PERSPECTIVES

Table 7.2 presents intercorrelations among teacher and parent trustworthy and untrustworthy communication variables and peer sociometric variables by gender.

Parents and teachers did not generally agree in their judgments of trustworthy and untrustworthy communication for either boys or girls. Table 7.2 presents nine correlation coefficients (three parent indices by three teacher indices of trustworthy–untrustworthy communication) for both sexes. Only 1 of 18 correlation coefficients presented in Table 7.2 reached statistical significance. That is, for girls, PTC rating was negatively correlated with TUTC.

Parents and peers likewise did not agree regarding trustworthiness of children. None of the parent indices correlated with the peer sociometric ratings for trust for either boys or girls.

Teachers and peers, in contrast, agreed strongly regarding trustworthiness in both sexes. All six correlation coefficients between teacher indices

TABLE 7.2. Intercorrelations among parent and teacher ratings of trustworthy communication and peer sociometric variables, by gender.

	1	2	3	4	5	6	7	8	9
1. PTTC	—	.92***	-.46*	.33	.23	-.40	.19	.18	.36
2. PTC	.95***	—	-.09	.36	.26	-.42*	.15	.19	.29
3. PUTC	-.93***	-.77***	—	-.03	.01	.06	-.15	-.03	-.27
4. TTTC	.29	.29	-.26	—	.94***	-.94***	.23	.32*	.49***
5. TTC	.30	.29	-.28	.97***	—	-.78***	.23	.32*	.47***
6. TUTC	-.25	-.26	.22	-.97***	-.87***	—	-.20	-.29*	-.46***
7. Play	-.09	-.15	.01	.46***	.45***	.44***	—	.82***	.71***
8. Work	-.06	-.14	-.04	.49***	.49***	-.46***	.93***	—	.80***
9. Trust	.10	.05	-.14	.73***	.70***	-.70***	.81***	.82***	—

PTTC, parents' total trustworthy communication; PTC, parents' trustworthy communication; PUTC, parents' untrustworthy communication; TTTC, teachers' total trustworthy communication; TTC, teachers' trustworthy communication; TUTC, teachers' untrustworthy communication; play, play peer sociometric; work, work peer sociometric; trust, trust peer sociometric.

Note. correlations above diagonal are based on data for girls; below diagonal are for boys.

$n = 65$ (boys) and 61 (girls) for correlations of teacher-rated variables with peer variables; $n = 28$ (boys) and 23 (girls) for correlations of parent-rated variables with peer variables.

* $p < .05$.
** $p < .01$.
*** $p < .001$.

of trustworthiness and peer sociometric trust were highly significant at the .001 level of significance. Teacher indices accounted for approximately half of the variance in peer trust for boys and about one quarter of the variance in peer trust for girls.

The pattern of correlations in Table 7.1 indicates that the degree to which parents, peers, and teachers agreed regarding trustworthiness in children varied widely. We found high degree of correspondence between teachers' and peers' judgments of trustworthiness, especially for boys. In contrast, parent judgments of trustworthiness did not agree with peer judgments, or teacher judgments for boys or girls. The lack of agreement between parents and peers, and parents and teachers, is not well understood, yet indicates the importance of collecting information in multiple settings and from different perspectives.

Discussion

These findings provide initial evidence that trustworthy–untrustworthy communication, though difficult to observe, can be reliably assessed in children. Analyses of both teacher and parent ratings on the TCS yielded high internal consistency reliability coefficients. Reliability data were consistent with factor-analytic results of teacher ratings that suggested that the TCS measured one variable.

Current results suggest that children's interpersonal trust and trustworthiness, as well as their overt, aggressive, and disruptive behavior problems, are important aspects of their peer relationships. Of particular note for this study was the finding that teacher ratings of trustworthy communication were highly predictive of peer status in boys and girls. This finding adds to recent evidence indicating that covert antisocial behavior predicts children's acceptance in the peer group (Patterson, 1986) and suggests that to gain a better understanding of children's peer relationships or to identify the behavioral dimensions of children's peer status, covert, as well as overt behaviors, must be assessed.

Results appear to be highly similar whether one uses positive items (trustworthiness) or negative items (untrustworthiness). Use of only positive items may increase rater willingness to complete the scale by significantly reducing the number of items to be rated and avoiding reluctance to assign undesirable behaviors or characteristics such as lying to a child.

The generally low levels of correspondence in judgments of trustworthiness between parents and teachers, and between parents and peers, is not well understood. Perhaps differences in the contexts in which children were observed by teachers, parents, and peers accounted for relatively poor consistency in ratings across perspectives. Teachers and peers observed students in the same context. Parents observed their children in quite different contexts. For example, the ratio of children to adults is different, relationships between adults and children are different, and standards for comparison vary widely.

The present findings provide evidence for the social validity of trustworthy and untrustworthy communication ratings. The high degree of correspondence between teacher ratings on the TCS and peer sociometric ratings for play, work, and trust was evidence for the social validity of trustworthiness ratings. A measure has social validity when it predicts important outcome variables (Gresham, 1986). Peer status measures are considered important outcome variables that are in turn predictive of indices of adjustment such as dropping out of school, criminality, and later psychopathology (Parker & Asher, 1987). Findings from this study suggest that children's trustworthiness is strongly related to their standing in their peer group. Children who are perceived as untrustworthy by teachers are less likely to be selected by their same-sex classmates as play partners or work partners. Further, children are less willing to share information with their untrustworthy peers, especially when the information is not trivial.

Additional evidence for social validity is found in the high correspondence between peer status indices. Peer sociometric ratings for play and for work have been used frequently in the study of peer acceptance and rejection, peer relationships, and social competence. They are well established measures of peer status. The trust sociometric index, a new measure, was highly related to both of these indices in both sexes. This suggests that children who cannot be trusted by their peers are highly unlikely to attract peers as play or work partners.

Summary and Future Directions

In this chapter we briefly reviewed research indicating that adults perceive lying as a serious behavior problem and that it is related to current and future adjustment problems. We indicated the obstacles to assessing lying and presented an index for measuring trustworthiness. We presented data on normal fifth-grade children's trustworthiness regarding: the reliability of adult ratings, gender differences, the correspondence among peer, teacher, and parent perspectives, and the social validity of trustworthy communication ratings. The present findings suggested that interpersonal trust and trustworthiness of communications are highly important aspects of children's lives. While we were encouraged by these findings, many questions remain regarding children's trustworthy communications. We outline some of those questions in the following discussion.

One set of questions regards developmental issues. For which age levels can trustworthy communication be assessed reliably via adult ratings? What is the frequency of lying at various ages, and does the frequency of lying change over time? Do the purposes served by lying (e.g., avoiding punishment, protecting friends, and gaining status and attention) change as children grow older? Do adult raters distinguish types of lies in children of different ages or view trustworthy/untrustworthy behavior more globally (e.g., honest/dishonest behavior) at all ages? Is there a significant relation between lying and peer status over the course of childhood? Studies that reliably assess perceptions of trustworthy communication over time need to be conducted.

Another set of questions regards the relation of trustworthiness to indices of current and future adjustment. How does reported or perceived trustworthiness relate to social skills, self-esteem, and to behavior problems such as aggression, anxiety, withdrawal, and attending problems? With what other indices does lying in childhood best predict specific problems in later childhood, adolescence, or adulthood?

A final set of questions regards the assessment of the effects of interventions for untrustworthy communications. Which intervention strategies can significantly reduce untrustworthy behavior or increase trustworthy communications? Does increased trustworthy communication have a positive effect on a child's social behavior, behavior problems, and peer status? What impact does intervention for untrustworthy communication have on risk for future maladjustment? Thus, while our research has focused on assessment of trustworthy and untrustworthy communications, we hope, of course, to contribute to identification of methods to increase trustworthy communication. We hypothesize that increasing truthful behavior will, however slowly, contribute to improved peer relationships. We believe that improvement in peer relationships may significantly reduce the risk of future behavior and adjustment problems. These larger hypotheses will require intervention research, research aided by improved measures of important but difficult to assess patterns of clandestine, untrustworthy behavior.

References

Achenbach, T.M. (1966). The classification of children's psychiatric symptoms: A factor analytic study. *Psychological Monographs*, *80*(7, Whole No. 615).

Achenbach, T.M., & Edelbrock, C.S. (1981). Behavioral problems and competencies reported by parents of normal and disturbed children aged four through sixteen. *Monographs of the Society for Research in Child Development*, *46*(1, Serial No. 188).

American Psychiatric Association. (1987). *Diagnostic and statistical manual of mental disorders* (3rd ed., rev.). Washington, DC: Author.

Asher, S.R., & Hymel, S. (1981). Children's social competence in peer relations: Sociometric and behavioral assessment. In J.D. Wine, & M.D. Smye (Eds.), *Social competence* (pp. 125–157). New York: Guilford Press.

Bard, J.A. (1980). *Rational emotive therapy in practice*. Champaign, IL: Research Press.

Behar, L., & Stringfield, S. (1974). A behavior rating scale for the preschool child. *Developmental Psychology*, *10*, 601–610.

Blackham, G.J., & Silberman, A. (1980). *Modification of child and adolescent behavior* (3rd ed.). Belmont, CA: Wadsworth.

Bok, S. (1978). *Lying: Moral choice in public and private life*. New York: Pantheon.

Burt, C. (1925). *The young delinquent*. New York: D. Appleton.

Carlson, C.L., Lahey, B.B., & Neeper, R. (1984). Peer assessment of the social behavior of accepted, rejected, and neglected children. *Journal of Abnormal Child Psychology*, *12*, 187–198.

Conners, C.K. (1969). A teacher rating scale for use in drug studies with children. *American Journal of Psychiatry*, *126*, 884–889.

Conners, C.K. (1970). Symptom Patterns in hyperkinetic, neurotic, and normal children. *Child Development*, *41*, 667–682.

Edelbrock, C., & Loeber, R. (1985). *Conduct problems in childhood and adolescence: Developmental patterns and progressions*. Unpublished manuscript.

Freud, A. (1965). *Normality and pathology in childhood*. New York: International Universities Press.

Gesten, E.L. (1976). A health resources inventory: The development of a measure of the personal and social competence of primary grade children. *Journal of Consulting and Clinical Psychology*, *44*, 775–786.

Goyette, C.H., Conners, C.K., & Ulrich, R.F. (1978). Normative data on revised Conners Parent and Teacher Rating Scales. *Journal of Abnormal Child Psychology*, *6*, 221–236.

Gresham, F.M. (1986). Conceptual issues in the assessment of social competence in children. In P.S. Strain, M.J. Guralnick, & H.M. Walker (Eds.), *Children's social behavior: Development, assessment, and modification* (pp. 143–179). Orlando, FL: Academic Press.

Group for the Advancement of Psychiatry. (1966). *Psychopathological disorders in childhood: Theoretical considerations and a proposed classification*. New York: Author.

Healy, W. (1917). *The individual delinquent*. Boston: Little, Brown.

Herbert, G.W. (1974). Teacher's ratings of classroom behaviour: Factorial structure. *British Journal of Educational Psychology*, *44*, 233–240.

Jensen, L.C., & Hughston, K.M. (1979). *Responsibility and morality*. Provo, UT: Brigham Young University Press.

Kim, Y., Anderson, H.E., Jr., & Bashaw, W.L. (1968). The simple structure of social maturity at the second grade level. *Educational and Psychological Measurement*, *28*, 145–153.

Kupfer, D.J., Detre, T., & Koral, J. (1974). "Deviant" behavior patterns in school children, application of KDS™-14. *Psychological Reports*, *35*, 183–191.

Langner, T.S., Gersten, J.C., McCarthy, E.D., Green, E.L., Herson, J.H., & Jameson, J.D. (1976). A screening inventory for assessing psychiatric impairment in children 6 to 18. *Journal of Consulting and Clinical Psychology*, *44*, 286–296.

Loeber, R., & Dishion, T.J. (1983). Early predictors of male delinquency: A review. *Psychological Bulletin*, *94*, 68–99.

Loeber, R., & Schmalling, K.B. (1985a). Empirical evidence for overt and covert patterns of antisocial conduct problems: A metaanalysis. *Journal of Abnormal Child Psychology*, *13*, 337–352.

Loeber, R., & Schmalling, K.B. (1985b). The utility of differentiating between mixed and pure forms of antisocial child behavior. *Journal of Abnormal Child Psychology*, *13*, 315–336.

McConnell, S.R., & Odom, S.L. (1986). Sociometrics: Peer-referenced measures and the assessment of social competence. In P.S. Strain, M.J. Guralnick, & H.M. Walker (Eds.), *Children's social behavior: Development, assessment, and modification* (pp. 215–284). Orlando, FL: Academic Press.

Miller, L.C. (1967). Louisville Behavior Checklist for males, 6–12 years of age. *Psychological Reports*, *21*, 885–896.

Mitchell, S., & Rosa, P. (1981). Boyhood behaviour problems as precursors to criminality: A fifteen-year follow-up study. *Journal of Child Psychology and Psychiatry*, *22*, 19–33.

Nay, R.W. (1979). *Multimethod clinical assessment*. New York: Gardner Press.

Nucci, L. (1981). Conceptions of personal issues: A domain distinct from moral or social concepts. *Child Development*, *52*, 114–121.

Oden, S., & Asher, S.R. (1977). Coaching children in social skills for friendship making. *Child Development*, *48*, 495–506.

Parker, J.G., & Asher, S.R. (1987). Peer relations and later personal adjustment: Are low-accepted children at risk? *Psychological Bulletin*, *102*, 357–389.

Patterson, G.R. (1986). Performance models for antisocial boys. *American Psychologist*, *41*, 432–444.

Piaget, J. (1968). *The moral judgment of the child* (M. Gabain, Trans.). New York: The Free Press. (Original work published 1932)

Pimm, J.B., Quay, H.C., & Werry, J.S. (1967). Dimensions of problem behavior in first grade children. *Psychology in the Schools*, *4*, 155–157.

Pulkkinen, L. (1983). Finland: The search for alternatives to aggresion. In A.P. Goldstein & M. Segall (Eds.), *Aggression in a global perspective* (pp. 104–144). New York: Pergamon.

Quay, H.C. (1979). Classification. In H.C. Quay & J.S. Werry (Eds.), *Psychopathological disorders of childhood* (pp. 1–42). New York: Wiley.

Quay, H.C., & Peterson, D.R. (1983). *Interim Manual for the Revised Behavior Problem Checklist*. Coral Gables: University of Miami.

Robbins, L.N. (1966). *Deviant children grown up*. Baltimore: Williams & Wilkins.

Roistacher, R.C. (1974). A microeconomic model of sociometric choice. *Sociometry*, *37*, 219–238.

Rutter, M. (1967). A children's behavior questionnaire for completion by teachers: Preliminary findings. *Journal of Child Psychology and Psychiatry*, *8*, 1–11.

Singleton, L.C., & Asher, S.R. (1977). Peer preference and social interaction among third-grade children in an integrated school district. *Journal of Educational Psychology*, *69*, 330–336.

Smith, G.M., Schwerin, F.T., Stubblefield, F.S., & Fogg, C.P. (1982). Licit and illicit substance use by adolescents: Psychosocial predisposition and escalatory outcome. *Contemporary Drug Problems*, *11*, 75–100.

Stouthamer-Loeber, M. (1986). Lying as a problem behavior in children: A review. *Clinical Psychology Review*, *6*, 267–289.

Stouthamer-Loeber, M., & Loeber, R. (1986). Boys who lie. *Journal of Abnormal Child Psychology*, *14*, 551–564.

Turiel, E. (1977). Distinct conceptual and developmental domains: Social convention and morality. In C.B. Keasy (Ed.), *Nebraska symposium on motivation* (Vol. 25, pp. 77–116). Lincoln: University of Nebraska Press.

Wile, I.S. (1942). Lying as a biological and social phenomenon. *The Nervous Child*, *1*, 293–313.

Wilson, J.M. (1985). *The identification of untrustworthy communication in children*. Unpublished master's thesis, Arizona State University, Tempe.

Wilson, J.M., & Carroll, J.L. (1985). *The evaluation of a measure of untrustworthy communication*. Paper presented at the annual convention of The National Association of School Psychologists, Las Vegas.

Appendix 7.1:
Trustworthy Communication Scale*

Student Name	Grade	Teacher

Part I Directions: Write the number that corresponds to the most appropriate response in the blank provided.

  0 = not at all descriptive of student
  1 = slightly descriptive of student
  2 = somewhat descriptive of student
  3 = very descriptive of student

1. Does not hesitate to speak untruthfully to get what he or she wants. ____
2. Lies to protect friends who have broken rules. ____
3. Accuses other individuals of things they actually did not do. ____
4. Brags and boasts untruthfully to gain status and attention and to appear better than he or she really is. ____
5. Lies about failures or breaking rules to avoid disapproval from parents, teachers, or peers. ____
6. Tells the truth even if he or she stands to gain something valuable by not telling the truth. ____
7. Denies wrongdoing to avoid punishment. ____
8. Never deliberately hurts another person by telling falsehoods about him or her. ____
9. Tells the truth about failing or doing wrong, even when it results in disapproval from parents, teachers, or peers. ____
10. Tells the truth about a failure although it may be personally embarrassing. ____
11. Seeks status and attention in appropriate (truthful) ways. ____
12. Tells the truth about a performance, even when lying about it would result in a valuable prize. ____
13. Lies about others' performances to make himself or herself appear better. ____

*Copyright 1991 by John M. Wilson. Reprinted by permission.

14. Denies performance to avoid feeling embarrassed.   _____
15. Cannot be trusted to tell the truth about a friend's wrong-doing, especially when the friend might be punished.   _____
16. Makes false statements about other persons just to hurt them.   _____
17. Admits wrongdoing, even when there is a good chance he or she will be punished.   _____
18. Does not falsely accuse others.   _____
19. Lies about a performance to receive a reward that has not been earned.   _____
20. Speaks untruthfully about failures in order to avoid embarrassment.   _____
21. His or her untruthful statements often cost other persons money, time, or energy.   _____
22. Knows when he or she is telling the truth.   _____
23. Does not distinguish truth from untruth in what he or she says.   _____
24. Can be trusted to supply truthful information about a friend who has broken a rule, even when the friend might be punished.   _____
25. Does not attempt to make himself or herself appear better by lying about other's performances.   _____
26. Attempts to tell the truth about an individual whether or not that individual is someone he or she likes.   _____
27. Attempts to accurately and truthfully describe his or her own abilities, attainments, activities, or possessions.   _____
28. Avoids punishment by blaming others for something bad he or she has done.   _____
29. Speaks truthfully about a friend's misdeed even if a friendship might be lost or the friend might be punished.   _____
30. Deliberately misleads you or others when speaking about his or her abilities, attainments, activities, or possessions.   _____

Part II Directions: Please write the letter that corresponds to your response in the blank provided. Base your judgments on the actual observations you have made.

    A = 0 times
    B = 1 times
    C = 2–4 times
    D = 5 or more times

31. In the past 10 days, how many times have you had to speak to this child or take some action about his or her lying to avoid the consequences of some misbehavior?   _____
32. How many times in the past 10 days have you observed this child attempting to gain something by misleading you or others?   _____

33. How many times in the past 10 days have you observed this child making false claims about his or her abilities, attainments, activities, or possessions?   ____
34. How many times in the past 10 days have you observed this child lying to you or another person about a friend's misbehavior?   ____
35. How many times in the past 10 days have you observed this child covering up the truth to avoid feeling embarrassed?   ____
36. How many times in the past 10 days have you observed that this child's lies resulted in harm to other individuals?   ____

Part III Directions: Please put the number of the type of lie you are most likely to observe for this child in the top space. Continue to select the most often observed lie from the remaining types on the list until you reach the bottom line (least often observed type). For types *never* observed, enter the number(s) on the seventh line.

Types of lies   *Most likely*
1. Self-preservation: avoid punishment, blame, or disapproval.   1st ____
2. Self-preservation: avoid embarrassment   2nd ____
3. Self-aggrandizement: untruthful boasting or bragging   3rd ____
4. Loyalty: protect friends   4th ____
5. Selfishness: gain material advantage   5th ____
6. Antisocial: harm, falsely accuse   6th ____
7. Immaturity: misunderstand reality   7th ____
                                                            Least Likely

8
Betrayal Among Children and Adults

WARREN H. JONES, MIRAMAR G.COHN,
AND CURTIS E. MILLER

An ironic issue has emerged in research on the psychology of relationships. On the one hand, numerous theories and considerable research suggest that satisfying and intimate relationships with family members, friends, and loved ones not only contribute to happiness, well-being, adjustment, and perhaps even physical health (e.g., Bowlby, 1973), but indeed, such relationships may be critical for both individual and species survival (e.g., Hogan, 1982; Hogan, Jones, & Cheek, 1985). Similarly, it has been widely suggested that one's social support network—defined as the persons with whom one has more or less regular contact and who provide information, comfort, and assistance—mediates the effects of stress (Cohen & Syme, 1985; Sarason & Sarason, 1984).

On the other hand, it is becoming increasingly clear that a major source of stress in the lives of most people is conflict with one's close friends and loved ones (e.g., Fischer, 1982; Rook, 1984). For example, interpersonal betrayal (i.e., violations of trust and allegiance, intrigue, and treachery within close personal relationships) represents an important constraint to the rewards and pleasures of intimate relationships, either potentially or in fact. We conceptualize betrayal as a serious violation of the norms and expectations of a relationship (e.g., violations of trust, commitment, confidence, as well as disloyalty, deceit, unfaithfulness, harm-doing, etc.). As such, the potential for betrayal by an intimate partner is the "price" one pays for the benefits of intimacy. In the interpersonal sense, one can be betrayed only by a partner one trusts and with whom one is close, whereas the ultimate protection against betrayal is to have no relationships, or only superficial ones.

Previous research on topics related to betrayal such as deception have demonstrated their relevance to interpersonal and relational outcomes (cf. Eckman, 1985; Metts, 1989; Miller, Mongeau, & Sleight, 1986). The focus on betrayal, however, emphasizes the diversity of experiences that may undermine the trust on which mutually satisfying and close relationships are presumably built. For example, beyond lies and deception, relational satisfaction and commitment may be damaged by angry words, physical

118

abuse, lack of attention and affection, and so on. Indeed, one may damage or destroy a close personal relationship by telling the truth as in betraying a confidence or "brutal honesty."

We begin this chapter with an overview of our ongoing research on betrayal including the research methodologies we have used in studies involving a variety of participant populations. Next, we survey selected results regarding betrayal among college students and noncollege adults including, for example, personality and demographic differences, types of betrayal, types of relationships involved in instances of betrayal, consequences of betrayal, and what might be called perspective differences (i.e., differences arising from being the victim of a betrayal or the betrayer). In addition, preliminary analyses of betrayal data obtained from two distinct samples of 9- to 12-year-old boys will be briefly presented and discussed. Finally, we will summarize our findings and discuss points of convergence and differences in betrayal among children as compared to older age cohorts.

Research on Betrayal

Several observers (c.f. Werner, Altman, Oxley, & Haggard, 1987) have argued that dyadic relationships emerge in the context of broad social and interpersonal processes in which competition for interpersonal and material resources, mixed-motives, and transitory purposes seriously complicate the path from interpersonal intentions to interpersonal outcomes. Thus, people must deal with limitations on the time, energy, attention, and affection they can devote to any given relationship; therefore, they must often choose one relational partner over another and choose also between satisfying their own interests and needs versus those of others. Competition and limited resources mean that friends and loved ones often will be openly opposed, or when that is not possible, occasionally deceived and plotted against. Conflicting motives and shifting allegiances increase the probability that trust, promises, and solemn vows will be broken, and quite often the simple need for conversation or diversion means that gossip— even when imaginary and malicious—will be presented as truthful and harmless. In short, in a complex interpersonal world, sooner or later, many people will betray or will be betrayed by at least some of their closest friends and loved ones.

To date, we have conducted several surveys and related studies on betrayal. In these studies we have operationalized betrayal in three ways. Our initial efforts involved respondent-generated accounts of betrayal— what have been termed *micronarratives* (Baumeister, Stillwell, & Wotman, 1990). Specifically, participants were asked to write about their relevant experiences in an open-ended response format. The primary goal in these studies was to learn what sorts of actions and events are judged to be instances of betrayal. In addition, these accounts contained a variety of suggestions as to who betrays whom, why, and with what effect. Such autobiographical narratives are typically seen as attempts to understand one's own experiences (Gergen & Gergen, 1988) and have the benefit of providing information regarding the presumed motivations for important experiences as well as the respondent's recall of the details of such experiences.

Second, we have examined betrayal as an individual difference variable by constructing and validating a self-report scale. The purpose of this approach was to assess the personality, demographic, and attitudinal correlates of the self-reported propensity to betray and also the impressions that significant others form of persons who vary in their personal histories as betrayers.

Third, we have examined the issue of betrayal as a dimension of the social network. These studies afforded the opportunity to explore the apparent consequences of betrayal within a broader interpersonal context. For example, these data addressed questions such as whether people who betray their relationships report smaller and less satisfying networks, as common sense would suggest, and how people feel about persons whom they believe have betrayed them. Similarly, these data also provided the opportunity to examine how perceptions of betrayal are related to other interpersonal judgments, such as jealousy and perceived reciprocity.

Betrayal Narratives

At the outset one of our primary questions was, does betrayal constitute only certain interpersonal transgressions or will any offensive behavior be viewed as an instance of interpersonal betrayal? Consequently, we instructed samples of adult respondents to provide written accounts of betrayal from each of two perspectives: (a) the most significant experience in their life in which they had betrayed someone else and (b) the most significant incident in which they had been the victim of betrayal. In these studies, we also asked participants to provide certain details of the incident such as their relationship to the victim or perpetrator, when the betrayal occurred, whether the victim was aware of the betrayal, the presumed motives involved, and the effect, if any, on the relationship in question.

Results of studies among adults (Hansson, Jones, & Fletcher, 1990; Jones, 1988; 1989) indicated that, among women, betrayal (as both victim and perpetrator combined) that was due to an extramarital affair was more common than any other type, followed by lies, which included both lies told to and lies told about someone. For men, lies and extramarital affairs were more-or-less equally common, followed by betraying a confidence. A second issue of importance concerned who betrays whom. For both men and women, the most common type of relationship involved in betrayal was one's marital partner, after which there were gender differences in the rank order of betrayed relationships. For example, men reported more betrayals involving work relationships (i.e., work colleagues, bosses, subordinates, etc.), whereas women reported more betrayals involving friends, particularly same-sex friends. Also, approximately 75% of the men in these studies said that the person they had betrayed was a woman, whereas only half of the persons who had betrayed them were identified as women. For female respondents, roughly 55% of both the victims and perpetrators of the betrayals they described were identified as men. In addition, for both men and women, incidents of betraying another were reported to be significantly more recent than incidents involving having been betrayed (Hansson et al., 1990).

Finally, this procedure asked how the betrayal influenced the development of the relationship in question, if at all. We coded as "worse" those responses that indicated the relationship had terminated by virtue of divorce, breaking up, or never again speaking to one another, as well as responses indicating that the relationship had been harmed by lingering doubts and negative feelings. These were often expressed by respondents as "we are now less close," "the relationship is strained," and "there has been less trust between us since this happened." The category "same" referred to responses indicating either that the relationship was not changed by the betrayal or that its effects were only temporary, after which the relationship returned to what it had been. The category "better" referred to respondents who actually claimed that the relationship was enhanced following the betrayal, for example, by becoming more intimate or improving the couple's sex life. Results indicated that when describing being betrayed by others, respondents overwhelmingly (>90.0%) said that the relationship was worse than before. By contrast, when they betrayed someone else, in approximately half of the cases, the relationship was seen to remain the same or even to improve!

Individual Differences in Betrayal

MEASUREMENT

Our second approach to the study of betrayal involved the development of a self-report scale. Items were generated from the betrayal accounts elicited in the free-response narratives. The basic idea of many of the most frequent accounts was converted to a brief, single-sentence statement such as the following: "avoiding a friend when with people I want to impress," and "lying to a family member." These items were then administered to groups of college student and adult respondents with instructions to respond to each item on a 5-point rating scale anchored by statements referring to the frequency with which one has engaged in the behavior in question. Examples of the anchors were "I have never done this," and "I have done this many times."

Internal reliability analysis retained items such as "gossiping about a close friend behind his or her back," "complaining to others about your friends or family members," "making a promise to a family member with no intention of keeping it," and "failing to stand up for a friend when criticized or belittled by others." In addition, this analysis retained a few items referring to ingratiation and false expressions of acceptance. Items illustrative of this theme included "agreeing with people so that they will accept you" and "pretending to like someone you detest." Fifteen items with substantial item–total correlations were retained to make up the final version of the Interpersonal Betrayal Scale (IBS).

Subsequent analyses suggested that the IBS was internally reliable, for example, coefficient alpha was .87 in one sample. Also, preliminary evidence suggested the validity of scale interpretations. Scores on the scale were inversely correlated with self-ratings of respondent's moral standards, for example. Scores on the IBS were modestly contaminated with social desirability. On the other hand, there was some evidence for discriminant validity; for example, IBS scores did not correlate strongly with measures of delinquency and antisocial personality.

BIOGRAPHIC CORRELATES

To date, the IBS has been administered to over 1,000 respondents along with measures of a variety of constructs (Jones, 1988). In general, significant inverse relationships have been found between IBS scores and age, education, and marital length. Similarly, divorced persons score higher than married persons. Not surprisingly, there were particularly strong connections between self-reported betrayal and indices of both personal and relational problems. Alcoholics and psychiatric patients scored especially high, as did those who reported either having been the victim or instigator of physical and/or sexual abuse. Other groups with higher than average scores on the IBS included adult children of divorced parents, adult children of alcoholics, adjudicated delinquents, and adolescents permanently expelled from the public schools. On the other hand, analyses of several biographic variables were not related to scores on the IBS; the most notable of these was gender.

PSYCHOLOGICAL CORRELATES

In psychological terms, betrayers presented themselves as sullen, vengeful, and prone to jealousy and suspicion. In one study (Jones, 1988), college students completed the IBS and selected self-descriptive adjectives from a list that was provided. Results indicated that the self-portraits of high, as compared to low scorers on the IBS were more likely to include terms such as sulky, envious, cynical, doubting, solitary, aloof, morose, regretful, guilty, exploitive, gossipy, pompous, jealous, and suspicious; conversely, these self-descriptions were less likely to include terms like truthful, pleased, relaxed, involved, trusting and courageous.

Jones (1989) confirmed and extended this image of frequent betrayers using comparisons with standardized measures of personality. For example, scores from the IBS were related to measures of shame, guilt, suspiciousness and, in particular, resentment. Similarly, using a measure of personality disorders, Jones found that higher scores on the IBS were also associated with higher scores for borderline, paranoid, passive-aggressive, and, to a lesser extent, avoidant and histrionic personality disorder dimensions. Additional research indicated that IBS scores were significantly related to various dimensions of normal personality as measured by the California Personality Inventory (CPI) including inverse relationships with independence, self-control, good impression, well-being, self-realization, responsibility, tolerance, intellectual efficiency, psychological mindedness, and communality (Montgomery & Brown, 1988).

INTERPERSONAL CORRELATES

Interpersonal Betrayal Scale scores have also been compared to various measures of relationship functioning and satisfaction. For example, among a sample of noncollege adults (Monroe, 1990), these scores were inversely related to loneliness, satisfaction with one's family of origin and, for men only, marital commitment. Married betrayers reported experiencing more marital problems, in particular, loss of interest in the marriage, extramarital affairs, dissatisfying sexual relations, lying, negative emotions, and impatience. They were also more likely to blame their spouses for these and other problems rather than themselves or the couple jointly. By contrast, self-reported betrayal was unrelated to marital satisfaction for either men or women.

Social Network Analyses

Our third approach to the study of betrayal has used social support methodology. Specifically, respondents were asked to complete a modified version of the Social Network List (cf. Jones & Moore, 1987). This inventory requests the identification (by initials of persons) of significant others who provide social support and then the completion of a series of questions regarding each person on the list from which network characteristics such as size, composition, and quality can be calculated. Thus, respondents were asked to identify the age, gender, type of relationship, and length of acquaintance of each member of his or her social network. In addition, respondents rated on 4-point scales, whether they, for example, could confide in, were satisfied with, and felt equally important to each person listed along with several additional items. This generic procedure for assessing network characteristics and social support became a method of operationalizing betrayal by asking respondents to also identify network members they had betrayed or who, in their estimation, had betrayed them.

In one study, Jones (1988) found that almost half (45.2%) of the adult respondents indicated that they had betrayed at least one member of their current social network, and a somewhat higher percentage (52.4%) indicated that they had been betrayed by at least one network member. A few persons indicated that they had betrayed or been betrayed by every member of the network. By contrast, the average proportion of the social network who had betrayed the respondent was 18.8%, and the average proportion of network members who had been betrayed by the respondent was 20.3%. Many of the results using the Social Network List procedure replicated earlier findings regarding, for example, the types of relational partners cited as victims or perpetrators of betrayal. Also, as before, there was a tendency for network members identified as targets of betrayal to be cited as instigators as well.

In addition, and consistent with earlier results, the difference between men and women in terms of the proportion of relationships involving betrayal was not significant. On the other hand, correlations between responses to the two network betrayal items and other interpersonal judgments on the network list revealed an important gender difference. For men, there were numerous correlations, in expected directions, between betrayal from both perspectives and other interpersonal judgments. For example, the extent of betraying and having been betrayed by a network member were both inversely related to ratings of satisfaction with the relationship, love of the person, similarity to the person, and positively correlated with extent of disagreements with the person and regrets over the relationship. By contrast, for women, the significant relationships were limited to the item assessing having been betrayed. In other words, men expressed consistently negative judgments regarding those persons they had betrayed and persons by whom they had been betrayed. Women held a similarly negative view of persons who had betrayed them. However, for women, the covariations between having betrayed someone and the respondent's judgments about that person were unreliable.

Results from our previous studies have been largely consistent in suggesting the following conclusions: (1) betrayal is a common experience in the context of many types of close personal relationships, most particularly, romantic and marital relationships, friendship, and other family relationships; (2) although there are interesting gender differences in terms of the type and target of betrayal, for the most part, both male and female respondents report similar experiences and propensities toward betrayal; (3) there appear to be stable individual differences in betrayal that are associated with both biographic and personality characteristics; (4) betrayals occur primarily within the context of the current social network, and the perception of betrayal is related in predictable ways to other interpersonal judgments; and (5) the issue of perspective (i.e., whether one is the betrayer or the betrayed) is of paramount importance in relation to the perceptions and consequences of betrayal. Furthermore, this general pattern of results has appeared to be relatively stable across samples of varying ages and life circumstances including college students (Jones, Sanchez, & Merrell, 1989; Montgomery & Brown, 1988); married adults (Monroe, 1990); adults-in-general (Jones, 1988, 1989); and among the elderly (Hansson et al., 1990).

It is not clear, however, whether these results would generalize to the experiences of children, particularly in that developmental changes in experience and expectations associated with specific relationships such as friendship have been noted in previous research (Bigelow, 1977; Furman & Bierman, 1984; La Gaipa, 1981). For example, even in late childhood, opportunities for interpersonal relationships are typically more structured and determined by parental and adult supervision and guidance than is the case for persons who are older. Restricted interpersonal opportunities may result in fewer opportunities to betray and to be betrayed. On the other hand, research suggests that children as young as 3 years of age not only are capable of relevant betrayal behaviors such as deception but are capable also of suppressing emotional expressions that may lead to the detection of betrayal (e.g., Lewis, Stanger, & Sullivan, 1989). Furthermore, even if restricted in interpersonal opportunities, children may still betray and be betrayed by family members (parents, siblings, etc.), and the consequences of such betrayals might be expected to be greater during childhood as compared to later ages as a result of the presumptive influences of initial interpersonal involvements on later relationships (Hartup, 1986).

Moreover, research on children's friendship suggests, in a variety of ways, the relevance of betrayal experiences in interpersonal development. For example, as early as kindergarten, children show restrictive disclosure to friends by revealing more high-personal as opposed to low-personal information to friends than to nonfriends (Rotenberg & Sliz, 1988). Further, research suggests that the reasons for termination of children's friendships are largely age-appropriate variations of the betrayal experiences cited by college student and adult respondents, including aggression, rule and expectation violations, disloyalty, and ego-degrading (e.g., name-calling) experiences (Hayes, 1978; La Gaipa, 1981). Younger children might be particularly vulnerable to betrayal experiences because of difficulties in understanding that violations of friendship can be corrected in some cases (Yoniss, 1980). Indeed, some researchers have characterized the friendship concerns of children as revolving around their potential to be hurt, rejected, ridiculed, and exploited (Bigelow & La Gaipa, 1980).

Method and Results

To further explore the relevance of betrayal to late childhood (ages 9 to 12), we assessed two small samples of boys as a part of a larger study. One sample ($n = 20$) consisted of boys who had been placed in a residential facility for delinquent and neglected children and adolescents. Although approximately half of the sample had been placed in the facility following a pattern of delinquent behavior, and the remainder were found to have been neglected in the home environment, both conditions for placement were present in the majority of the sample. A "control" sample ($n = 20$) consisted of boys living at home with both biological parents. The two groups were comparable in age and education level but not socioeconomic status. Specifically, control participants were from higher socioeconomic families than the institutionalized participants, as would be expected. We presented participants with the three methods for assessing betrayal briefly outlined previously, with two major differences: (1) we obtained betrayal narratives in interview rather than written form; and (2) we modified the reading difficulty level of all instruments to accmmodate younger respondents, some of whom in the institutional samples were below grade level in reading and vocabulary comprehension. For example, the concept of betrayal was described as "doing something to a friend, family member, or someone you know which is 'against the rules' and 'hurts' the other person in some way."

BETRAYAL NARRATIVES

Table 8.1 presents comparisons of the institutionalized children and normal counterparts with respect to the several analyses of the betrayal narratives. Columns headed by %OF represent betrayal narratives in which the respondent described having betrayed someone else, whereas %BY refers to experiences as the victim of betrayal. As would be expected, institutionalized boys much more frequenty cited instances of betrayal from both perspectives involving acts that were clearly illegal (i.e., crime, delinquency, e.g., stealing). This group also frequently cited disappointments and broken promises as illustrated by failing to stop using drugs, failing to stop seeing "undesirable" friends, and school failure. Also, note that some children in the institutional group said that they had been betrayed by virtue of having been ignored, avoided, and/or abandoned, in each case by a parent. By contrast, the betrayals from both perspectives of the normal group fell largely into three categories: teasing, telling lies or making false accusations, and gossiping and betraying confidences. Thus, both the betrayals perpetuated by the institutional group as well as the betrayals they experienced apparently were more serious violations of interpersonal norms than those of the control group. This expectation was confirmed by an analysis in which two raters (unaware of the participants' group) rated the "seriousness" of each betrayal account on a 5-point scale, with higher scores reflecting more serious violations of relational norms. Analyses indicated that mean "seriousness" scores for the institutional group were significantly higher than for the noninstitutional group for both betrayals of others and betrayals by others.

TABLE 8.1. Percentage of betrayal categories cited in narratives by group.

Category/Variable	Institutional		Normal	
	%OF	%BY	%OF	%BY
Type of betrayal				
Lies/false accusations	15	0	15	25
Disappointment/broken promises	15	30	5	5
Teasing	0	0	30	30
Crime, delinquency	25	25	5	0
Gossip/betrayed confidence	15	0	15	20
Alienation of affection	15	5	0	5
Criticism/verbal abuse/arguments	0	5	15	5
Physical abuse/fighting	0	5	5	10
Two-timing/rejection/jilting	5	5	5	0
Ignoring/avoiding/abandonment	0	25	0	0
Destruction of property	5	0	5	0
Type of relationship				
Male friend	25	40	45	45
Sibling	40	5	35	40
Parent	15	40	10	0
Other relative	10	5	5	0
Other person (e.g., teacher)	10	0	5	10
Female friend	0	10	0	5
Change				
Improvement	25	5	25	0
None/temporary	55	40	60	50
Worse/ended	20	55	15	50
Blame				
Self	80	0	40	5
Other	20	100	60	95
Gender				
Male	55	70	75	75
Female	45	30	25	25

%BY, respondent victim of betrayal; %OF, respondent betrayed other.

Table 8.1 also indicates the types of relationships involved in the betrayal accounts of these respondents. As indicated, there were relatively few differences between the groups in this rgard, except that the institutionalized males were more likely to cite the mother and the father as the perpetrator of betrayals against them as compared to the normal group. Also, normal respondents more frequently indicated betrayals of and by one's siblings, especially brothers. Otherwise, both groups cited male friendships as the most common relationships involving betrayal.

Regarding change, both groups were more likely to indicate that their betrayals of others had resulted in improved relationships than instances where they had been betrayed. By contrast, although respondents in both groups were more or less equally likely to blame the other person, when they had been betrayed, normal, as compared to institutional children were only half as likely to blame themselves when they had been the per-

TABLE 8.2. Mean Interpersonal Betrayal Scale scores for selected groups.

Group description	N	Mean
Alcoholics	62	45.84
Psychotherapy clients	31	44.10
Institutionalized adolescent boys (ages 13–18)	22	43.50
Institutionalized boys (ages 9–12)	20	37.07
Normal adolescents (ages 13–18)	69	36.60
Normal boys (ages 9–12)	20	36.45
College students	109	35.91
Adult males	496	35.04
Adult females	523	34.96
Elderly adults (age > 65)	78	27.57

petrator of the incident. Also, there was a slight tendency for the institutional sample to more frequently cite having betrayed and having been betrayed by female rather than male relational partners as compared to the normal sample. Additional analyses failed to yield significant differences between the respondent groups.

INDIVIDUAL DIFFERENCES IN BETRAYAL

Table 8.2 presents the means for self-reported betrayal using the IBS. Groups presented include the institutionalized and normal children from the present sample as well as institutionalized male adolescents (from the previously cited facility) and normal male adolescents. Also, Table 8.2 contains means from selected age cohorts obtained in previous studies. As may be seen, the institutional and normal children in this sample yielded roughly equal scores on the IBS. Also, whereas these scores were modestly higher than those obtained from normal adults and college students, they do not differ significantly from one another nor from a previous sample of normal adolescents. Consequently, neither group appeared to be dispositionally more prone to betrayal.

Betrayal and the Social Network

Analyses of the data obtained using the modified Social Network List indicated that the instituationalized boys reported having betrayed a mean of 46.6% of their current social network members, whereas 24.7% of social network members were seen as having betrayed them. The corresponding figures for noninstitutionalized boys were 44.5% and 33.8%, respectively, and neither difference between the groups was significant. Thus, the two groups were similar in the proportion of network members they indicated having betrayed and having betrayed them. Also, the correlation between IBS scores and the proportion of the network betrayed by the respondent was ($r[18] = .47, p < .05$) for normal boys and ($r[18] = .63, p < .05$) for the institutionalized sample. The corresponding anlayses between IBS scores and the proportion of the network listed as having betrayed the respondent were not reliably different from zero in either case, however.

In addition, we compared IBS scores to network characteristics and interpersonal judgments within each group. Among institutionalized boys, higher scores on the IBS were associated with fewer adults in the social network, $r(18) = -.47, p < .05$; and fewer long-term relationships, $r(18) = -.35, p < .10$; as well as lower proportions of network members perceived as similar, $r(18) = -.42, p < .05$; and greater proportions of network members whose relationships were characterized by respondents as involving jealousy, $r(18) = .41; p < .05$; disagreements, $r(18) = .56, p < .05$; and regret, $r(18) = .35, p < .10$. Among normal boys, higher IBS scores were associated with a greater proportion of adults in the social network, $r(18) = .62, p < .01$; as well as greater proportions of network relationships characterized by jealousy, $r(18) = .63, p < .01$; and disagreements, $r(18) = .58, p < .01$.

Within the institutionalized group, having been betrayed by larger proportions of one's social network was associated with smaller proportions of the network characterized by "can turn to for help," $r(18) = -.45$, $p < .05$; "can confide in," $r(18) = -.30, p < .10$; and greater proportions of network relationships identified as involving disagreements, $r(18) = .77$, $p < .01$; and regret, $r(18) = .48, p < .05$. The proportion of network members betrayed was related to the proportion of disagreements, $r(18) = .46$, $p < .05$, and regret, $r(18) = .32, p < .10$, among this group. Similarly, among the noninstitutionalized group, greater porportions of network members characterized as having betrayed the respondent were reliably associated with greater proportions of jealousy $r(18) = .54, p < .05$; disagreements, $r(18) = .40; p < .05$; and regret, $r(198) = .32, p < .10$. Among normals, the proportion of the network betrayed was related only to the proportion of relationships involving disagreements, $r(18) = .72$, $p < .01$.

Summary and Conclusions

Results from this and previous studies suggest several related conclusions. First, betrayal is a common and pervasive phenomenon. Depending on whether betrayal is operationalized in terms of current network membership or as any relevant event, involving anyone, at any point in ones' life, in previous studies (Hansson et al., 1990; Jones, 1988, 1989) the proportion of respondents who cited instances of betrayal varied from a low of just under 50% to a high of over 90%. Data from the two samples of boys examined in the present study did not differ much from previous studies involving adolescents and adults in this regard. In short, betrayal experiences appear to be quite familiar in the lives of both children and adults.

Second, there are stable differences in the consequences of betrayal, depending on whether one betrays or has been betrayed. Undoubtedly, to a large extent, this simply reflects the impact of differences in self-interest and awareness associated with these two perspectives. It is not particularly surprising that respondents appear more willing to excuse their own transgressions than the offenses of their relational partners, for example. However, it should be noted that the issue of perspective involves more than simple self-interest. It is clear that a person can betray another person—even in an important way—without that person becoming aware of it. What is less obvious is that, for example, a person may feel betrayed by a relational partner even when that partner is unaware that he or she has done anything wrong. Furthermore, the partner may or may not be unaware of his or her betrayal because he or she is insensitive. Instead, the differences may derive in large measure from the perspective of the perceiver. Thus, this issue is also important because it emphasizes the extent to which judgments of betrayal can be embedded in and shaped by the individual perceptions, beliefs, and expectations of the observer, that is, in the unique perspective of the person who feels that an act of betrayal has occurred. As before, the present data on male children confirm the differential consequences of betrayal associated with the perspective from which the act of betrayal is viewed. Furthermore, these differential consequences may be exaggerated in children, in that once a betrayal is perceived, strategies for reconciliation may not be available (Yoniss, 1980).

Third, analyses involving social network and support methodologies suggest that betrayal occurs among one's closest relationships and is generally related, in predictable ways, to other interpersonal judgments and outcomes. It's an obvious point, but these studies confirm that perceived betrayals by others often lead to the termination of a relationship, or where that is not feasible, to smoldering distrust and ill-will. Similarly, the most devastating betrayals occur among the most important and intimate relationships. The counterpart of this truism is that one can be betrayed only after becoming vulnerable in an intimate relationship. Less obviously, betraying and being betrayed do not always appear to lead to either social isolation or pervasive dissatisfaction with one's social and intimate relationships. Instead, as operationalized in these studies, betrayal often seems to function more like an environmental stressor that is tolerated, avoided, or overcome, than the inexorable end to the relationship. This point is consistent with the present data as well. For example, both groups reported betraying and being betrayed by friends with whom, in the vast majority of cases, they were still involved. In addition, the noninstitutionalized group reported several betrayals by and of siblings, whereas the institutionalized sample cited several instances of betrayal involving parents. Even so, for both cases, most respondents indicated positive ratings of these persons as well (e.g., "can confide in this person," "love this person," etc.). Frequently, then, betrayal appears to result in mixed and ambivalent feelings toward relational partner rather than the termination of the relationship.

Fourth, although betrayal is a common feature in the interpersonal lives of most people, people also vary in the likelihood that they will betray their relational partners. Some betray less than the average, some betray more. The nonbetrayers tend to be older, better educated, and religious. On the other hand, it is too early to determine whether many of the biographical correlates of betrayal are substantive rather than the result of methodological or extraneous variation. For example, scores from the present study involving 9- to 12-year-old boys were slightly elevated as compared to scores obtained from college students and older adults in previous studies. It is not yet clear, however, whether the inverse correlation between age and IBS scores reflects the rapidly shifting allegiances and romantic involvements typical of youth or merely a greater willingness on the part of adolescents and children to admit to socially undesirable behaviors. On the other hand, the psychological characteristics of frequent betrayers are clear; they are jealous, suspicious, envious, and perhaps above all else, resentful. Although one cannot tell from these data, it seems reasonable to suppose that some people begin new relationships with chips on their shoulders, and resentful, suspicious types would seem to be likely candidates for doing so. This, in turn, makes betrayal virtually inevitable because of the way such people are likely to react to the natural fluctuations in intimacy and satisfaction that characterize long-term relationships.

Fifth, although not assessed in this preliminary study of children, stable gender differences appear to be associated with betrayal, and some of these follow: Men appear more likely to betray romantic partners (especially their wives), as well as business associates. Women appear more likely to betray other family members and friends. Men more frequently indicated that they had been unfaithful, women reported being more likely to betray a confidence (Jones, 1988, 1989). Also, among women, the consequences, feelings, and explanations associated with betrayal were less predictable than for men. On the other hand, little evidence suggests that one sex was more likely to betray than the other.

Despite considerable differences in life circumstances of the boys in the present study, with the exceptions noted, the two groups did not differ substantially on these measures of betrayal. Perhaps the most striking difference was that the betrayals (including both as victim and perpetrator) reported by the institutionalized, as compared to the normal, boys appeared to be more serious and devastating, as would be expected. Differences were also observed in the types of relationships most frequently involved in the betrayals of these boys. As a consequence, it seems reasonable to conclude on the basis of these and previous analyses that the causes and consequences of betrayal remain relatively stable across respondent groups, with differences attributable to individual and familial problems. On the other hand, it is also reasonable to conclude that more serious betrayals (e.g., abandonment) involving one's most critical relational partners (e.g., parents) would exert major influences on a variety of factors including identity formation and the subsequent development of relationships. Consequently, the observed differences between groups most likely contributed to the difference in living circumstance, as well as important variables not assessed in this study.

To summarize, our preliminary analyses suggest that the responses of the boys in the two present samples did not differ much from those of older age cohorts previously examined (Hansson et al., 1990; Jones, 1988, 1989; Jones et al., 1989 April). For example, although the types of betrayal cited in the narratives were more likely to involve age-relevant experiences such as teasing, these respondents yielded patterns very similar to college students and older adults, especially with respect to the proportion of social network members cited as involved in betrayals and the differential consequences associated with betraying as compared to being the victim of betrayal. Furthermore, analyses indicated relatively few differences in betrayal-related experiences between the institutionalized and normal samples, except in types of relationships and seriousness of betrayals.

Finally, in noting that betrayal is commonplace or more-or-less inevitable, we do not mean to suggest that it is justified or neutral in its consequences. On the other hand, we would like to offer one closing observation based on these studies. Far from being an aberration in human relationships, betrayal is both inherently and intimately bound up with fundamental modes of relating to one another. To enjoy the many advantages of close personal relationships, one must endure the risks that they entail, specifically, betrayal and rejection. In this sense then, betrayal represents one of the constraints or barriers to relationships; it is the dark side of trust, love, and commitment. Moreover, it always accompanies these interpersonal processes, at least as a potentiality. Thus, both the threat and reality of betrayal are part of what makes genuinely healthy and mutually satisfying relationships so problematical, but it is also part of what makes such relationships, when achieved, so rewarding.

References

Baumeister, R.F., Stillwell, A., & Wotman, S.R. (1990). Victim and perpetrator accounts of interpersonal conflict: Autobiographical narratives about anger. *Journal of Personality and Social Psychology, 59*, 994–1005.

Bigelow, B.J. (1977). Children's friendship expectations: A cognitive-developmental study. *Child Development, 48*, 246–253.

Bigelow, B.J., & La Gaipa, J.J. (1980). The development of friendship values and choice. In H.C. Foot, A.J. Chapman, & J.R. Smith (Eds.), *Friendship and social relations in children* (pp. 189–210). New York: Wiley.

Bowlby, J. (1973). *Attachment and loss. Vol. 2. Anxiety and anger.* London: Hogarth.

Cohen, S., & Syme, S.L. (Eds.). (1985). *Social support and health*. New York: Springer-Verlag.

Ekman, P. (1985). *Telling lies*. New York: W.W. Norton.

Fischer, C.S. (1982). *To dwell among friends*. Chicago: University of Chicago Press.

Furman, W., & Bierman, K.L. (1984). Children's conceptions of friendship: A multimethod study of developmental changes. *Developmental Psychology, 20*, 925–931.

Gergen, K.J., & Gergen, M. (1988). Narrative and the self as relationship. In L. Berkowitz (Ed.), *Advances in experimental social psychology* (Vol. 21, pp. 17–56). San Diego, CA: Academic Press.

Hansson, R.O., Jones, W.H., & Fletcher, W.L. (1990). Troubled relationships in later life: Implications for support. *Journal of Social and Personal Relationships, 7*, 451–463.

Hartup, W.W. (1986). On relationships and development. In W.W. Hartup & Z. Rubin (Eds.), *Relationships and development* (pp. 1–26). Hillsdale, NJ: Lawrence Erlbaum.

Hayes, D.S. (1978). Cognitive bases for liking and disliking among preschool children. *Child Development, 49*, 906–909.

Hogan, R. (1982). A socioanalytic theory of personality. In M.M. Page (Ed.), *Nebraska symposium on motivation: Personality—Current theory and research* (pp. 55–90). Lincoln: University of Nebraska Press.

Hogan, R., Jones, W.H., & Cheek, J.M. (1985). Socioanalytic theory: An alternative to armadillo psychology. In B. Schlenker (Ed.), *Self and identity: Presentation of self in social life* (pp. 221–242). New York: McGraw-Hill.

Jones, W.H. (1988, July). *Psychological and interpersonal issues in betrayal and treachery*. Paper presented at the Fourth International Conference on Personal Relationships, Vancouver, British Columbia, Canada.

Jones, W.H. (1989, April). *Betrayal and other pains of close relationships*. Paper presented at the meeting of the Southwestern Psychological Association, Houston, TX.

Jones, W.H., & Moore, T.L. (1987). Loneliness and social support. *Journal of Social Behavior and Personality, 2*, 145–156.

Jones, W.H., Sanchez, D., & Merrell, J. (1989, April). *Explanations of betrayal accounts*. Paper presented at the meeting of the Southwestern Psychological Association, Houston, TX.

La Gaipa, J.J. (1981). Chiidren's friendships. In S. Duck & R. Gilmour (Eds.), *Personal relationships: 2. Developing personal relationships* (pp. 162–186). London: Sage.

Lewis, M., Stanger, C., & Sullivan, M.W. (1989). Deception in 3-year-olds. *Developmental Psychology, 25*, 439–443.

Metts, S. (1989). An exploratory investigation of deception in close relationships. *Journal of Social and Personal Relationships, 6*, 159–179.

Miller, G.R., Mongeau, P.A., & Sleight, C. (1986). Fudging with friends and lying to lovers: Deceptive communication in personal relationships. *Journal of Social and Personal Relationships, 3*, 495–512.

Monroe, P.R. (1990). *A study of marital problems, marital satisfaction, and commitment*. Unpublished doctoral dissertation, University of Tulsa.

Montgomery R.L., & Brown, E.O. (1988, July). *Betrayal, treachery, the CPI, and the Jenkins Activity Survey*. Paper presented at the Fourth International Conference on Personal Relationships, Vancouver, British Columbia, Canada.

Rook, K.S. (1984). The negative side of social interaction: Impact on psychological well-being. *Journal of Personality and Social Psychology*, *46*, 1097–1108.

Rotenberg, K.J., & Sliz, D. (1988). Children's restrictive disclosure to friends. *Merrill-Palmer Quarterly*, *24*, 203–215.

Sarason, I.G., & Sarason, B.R. (Eds.). (1984). *Social support: Theory, research and applications*. Dordrecht, Netherlands: Martinus Nijhof.

Werner, C.M., Altman, I., Oxley, D., & Haggard, L.M. (1987). People, place and time: A transactional analysis of neighborhoods. In W.H. Jones & D. Perlman (Eds.), *Advances in Personal Relationships* (Vol. 1, pp. 231–275.). Greenwich, CT: JAI Press.

Yoniss, J. (1980). *Parents and peers in social development*. Chicago: University of Chicago Press.

9
Trust and Children's Developing Theories of Mind

MICHAEL CHANDLER AND SUZANNE HALA

Conspicuous among those whom "you can fool all of the time" are innocent children. This follows for the reason that mistrust, whatever else it
may be, is also something of an intellectual accomplishment, the achievement of which is neither quick nor automatic. Still, learning about deceit
and the broader possibilities for false belief is a standard part of what we
take growing up to mean. Our chapter is about this loss of innocence.
What will be said on this subject is meant to persuade you of two things.
One of these is that there are good reasons for believing that by 2 or 3
years of age, but not much before, young children first acquire those
cognitive competencies required to appreciate that persons can be misled
into taking as true what is otherwise known to be false. The other is that,
in addition to all of its otherwise uplifting effects, this same cognitive
accomplishment has the harsh consequence of also eroding an earlier and
more earnest faith in the simple truth of what others have to say. Something like this new prospect for bad faith is almost certainly a part of what
Erikson (1950) had in mind by his regular insistence that the issue of
trust, while held out as the centerpiece of only the first of his psychosocial
periods, is repeatedly taken up and reworked at each subsequent juncture
along the life-span developmental course. The present chapter will have
served its purpose if it succeeds in making clear why the course of young
preschool children's cognitive development contributes to this recursive
process by stripping them of an earlier naivety and confronting them with
the previously unenvisioned prospect of being dealt with dishonestly.

If interest in children's thoughts about the prospects of being deceived
was somehow unique to those directly concerned with the study of trust
and mistrust, then much less would be known about this subject than is
actually the case. As it happens, a serendipitous flurry of recent research
into the development of children's so-called "theories of mind" is respon-
sible for the accumulation of a substantial body of new evidence concerning the broad topic of false-belief understanding (e.g., Astington, Harris,
& Olson, 1988; Perner, in press; Wellman, 1990). These data, while still
subject to the usual range of alternative interpretations, go some important

distance toward establishing the existence of a definite watershed in children's cognitive developmental course, before which the prospect that someone might intentionally lead them into some false belief is simply unavailable. Why this is so, and approximately when in the ordinary flow of development such limitations are typically overcome, has a direct and obvious bearing on the kinds of interactions that could serve to undermine trust. That is, children who cannot even envision what it might mean to hold to a counterfactual belief, or who wouldn't recognize a lie or deceitful act if it ran over them, would appear to be insulated by their own immaturity from the corrosive effects of such dishonesties and can hardly be expected to take umbrage at being victimized in these ways.

Sensitive parents and child-care professionals already know these things to some approximation and eventually give up perpetrating convenient frauds on children altogether, or at least recognize the importance of crafting a better brand of lies. What is not commonly known, and the unsettled matter to which contemporary research into children's earliest theories of mind speaks directly, is more precisely *when* and *why* such changes come about. Selectively reviewing the available literature regarding these matter is the business taken up in this chapter. More specifically, attention will focus on the ability of children of different ages, not only to recognize, but also to perpetrate various forms of deception, and on the status of these abilities as a general marker of false belief understanding.

Step one of this recounting will be to (a) report on what is generally had in mind by those who have sought to characterize young preschool children as coming to real if fledgling theories about the workings of their own and other's minds and (b) to make clear the special role of so-called "false-belief understanding" in deciding who does and who does not "deserve" to be credited with such mentalistic theories. Step two, which is the real centerpiece of this effort, is more methodological and empirical in character, and attempts to arbitrate current controversies over when young children first understand the possibility of false belief. Because the upshot of this analysis is that measures of deceptive intent provide what appear to be the earliest window into children's grasp of the possibility of false belief, special attention will be devoted to providing a summary account of what is known about children's understanding of such lies and other deceptive practices. Finally, part three ends the chapter in a brief attempt to extract the potential relevance of all of these data for our own efforts to view trust in ways newly informed by contemporary developmental theory and research.

Beliefs about Beliefs

On Having a "Theory of Mind"

Because the job of building some cohesive theory capable of organizing and extending our knowledge regarding the intricacies of mental life is usually understood to be the unfinished business of grown-up philosophers and social scientists, all of the recent talk about young children's so-called "theories of mind" that has sprung up in the cognitive developmental literature has appeared to many to be needlessly hyperbolic, if not downright mistaken. There is, consequently, some need to begin this discussion by defending the appropriateness of such top-lofty talk about children's mentalistic "theories."

One way of doing so is to stress that the closest continuers to children's theories of mind are not the bookish efforts of professional psychologists but the "folk psychologies" common to ordinary adults (Forguson & Gopnik, 1988; Gopnik, 1990). One remarkably widespread, and perhaps even universal, common core of such folk theories is that "belief-desire" framework by means of which we routinely undertake to explain one another's behaviors by viewing all voluntary actions as some cross-product of (a) what we want or desire and (b) what we think or believe to be the case (Wellman, 1988, 1990). Although providing only the most rudimentary of building blocks to what, for most adults, quickly becomes a much more elaborated accounting system (Chandler, 1987, 1988), even in its simplest form such a belief–desire psychology shares with scientific theories more generally (a) the invention of certain constructs, which (b) along with definite rules for their interrelations, (c) permit the making of novel predictions (Wellman, 1988). It is the origins of precisely this sort of rudimentary theory of mental life that numerous contemporary cognitive scientists have been interested in pinning down.

The Methodologic Superiority of False as Opposed to True Beliefs

In principle, the task of deciding when young persons first warrant being credited with some such fledgling theory of mind is conceptually straightforward and amounts to no more than settling on what should stand as evidence of their ability to attribute beliefs or desires to others. In practice, agreement about these matters has proven devilishly hard to achieve. This discord has arisen primarily as a consequence of serious differences of opinion over what should count as instances of first and higher order beliefs.

Clearly, infants-in-arms hold to beliefs about the world, as do so-called "lower" animals of almost every stripe. That is, if we mean by the term *belief* something like a working mental representation of how things are, then any organism capable of learning from experience harbors such beliefs. By contrast, attributing to others anything quite as elaborate as even a beginning "theory of mind" would seem to presuppose some still higher order abilities of the sort required to entertain beliefs about beliefs (Olson, Astington, & Harris, 1988). Many of the interpretive problems that have arisen in the literature concerned with the early acquisition of such mental models stem from difficulties in distinguishing such "true" metarepresentations from the primary beliefs that they are about. Shortly after their first birthday, for example, children often engage in acts of declarative pointing (Leung & Rheingold, 1981) and otherwise struggle to bring to the attention of others matters of interest what would otherwise be overlooked (Lempers, 1979). Although few would be prepared to regard these behaviors as clear evidence of an early theory-like understanding of the mind, they do seem to suggest at least a premonition about such mental events. Similarly, the penchant of 2- and 3-year-olds for collusive games of social pretence (Dunn, 1988; Howes, 1985; Leslie, 1988), with their conspiratorial commitment to the counterfactual, are difficult (we would argue impossible) to account for if toddlers truly lacked any capacity to form beliefs about the beliefs of others. By the same token, children of this age regularly and appropriately salt their earliest conversations with various intentional state terms such as *think*, *know* and *want* (Bretherton & Beeghley, 1982). How the usage of such terms could arise if such young persons were as ignorant of the epistemic states of others as some would have it is far from clear.

Pitted against all of the foregoing lines of evidence in favor of the possibility that 2- and 3-year-olds, and perhaps still younger children, already subscribe to some real if fledgling theory of mind are a series or reductive readings of these same facts. Perhaps, it is argued, all supposed instances of declarative pointing are no more than elaborate shows of enthusiasm, all apparent references to intentional states only the mindless repetition of pat phrases, and all apparent acts of social pretense no more than the unwinding of well-polished social scripts. None of this, of course, is proven, but the doubts are there, and out of this uncertainty has grown the special interest in children's grasp of the possibility of false belief. The obvious logic here is that, because it is constitutive of what it means to hold to a belief that such notions can be in error, anyone who lacks an appreciation of the fact that beliefs can be false simply fails to understand what holding a belief is all about. Thus, unless or until young persons satisfy this litmus test (Wellman, 1988) of understanding, any attempt to attribute to them a beginning theory of mind is now commonly seen to be premature. The open question, to which we turn in the section to follow, is precisely what sorts of behaviors on the part of young children can taken as evidence of their emerging grasp of the possibility of such false beliefs.

Alternative Criterion of False-Belief Understanding

Although the contemporary research literature on developing theories of mind is literally awash in candidate procedures meant to assess young children's earliest understanding of the possibility of false beliefs, all of these alternatives ultimately devolve into measures of one or the other of two generic types. One of these, commonly referred to as measures of "unexpected change," focuses on the ability of subjects to recognize and directly comment on the fact that ignorance can lead persons (usually hypothetical story characters) to act on beliefs that are objectively false. The second of these two classes of procedures avoids the pitfalls associated with such discursive accounts by accepting as equal coinage the efforts of young persons to actively lead others into believing to be true what they themselves know to be false. The evident logic here is that all attempts to execute such deceptive practices naturally presuppose some capacity on the part of others to be misled. By this standard, clear evidence that young persons somehow intend to deceive, no matter whether they do so well or badly, is seen to count as unimpeachable proof that they already understand the possibility of false belief and, consequently, harbor at least some fledgling theory of mind.

Were it the case that these alternative measurement strategies yielded closely comparable results, then there would be little to choose between them. As it is, these classes of measures paint radically different pictures of young children's grasp of the possibility of false belief. As subsequent sections will seek to show, investigators who have relied exclusively on measures of unexpected change regularly report that only 4- or 5-year-olds, but not still younger children, truly appreciate the possibility of counterfactual beliefs. By contrast, others (e.g., Lewis, Stanger & Sullivan, 1989), including ourselves (Chandler, Fritz & Hala, 1989; Hala, Chandler & Fritz, 1991), who have relied instead on more direct measures of children's capacities to engage in deceitful practices, typically report evidence indicating that children as young as 2 or 3 are capable of taking active steps to disinform others and so must already appreciate the possibility of false beliefs.

Before attempting to arbitrate this dispute, or otherwise endorsing one of these accounts of preschool children's emerging theories of mind as more in the running for the truth, it is important that we begin by shedding any pretense of personal disinterest in how this matter is resolved. Along with our research colleague Anna Fritz, we are already on record (e.g., Chandler et al., 1989; Hala et al., 1991) as having actively championed the "early-onset" view that children as young as 2 or 3 are in fact capable of recognizing the possibility of false beliefs and of employing this knowledge in carefully crafting elaborate frauds purposefully meant to mislead others. Making clear why we hold to such views is best achieved, however, by first carefully examining the evidence that speaks against them, most of which has arisen from the application of various unexpected change measures of false-belief understanding.

Unexpected Change Measures

If one wishes to learn something about the ability of young children to entertain beliefs about the beliefs of others, then the most natural move would seem to be to simply ask them what they imagine someone else might be thinking about some simple matter or fact. Unfortunately, no such straightforward approach is workable for the reason that there is no way of deciding whether children actually understand such questions as they are intended. This follows for the reason that, in the case of true beliefs, questions about what another thinks about X and what is factually true about X admit to exactly the same answer. Such doubts hold little sway in the case of adults, whom we have every reason to assume are able to successfully hear and maintain the distinction between reality and beliefs about it, and for whom it seems entirely appropriate to suppose that they also preserve the difference between questions about thoughts and their possible referents. By contrast, when the subjects of one's investigations are children, and the topic of inquiry happens to be just whether they can or cannot grasp the distinction between beliefs and what those beliefs are about, then their responses to ordinary questions concerning the mental processing of self-evident truths tells us nothing whatsoever about the status of their developing theories of mind.

One available route around this interpretive impasse is simply to arrange matters in such a way that those target individuals whose possible beliefs are to be commented on would ordinarily get things wrong. By gerry-mandering information in this way, and consequently forcing a wedge between the way things are and how some stimulus person would imagine them to be, the identity that typically obtains between states of the world and those mental states that are imagined to reference them is broken by requiring different responses to the questions "what is true about Y?" and "what does X believe to be true about Y?".

Numerous recent studies (e.g., Hogrefe, Wimmer & Perner, 1986; Perner, Leekam & Wimmer, 1987) into the course of children's developing theories of mind have capitalized on the divide-and-conquer strategy detailed here previously by introducing what have come to be referred to as "unexpected change measures" of false-belief understanding. A clear prototype for such procedures is to be found in the germinal work of Heinz Wimmer and Joseph Perner. In their original flagship study (Wimmer & Perner, 1983), these investigators required young subjects to comment on the likely beliefs of a doll figure named "Maxi," whose ideas regarding the whereabouts of a chocolate bar came to be dated as a consequence of his having been out of the room when it was unexpectedly moved from one location to another. The ability of children of various ages to appreciate that Maxi's ignorance of these events would lead him into error about the true current location of the chocolate was taken as hard evidence of their ability to entertain the possibility of false or counterfactual beliefs. In more than 20 subsequent variations on this simple theme, Wimmer and Perner and their colleagues (Perner, in press) have accumulated an impressive store of data, all of which support their conclusion that children younger than approximately 4 years of age suffer some previously unrecognized cognitive deficit that wholly blocks them from the possibility of false-belief understanding and, consequently, prevents them from subscribing to even a rudimentary theory of mind.

Although in many respects, these several studies are all models of a certain brand of methodological rigor, and although together they form an all but impenetrable thicket of self-citations documenting the supposed cognitive incompetencies of young preschoolers, there are, nevertheless, good reasons to doubt the representativeness of the data on which they rely. There is reason, for example, to wonder aloud whether such unexpected change tasks make the kind of "immediate human sense" (Donaldson, 1978) to preschoolers that one has a right to demand of procedures held out as "minimally complex" measures of false-belief understanding (Freeman & Doherty, 1989). Such procedures are, in fact, remote from children's own immediate interests; cast subjects in the role of passive observers of hypothetical third-party scenarios; are semantically dense and temporally ill marked; and require children to comment on, rather than otherwise act with reference to situations, the episodic structure and computational requirements of which are both needlessly complex. For all these reasons, 2- and 3-year-olds may very well fail such tasks, not because they lack those metarepresentational skills necessary to support beliefs about beliefs, but rather because their best abilities and interests are not engaged, their problem-solving efforts are derailed by incidental inference tasks, and their thinking is otherwise muddled by uncertainties as to precisely what they are being asked to comment on. While piecemeal efforts have been made to redress one or another of this list of failings (e.g., Lewis & Osborne, 1989; Moses, 1990; Zaitchik, 1989), what actually seems required is some more wholesale attempt to rewrite such procedures from the ground up. One means of doing so is to substitute for such unexpected change procedures an entirely different class of measures that approach the question of children's false-belief understanding by monitoring instead their developing abilities to deceive or purposefully mislead others into taking as true what they themselves believe to be false.

Deception as a Possible Marker of False-Belief Understanding

What, for the purpose of this chapter, makes the study of early deceptive practices of special interest is the fact that it jointly contributes to our knowledge of the roots of mistrust, on the one hand, and the development of false-belief understanding, on the other. That is, at least two things must be true of persons newly initiated into the prospects of deceit. One of these is that, having themselves acted in bad faith, they are now better positioned to first entertain the possibility that others may respond in kind with dishonesties of their own. The other is that there is no longer room for any serious doubt that they must appreciate the possibility of false beliefs and, consequently, deserve to be credited with at least a rudimentary theory-like understanding of the mind. This follows for the evident reason that there would be little point in struggling to disinform others unless one could also understand that the upshot of doing so would be persuading them to take as true what one knew to be false.

It is on the strength of the foregoing rationale that developmentalists, along with everyone from ethologists and comparative psychologists to military strategists (Sexton, 1986) and students of charlatanry (Hyman, 1989), have been interested in working out the conditions that make deception possible. Three pieces of this large but scattered literature bear directly on our topic. Two of these, which deal in turn with the topics of possible deception in so-called "lower" animals and the pointed lies of older children, bracket and will serve to introduce our own (e.g., Chandler et al., 1989; Hala et al., 1991) and other's (e.g., Lewis et al., 1989) more recent work on nonverbal deception in preschool children.

DECEPTION ON A PHYLOGENETIC SCALE

The question of whether animals other than humans have the capacity to purposefully lead others into false beliefs, while interesting in its own right, is relevant in the present context primarily because the research it has generated has served to bring to the surface certain conceptual problems that any workable definition of deception must attempt to sort out. Central among these are the degrees to which various ways of acting or of being in the world must register as purposeful, communicative, disinforming, and digital to qualify as genuinely deceitful.

For much the same reasons that have led contemporary developmentalists into the study of children's first deceptive practices, comparative psychologists also recently have begun to reassess the prospects of deceit in other species (e.g., Byrne & Whiten, 1988; Mitchell & Thompson, 1986; Premack 1988; Premack & Woodruff, 1978). Historically, turn-of-the-century representatives of both of these groups managed to embarrass themselves by trafficking in unwarranted mentalistic attributions regarding their subjects, precipitating what amounted to a 50-year dark age in the study of all higher mental processes. More recently, however, the same "cognitive revolution" that has swept the rest of the field also has empowered an equivalent movement among comparative psychologists aimed at searching out possible theories of mind in everything from shore birds (Sordahl, 1986) to chimpanzees (Chevalier-Skolnikoff, 1986; deWaal, 1988; Premack & Woodruff, 1978). Unlike their developmental counterparts, however, serious doubts still are to be had among mainstream ethologists as to whether members of any other species ever get to the point of actually holding to beliefs about beliefs (Premack, 1988), thereby ensuring the need for special vigilance against the prospect of being too quickly led into easy presumptions about possible metarepresentational abilities. Consequently, there is much to be learned from the character-istically cautious approaches to these matters taken by those concerned with such cross-species comparisons.

First among these cautionary moves has been the efforts on the part of ethologists to distinguish between those various genetically "designed" appearances or automatic ways of being that have the unintended effect of misleading others and those other more clearly premeditated and dis-ingenuous acts purposefully meant to engender false beliefs. The animal kingdom, is in fact, literally alive with various sorts of Batesian mimicries and camouflage artistry of the first sort that serve various species in their efforts to be taken for something that they are not. There are, for example, plants that manage to pass themselves off as stones (Mitchell, 1986), butterfly wings patterned after the eyes of predatory birds (Byrne & Whiten, 1988), and endless other tricks of the animal trade, all meant to keep small things from being eaten by larger things. Contrapuntally, just as many creatures (e.g., angler fish and cannibal fireflies (Lloyd, 1986), seek to lure their prey by appearing to be something that they are not. While genetically programmed ruses of this sort often do succeed, it is just as obvious that there is nothing about these matters to suggest that they represent acts of bad faith or are meant as communications in any ordinary sense. In much the same way that the moon illusion goes on tricking our sensory system without even the possibility of deceptive intent, so do rock plants go on looking like stones, whether anyone who might otherwise graze on them happens to be looking or not. The useful point to be taken from all of this is that it is obviously not enough that someone has been deceived for a particular behavior to qualify as truly disingenuous. In addition, such acts must somehow also qualify as truly conversational and be *meant* to have the misleading effect that they sometimes do.

SINS OF OMISSION AND COMMISSION

A second and related issue that has emerged from available studies con-cerning the possibly deceptive acts of other species is the importance of distinguishing between behaviors that serve to *withhold* useful information as opposed to acts more explicitly aimed at *disinforming* others by sup-plying them with information that is patently false. Small animals, for example, are often very good at going all quiet when there are grounds for hope that their presence will thereby remain undetected. Although it is altogether possible that such secretive attempts to withhold information represent carefully executed plans intended to lead others into false beliefs, other less Machiavellian interpretations can be made to work equally well. What, for instance, are we to believe when the quarry freezes in its tracks at the snapping of some proverbial dry twig, and are we enti-tled to change our minds when we learn that it is Natty Bumpo and not some mindless furry thing (Chandler, Fritz, & Hala, 1989)? What is made apparent by such examples is that, by itself, simple secret keeping can be a poor substitute for more sturdy evidence of deceptive intent. Consequently, one is probably on safer methodologic grounds to discount most such acts as too interpretively ambiguous and to hold out instead for the more positive evidence provided by behaviors that are explicitly disinforming.

MANIPULATING BEHAVIOR VERSUS MANIPULATING BELIEFS

Even the conservative stance promoted previously does not go far enough, however, in warding off reductive assaults from still other quarters. One such further interpretive ambiguity arises out of the fact that it is still possible to actively engineer information for the purpose of manipulating the *behaviors* but not the *minds* of others. Many species of animals that would not otherwise be suspected capable of forming a deceptive intent do, for example, apparently manage to mislead in this fashion. Injury-feigning birds (Sordahl, 1986) or Dennett's (1987) often-repeated example of the family dog that limps for attention or scratches at the door as a ruse for unseating someone from its favorite chair are familiar cases in point. What need not be, and likely is not, present in such manipulative actions is any "notional" (Sexton, 1986) appreciation of the sorts of wrong-headed beliefs that might be attached to them by others. As Morgan (1894) long ago pointed out, it is enough in such instances to assume that in the past, such behaviors have been unwittingly associated with favorable outcomes and are simply learned and run off without any recognition of what others may or may not happen to think about them. What this teaches us is that, in our search for some minimally complex but defensible standard of deceptive practices, only those actions clearly undertaken for the specific purpose of manipulating thoughts rather than behaviors unambiguously qualify. The hard part, as we will go on to show, is to know when thoughts and not behaviors are being targeted.

DIGITAL VERSUS ANALOGICAL DECEITS

Having agreed on this much, there still remains an unwieldy variety of disinforming behaviors that, while being equivalently purposeful and communicative, still manage to be dissimilar in most other important respects. In fact, almost any information that persons regularly employ in sorting out what is true or false about their environment can be strategically perverted by those intent on leading others down some garden path. In light of this diversity, some taxonomic scheme for further partitioning the range of possible deceptive acts is frequently sought (Hyman, 1989). One popular convention has been to distinguish lies from all other more behavioral feints, ruses, bluffs, and so on. Although there is some merit to this way of packing things up, it does have the serious demerit of leaving unsettled the question of what to do with behaviors such as deceptive pointing that manage to be declarative and semantical without qualifying as truly lexical. A promising alternative proposed by Anderson (1986) is to distinguish between deceits that employ "digital" as opposed to "analogical" codes. What is at stake in this dichotomy is a distinction that divides those communicative forms that rely on arbitrary but socially sanctioned symbol systems (e.g., both language and declarative pointing) from analogic codes that somehow simulate actual objects or events in the physical or psychological environment. Dummy TV monitors and false smiles qualify by these standards as instances of falsely fashioned analogical codes, as do stealth and bluffing one's way through a poor hand of cards. In all these instances, some misleading structural or functional piece of the naturally occurring environment is brought into communicative play by substituting it for the true objects or events they are made to mimic. By contrast, digital deceptions, such as lying through one's teeth or falsifying one's tax return, succeed, not by literally changing the environment to resemble some counterfactual situation, but by altering the way such environments are coded within some arbitrary, (though not necessarily verbal) signal system that declares, but does not demonstrate, some counterfactual state of affairs.

For each of these alternatives, a certain list of pros and cons can be identified. It follows on this distinction, for example, that the opportunities to counterfeit digital codes are often less constrained by their context than are analogical deceptions. One may, for instance, lie about almost everything under the sun, whereas the negotiation of a successful trompe l'oeil is a more problematic affair, heavily dependent on the right mixture of available environmental resources. At the same time, however, digital deceits, which always hinge on some form of secondhand report, are rarely successful when the persons they are meant to deceive are in a position to check out what is being said on their own. That is why a well-crafted lie is one that is hard to verify and the claim that "there is nobody here but us chickens" rarely works.

On the plus side for analogical deceptions is the fact that, because they are typically nonverbal and closer to direct action or imitation than are socially transmitted digital codes, fewer extraneous performance factors may be required for their successful execution. This becomes a matter of prime importance in subsequent sections where the emphasis shifts to a consideration of the earliest ages at which human deception is possible. The immediate purpose to which the distinction between analogical and digital deceit will be put, however, is as an analytic wedge with which to divide the balance of this chapter into its remaining sections. The first and shortest of these sections deals with lying or deceptive pointing and selectively reviews a part of what is known about this and related forms of digital deceit. The second concerns deceits of a more analogical sort and principally deals with our own and other's recent research into children's strategic efforts to mislead others in games of hide-and-seek.

Lying and Other Forms of Digital Deceit

Children are notorious for verbally misrepresenting things in ways that are often patently self-serving and clumsily transparent. Although to what degree such "romancing" (Piaget, 1932/1965) deserves being thought of as actual lying remains a matter for debate (Chapter 2), its essential universality has prompted a good deal of research interest in the questions of precisely when young persons do in fact first begin to appreciate the meaning of, or develop any real talent for the telling of full-fledged lies. Other chapters in this volume provide extensive reviews of a literature intended to answer these question, most of which need not be repeated here. Still, because of their bearing on what is to follow, two or three especially pertinent conclusions from these and other summary accounts warrant some retelling.

Central among these take-home messages is the well-documented fact that young children are typically a very long way away from any proper *definitional* understanding of what is entailed in labeling something as a lie. More than half a century ago, Piaget (1932/1965) provided what may have been the first systematic evidence relevant to this point by presenting data meant to show that children younger than approximately 8 years of age are "moral realists" who discount or ignore the intentions of other speakers and decide whether they have lied or been truthful solely on the basis of the factual accuracy of their claims. The standard form that such semantical confusions take is that young preschool- and school-aged children commonly collapse the essential distinction between truth and truthfulness and wrongly imagine that any statement that is objectively false is also a lie.

More recently, other investigators (e.g., Chapter 2; Strichartz & Burton, 1990; Vasek, 1988; Wimmer, Gruber, & Perner, 1985) have succeeded in replicating most of Piaget's original empirical findings, although without always reaching the same conclusions concerning the course of children's moral development. What has become clear as a result of these more contemporary studies is that certain of the failings of such young persons are more "lexical" (Wimmer et al., 1985) than moral and hinge not so much on any ignorance of the possibility of malicious intent as on a failure to appreciate that the intention to wrongly inform is itself constitutive of what the term *lying* is conventionally understood to mean.

What somewhat obscures the developmental significance of these common lexical confusions is the body of recent evidence showing that children are not unique in their susceptibility to such interpretive errors. As Peterson (Chapter 2) and Strichartz and Burton (1990) have shown, many older children and even adults similarly confuse the notions of truth and truthfulness, especially when the false statements to be evaluated have serious negative consequences or mislead persons in high places.

Quite apart from the remaining uncertainty about just how age dependent such lexical confusions may eventually prove to be, however, what all of this evidence does do is serve to remind us that getting a firm grip on the slippery terminological differences that divide lies from other sorts of untruths is an extremely problematic business that commonly gets off to a slow start and a late finish. What some have failed to appreciate, perhaps because of the importance of these findings for other purposes, is that all of these otherwise interesting data actually tell us absolutely nothing about the altogether different question of when children first begin entertaining the idea that words can be used deceptively.

Fortunately, within the contemporary literature on lying, a second stream of research is more directly relevant to questions concerning the extent to which children of various ages actually recognize and seize on available opportunities to verbally misrepresent the truth. In attempting to make some sense of this often-confusing body of evidence, three issues that overlap in practice need to be kept conceptually distinct. One of these concerns the measurement or observational contexts within which such data are collected. The second relates to the specific sorts of things subjects are expected to lie *about*. Finally, it is essential to decide from the outset just how convincing or well crafted a verbal misrepresentation has to be before it can be judged to qualify as a full-fledged lie. Each of these separate matters is taken up briefly in the following discussion.

THE CONTEXT OF MEASUREMENT

With reference to the first of these matters, it is generally agreed on in theory, but not always honored in practice, that the best tests of this or any other early competence are those that maximize children's readiness to perform, while holding to a minimum all other extraneous task demands. In the case of efforts to assess children's earliest abilities to lie, sticking with these otherwise simple rules of thumb is complicated by two facts. One of these is that young persons should perhaps be forgiven if they proceed with extreme caution when prompted by strange adults to lie for the record. Whether children who fail to rise to such bait actually lack those fundamental capacities required for conceiving of the very possibility of a lie or are more simply exercising reasonable discretion, is often far from clear. In a recent study by LaFreniere (1988), for example, few 3-year-olds were found to be willing or able to lie to an examiner about the location of an object they had just hidden. As the author of this study was quick to acknowledge, however, the fact that these young subjects quickly withered under direct questioning or cheerfully gave up their secret rather than risk an easily verifiable lie, may tell us little about their ability to misrepresent the truth under less intimidating circumstances. Additional support for this interpretation is to be found in a more recent study by M. Lewis, Stanger, and Sullivan (1989), in which more than 60% of a group of 3-year-olds either lied or refused to answer questions about whether they had peeked at a forbidden toy. The good performance of these young subjects in a testing situation where the truth was seemingly hard to verify adds further credence to the suspicion that previous failures to find experimental evidence of lying among 3-year-olds may simply reflect their preference for the truth or their understandable reluctance to get caught.

As the evidence just cited helps to demonstrate, at least half of the battle in settling the question of who is or is not grown-up enough to lie is won or lost in the struggle to persuade young subjects that bending the truth is both safe and profitable. The other half seems largely determined by one's success in finding assessment tasks that effectively minimize extraneous task complexities, without also rendering these procedures susceptible to solution by other more rudimentary problem-solving means. Unfortunately, most available studies appear to have waged a losing campaign on one or the other of these fronts. Studies by Selman (1980) and Shultz and Cloghesy (1981) provide interesting cases in point. In both of these studies, the authors found that preschool and early school-aged children regularly failed to lie effectively or otherwise act deceptively in various laboratory-based competitive game situations. What remains unclear in these and similar studies, however, is the degree to which such task failures are actually traceable to a general ignorance of the possible role of lies in provoking false beliefs or were instead simply the by-products of other less interesting failures on the part of such subject simply to understand or agree to the rules of such novel competitive games.

Deceiving About What?

Of at least equal importance to the foregoing concerns regarding the contexts of measurement is a second, largely unexplored, design issue having to do with exactly what it is that research subjects are being asked to be deceptive *about*. Intuitively, the job of misleading others about some physicalistic matter of fact, such as under which shell the pea is hidden, or where "Maxi" last saw the chocolate, would seem an altogether simpler and more straightforward matter than trying, for example, to deceive others about one's emotions or purposes of sentiments. That is, by any conceivable counting strategy, the task of formulating personal beliefs about what some second individual might think about one's own or other's intentional states would seem at least one recursive step further removed from ordinary experience than are still lower order thoughts about thoughts that directly concern concrete matters of fact. It follows from all of this that those threshold abilities required to conceive of the very possibility of deceptively leading others into false beliefs ought to predate what ever more elaborate skills are necessary to deceive others about one's own goals or intentions.

We are aware of two studies that lend some support to these expectations. In one of these (Peskin, 1989), the examiner engaged 3- and 4-year-olds in a game and encouraged them to express their *preferences* for one or the other of two decorative stickers, of the sort that children like to collect. The special demonic twist to this procedure was that subjects were made to compete with a puppet figure who got first pick and who always kept for itself whichever sticker the child subject indicated that he or she preferred. At least for an adult, the obvious way out of this annoying situation would be to simply lie about one's true preferences. Only a few 4-year-olds, and almost no one as young as 3, were found to hit on this strategy for disinforming others about their true sentiments.

In a related experiment, Russell, Sharpe, and Mauthner (1989) involved preschoolers in a superficially simpler zero-sum game that required only that they point incorrectly as a way of disinforming an opponent about which of two boxes contained a prize. Although not required to comment explicitly on their own preferences, as was the case in Peskin's (1989) procedure, any reasoned solution to this problem obviously hinges on the ability to frame a deceptive strategy involving a miscommunication, not simply about which box is empty or full but about which of the two boxes one *hopes* the opponent will choose. Were this not the case—that is, if all that was required for subjects to secure a "reward" was to respond in ways that ran counter to their own initial impulses—then a few trials should have proven sufficient to get subjects headed in the right direction. As it was, the young subjects of Russel et al. continued, trial after trial, to act against their own best interests.

Interesting as these findings are, they do not warrant the conclusion reached by Peskin (1989) and Russell et al. (1989) that 3-year-olds are unable to act deceptively at all. An alternative explanation is that children of this tender age simply lack the apparently higher order ability to deceive others about their own *intentions*. Whether or not children as young or younger than 3 are able to act deceptively with regard to simpler matters having to do, for example, with the physical location of material objects, is another issue entirely, to which we will shortly turn. Before doing so, however, what still remains to be dealt with here is the last in our list of procedural matters concerning children's lies; the matter of variable expertise.

LYING WELL VERSUS LYING AT ALL: THE ISSUE OF EXPERTISE

Whether children of a particular age should or should not be credited with a talent for telling lies depends, of course, on just how tall or convincing a tale must be to qualify. Somewhere near the upper reaches of this dimension of expertise are all of those especially credible and well-crafted lies that manage to fool most of the people most of the time. Near the opposite extreme are badly bungled lies of the sort told by one of Vasek's (1988) 3-year-old subjects who announced to her mother that "I didn't break the lamp and I won't do it again." The point that such a poorly conceived effort brings home is that, however generous one's inclusion criterion might be, there undoubtedly exist other attempts to misrepresent the truth that fall even shorter of acceptable standards and for which the term *lie* cannot be stretched to reasonably fit. Clearly, certain of young children's earliest "I don't know's" or "I didn't mean too's" are proto-lies of this dubious sort and so probably deserve to be lumped together into some throw-away category.

What such examples help to make clear is that precisely where appropriate definitional lines ought to be drawn will ultimately depend on what sorts or research questions one is of intending to answer. For certain investigators such as Feldman (Chapter 6), for example, what is particularly at issue are the ages at which young persons begin getting a grip on those subtle nonverbal give-away cues that otherwise prevent them from being truly accomplished liers. A lifetime can obviously be spent in perfecting such Machiavellian skills. By contrast, when the telling of intentional falsehoods is of interest primarily because of the insights they provide into children's theories of mind, as it is here, then almost any sort of shabby, ill-kept lie will do. Our own data suggest that, by the time they are 2 or 3, most children already know enough about the mental lives of others, and about their capacity for being led into false beliefs, that lies of this minimal sort are technically possible. It is also true, as we will go on to show, that such young persons are still too inexperienced in their use of language to warrant our relying on their predisposition to *tell* lies as an appropriate standard against which to evaluate their capacity to conceive of, or practice deceit.

Nonverbal Measures of Deceptive Intent

Apart from the several studies cited (i.e., Feldman (Chapter 6); Peskin, 1989; Russell et al., 1989; Vasek, 1988), most of which have relied exclusively on verbal response indicators, the only other work directly concerned with identifying the earliest ages at which preschool children engage in various deceptive practices is the series of studies that we have initiated (Chandler et al., 1989; Hala et al., 1991) and the derivative efforts of others (e.g., Peskin, 1989; Russell et al., 1989; Sodian, in press), undertaken in an attempt to prove us wrong. Although not all of the smoke generated by the rubbing together of these competing accounts has cleared, the weight of available evidence now appears to come down heavily on the side of what we will describe as our own "early-onset" view. The program of research that supports this conclusion is summarized briefly in the following discussion.

EARLY VERSUS LATE-ONSET VIEWS

As already summarized earlier in this chapter, a large number of recent studies, all of which have relied on some variation of Wimmer and Perner's (1983) standard "unexpected change" measure of false-belief understanding, has contributed to a premature consensus that children younger than approximately 4 years of age all suffer from some previously undiagnosed cognitive deficit that wholly blocks them from holding to beliefs about the beliefs of others. Loosely arrayed against this well-consolidated "delayed-onset" view is a much more scattered collection of distantly related investigators, bound together by little more than their shared commitment to the idea that any such premature talk of cognitive deficits practices a serious disservice on 2- and 3-year-olds, all of whom are taken to know a great deal more about the workings of other people's minds than their poor performance on various "unexpected change" measures of false-belief understanding would indicate. The good use that such young children make of various intentional state terms, their skills at games of social pretence, and their apparent knowledge of the rules governing perceptual access to knowledge are all counted, by proponents of this early-onset view, as evidence in their favor.

We, along with our colleague Anna Fritz, intruded ourselves into this controversy by arguing that what was needed as a means of potentially resolving this debate was some new way of testing young children's grasp of the possibility of false beliefs that did not obscure the best abilities of 2- and 3-year-olds by burdening them, as do standard "unexpected change" measures, with the necessity of verbally commenting on the comings and goings of third-party story characters. Such traditional procedures, we reasoned, unnecessarily transformed subjects into passive observers, and confronted them with hypothetical, narratively and inferentially complex word problems that prevented them from putting their best foot forward (Chandler et al., 1989). What we eventually came to as a way around such procedural handicaps was a hide-and-seek task engineered in such a way as to allow young subjects to set about to actively disinform their opponents if they had it within themselves to do so.

The Hide-and-Seek Task

Our own version of this popular children's game involved the use of a large playing board on which we encouraged subjects to hide a "treasure" from a second experimenter (E2) in one of several differently colored containers (see Figure 9.1). The wrinkle in this otherwise straightforward task was that we required participants to carry out their hiding efforts with the "aid" of a puppet figure outfitted with a set of rotating feet that left behind an inky trail of footprints wherever it was pushed across the playing surface. After first taking one turn in a "finders" role, which served to demonstrate how the puppet's tracks clearly betrayed any simple hiding effort, subjects were then encouraged to complete at least two trials in which their task was to hide the treasure in ways that would "make it hard for E2 to find." Among the several potential means at their disposal for doing just this, subjects were counted as having acted deceptively if they either (a) laid additional false and misleading sets of the tracks to empty con-

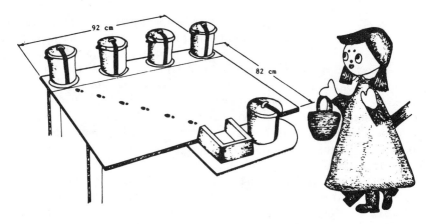

FIGURE 9.1. Hide-and-seek materials.

tainers; (b) wiped away the original set of tell-tale footprints, while also adding one or more sets of misleading tracks of their own: or (c) otherwise lied about the true location of the treasure.

STUDY 1

In our first study using this hide-and-seek procedure (Chandler et al., 1989), we employed a sample of 50 young boys and girls between the ages of $2\frac{1}{2}$ and 5. Each subject completed two separate hiding trials and was credited with having acted deceptively if he or she either lied or otherwise actively disinformed their opponent by laying sets of misleading trails on either or both of these occasions. The results that we obtained were very clear. Overall, more than 80% of these subjects evidenced the ability to lead others into false beliefs, and no significant differences were observed across the several age groups tested. Interestingly, only 20% of those subjects who succeed on this task did so by actually lying, adding credence to our suspicion that the poor showing of young subjects on other tasks may have been an artifact of an exclusive reliance on verbal response indicators. While these results were seen to provide promising support for our early-onset view, several alternative interpretations of these data still existed, and certain of our subsequent research efforts (i.e., Hala et al., 1991) have been directed to evaluating these potential alternative readings of our findings.

STUDY 2

First, it could be argued that, just as young children provided with hammers often end up hammering everything in sight, so too, when provided with a track-laying puppet, they might well be expected to lay tracks at every opportunity. Study 2 was intended as a check on this *random motion* interpretation. Here, we reasoned that if subjects could make appropriate and differential use of these same materials when instructed to *help* E2 find the treasure, as opposed to preventing her from doing so, then any suspicion that the participants in our first study had acted automatically or without reason would be undermined.

To this end, we tested another twenty 3-year-olds on both a "helping" and a "deceiving" version of the hide-and-seek task, employing the same materials described in study 1. The "deceptive" condition was carried out exactly as described for study 1. By contrast, in the "helping" condition, a different experimenter initially hid the treasure in the presence of the subject, without using the puppet and thus without leaving trails to the treasure's location. We then asked subjects, before the return of E2, to take whatever steps were necessary to make it "easy" to find the treasure.

The results of these efforts clearly corroborate the findings of our first study, in that all but one of these 20 subjects took active steps to deceive their opponent when instructed to make the task of finding the treasure difficult. More to the present point, when asked to be helpful, again 19 out of 20 of these same 3-year-old subjects spontaneously used the puppet to leave a clear set of tracks leading to the true location of the treasure. This set of differential findings, we believe, goes some important distance toward discounting the possibility that these or previous subjects somehow mindlessly exercised the materials placed at their disposal and suggests instead that they did in fact know what they were doing in employing their various deceptive strategies.

Study 3

A second and potentially more serious reductive reading of our previous findings is that although our subjects may very well have been attempting to influence their opponent in the hide-and-seek task, their efforts might have been aimed simply at manipulating the *behavior* but not the *beliefs* of the experimenter, by merely luring them away from the actual hiding places they had chosen.

An adequate defense against any such reductive reading of our earlier findings requires some demonstration that these young subjects had in fact understood the likely impact of their actions on the actual thoughts of their opponents. An easy opportunity to attempt such a demonstration was provided by certain parallels that exist between our own hide-and-seek task and other "unexpected change" measures of false-belief understanding. In both cases, someone leaves the room at a crucial moment when the location of an object is being changed. This partial symmetry allowed us to interrupt the procedures that we had followed in our first two studies by introducing a version of the "false-belief prediction" question that forms the centerpiece of standard "unexpected change" measures (e.g., Hogrefe, Wimmer, & Perner, 1986; Perner, Leekam, & Wimmer, 1987). Using this opportunity we again tested a new group of thirty 3- and 4-year-olds. After these subjects had completed their hiding efforts, but before their opponent returned to the room, we asked them "where will E2 look for the treasure?"

In line with our previous findings, all but 2 of these 30 subjects again acted deceptively. More importantly, for present purposes, the great bulk of subjects in all of these age groups successfully *predicted* that their opponent would search, not where they had actually hidden the treasure, but rather in that mistaken place that their disinforming clues falsely suggested it to be. The failure to find any age difference in these data, we believe, offers persuasive evidence that our subjects did in fact undertake their deceptive strategies with the aim of manipulating the *thoughts* and not just the *behaviors* of their opponents.

STUDY 4

As persuasive as the good performance of the subjects in study 3 may be, one last-ditch reductive interpretation of these findings remains. That is, it could still be argued that, in asking our subjects to report on where their opponent would "look for" the missing treasure, we had not gotten as directly as we might at precisely what they imagined E2 would actually be *thinking*. By these lights, the ability of our 3-year-olds to anticipate the likely search pattern that E2 would follow still could be seen to be about the *behavior* of E2 and not his or her *beliefs*.

We designed study 4 to evaluate this last reductive possibility by requiring a new group of subjects to make predictions not only about the likely behavior of their opponents but also about exactly what they might be thinking. To this end, we tested another 20 3-year-old subjects on our hide-and-seek task, this time by asking them on one trial where their opponents would "look for" the hidden treasure and on another where that same individual would actually "think" the treasure was located.

In line with our three preceding studies, all of these 3-year-olds took active and convincing steps to mislead their opponents, and similar to the results from study 3, 85% of these subjects also went on to appropriately predict that their opponent would search for the treasure in that place nominated by the presence of misleading clues. Finally, and most importantly, a full 90% of these subjects also specifically predicted that their opponent would actually *think* that the treasure was where they had deceptively led them to believe it would be.

Figure 9.2 provides a short graphic summary of the results of these four studies. As can be seen from an inspection of this figure, we so far have tested over 100 young preschool children, the great bulk of whom clearly show a special nack for leading others into false beliefs. In addition, these subjects were also able to turn these deceptive skills into helpful gestures when the circumstances warranted their doing so and seemed perfectly

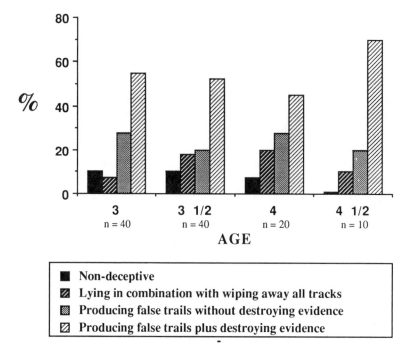

FIGURE 9.2. Percentage of subjects relying on different deceptive strategies across studies (Chandler et al., 1989; Hala et al., 1991).

at home in anticipating the consequences of their deceptive efforts, by reasonably predicting where their opponents would be led to "look for" or "think" the hidden treasure was located. On the strength of this evidence, we have succeeded in persuading ourselves, and perhaps others, that by 3 years of age children do in fact already have a working understanding of the possibility of false beliefs and thus deserve to be credited with some real, if fledgling, theory of mind.

Discussion and Conclusion

Among those investigative groups seriously committed to testing the controversial conclusions of our own earlier studies against potentially simplifying counter explanations, we have ourselves perhaps been the most ruthless. Studies 2, 3, and 4, as reported here, were all carried out in a systematic effort to explore the alternative possibility that what initially looked like hard evidence, indicating that 2- and 3-year-olds are already capable of deceitful practices, was in reality traceable to some still simpler ability, or was otherwise an artifact of our new procedures. What we learned instead was that none of these counter explanations could be made to wash and that such young preschoolers have in fact mastered a wide variety of verbal as well as nonverbal strategies for leading others into believing to be true what they themselves know to be false. This is not to say that they do not still have a lot to learn. As the work of Peskin (1989) and Russell et al. (1989) indicates, 3- and even 4-year-olds are not yet sufficiently expert at deception that they can reliably misinform others about their goals or preferences. Nor, as a study by Sodian (in press) demonstrates, are they even skilled enough to typically succeed at more pedestrian hide-and-seek games when the means for their doing so are made sufficiently round-about and obscure. Finally, our own work (e.g., Chandler et al., 1989) and that of numerous others (e.g., Vasek, 1988) makes it clear that children of this young age rank as amateurs when it comes to telling well-crafted lies or engaging in other complex forms of "digital" deceit.

Important as the foregoing qualifications are, what they do not do is in any way call into question the kernel ability of such young preschool children to recognize the very possibility of deceit. It is, we want to argue, the emergence of this novel insight that fundamentally alters, for such young persons, the future possibilities for trust. By common definition, to be trustful of others requires a firm belief in, or confident expectation of, not just the friendship, but also the fairness and honesty of others. As Erikson (1950) has helped to make clear, the consistent care and concern of others is absolutely "basic" to fostering in infant children any confident expectations regarding such matters of friendship and mutual affection. Nor does contemporary research into the cognitive capabilities of such babes-in-arms lead us in any way to doubt their ability to process information of the sort that would cause them into becoming increasingly trustful or mistrustful with regard to this key affective issue. Uncashed promissory notes issued by Erikson and others also have led us, however, to believe that related issues of trust will continually reemerge at each subsequent stage in the life cycle. What the research summarized in this chapter affords us is some new way of better understanding how and why new problems of trust might surface during the early preschool years. Available evidence now suggests that before the ages of 2 or 3, children lack those cognitive abilities necessary to grasp the very possibility of false belief. With the emergence of this competence, a new door is opened on a previously unrecognized corridor marked by possible dishonesties and deceitful practices. In making shame and particularly self-doubt the centerpieces of his second psychosocial stage, Erikson hints at, but doesn't begin to exhaust, the ways in which preschool children's developing "theories of mind" may contribute to their doubting for the first time, not just the friendliness, but also the honesty and fairness of others. In short, although ignorance may not be exactly bliss, it appears to insulate very young children from an awareness that others sometimes may act in ways meant to lead them astray. Available evidence now suggests, however, that 2- and

3-year-olds are already too sophisticated about the prospects of deceit to be fooled in this way "all of the time."

References

Anderson, M. (1986). Cultural concatenation of deceit and secrecy. In R.W. Mitchell & N.S. Thompson (Eds.), *Deception: Perspectives on human and nonhuman deceit* (pp. 323–348). Albany: State University of New York Press.

Astington, J.W., Harris, P.L., & Olson, D.R. (1988). *Developing theories of mind.* New York: Cambridge University Press.

Bretherton, I., & Beeghly, M. (1982). Talking about internal states. The acquisition of an explicit theory of mind. *Developmental Psychology, 18,* 906–921.

Byrne, W., & Whiten, A. (1988). *Machiavellian intelligence: Social expertise and the evolution of intellect in monkeys, apes, and humans.* Oxford, UK: Claredon Press.

Chandler, M.J. (1987). The Othello effect: An essay on the emergence and eclipse of skeptical doubt. *Human Development, 30,* 137–159.

Chandler, M.J. (1988). Doubt and developing theories of mind. In J.W. Astington, P.L. Harris, & D.R. Olson (Eds.), *Developing theories of mind* (pp. 387–413). New York: Cambridge University Press.

Chandler. M.J., Fritz, A.S., & Hala, S.M. (1989). Small scale deceit: Deception as a marker of 2-, 3- and 4-year olds' early theories of mind. *Child Development, 60,* 1263–1277.

Chevalier-Skolnikoff, S. (1986). An exploration of the ontogeny of deception in human beings and nonhuman primates. In R.W. Mitchell & N.S. Thompson (Eds.), *Deception: Perspectives on human and nonhuman deceit* (pp. 205–220). Albany: State University of New York Press.

de Waal, F. (1988). Chimpanzee politics. In W. Byrne & A. Whiten (Eds.), *Machiavellian intelligence: Social expertise and the evolution of intellect in monkeys, apes and humans* (pp. 122–131). Oxford, UK: Claredon Press.

Dennett, D.C. (1987). *The intentional stance.* Cambridge, MA: MIT Press.

Donaldson, M. (1978). *Children's minds.* New York: W.W. Norton.

Dunn, J. (1988). *The beginnings of social understanding.* Cambridge, MA: Harvard University Press.

Erikson, E.H. (1950). *Childhood and society.* New York: W.W. Norton.

Forguson, L., & Gopnik, A. (1988). The ontogeny of common sense. In J.W. Astington, P.L. Harris, & D.R. Olson (Eds.), *Developing theories of mind* (pp. 226–243). New York: Cambridge University Press.

Freeman, N.H., & Doherty, M.J. (1989). *Preschoolers solve a false-belief problem on a need-to-know basis.* Unpublished manuscript, University of Bristol, UK.

Gopnik, A. (1990). Developing the idea of intentionality: Children's theories of mind. *Canadian Journal of Philosophy, 20,* 89–114.

Hala, S., Chandler, M., & Fritz, A.S. (1991). Fledgling theories of mind: Deception as a marker of 3-year-olds' understanding of false belief. *Child Development, 62,* 83–97.

Hogrefe, G.J., Wimmer, H., & Perner, J. (1986). Ignorance versus false belief: A developmental lag in epistemic states. *Child Development, 57,* 567–582.

Howes, C. (1985). Sharing fantasy: Social pretend play in toddlers. *Child Development, 56,* 1253–1258.

Hyman, R. (1989). The psychology of deception. *Annual Review of Psychology*, *40*, 133–154.

LaFreniere, P. (1988). The ontogeny of tactical deception in humans. In R.W. Byrne & A. Whiten (Eds.), *Machiavellian intelligence: Social expertise and the evolution of intellect in monkeys, apes, and humans* (pp. 238–252). Oxford, UK: Clarendon.

Lempers, J.D. (1979). Young children's productions and comprehension of non-verbal deitic behaviors. *The Journal of Genetic Psychology*, *3*, 253–272.

Leslie, A. (1988). Some implications of pretense for the development of theories of mind. In J.W. Astington, P.L. Harris, & D.R. Olson (Eds.), *Developing theories of mind* (pp. 19–46). New York: Cambridge University Press.

Leung, H.L., & Rheingold, H.L. (1981). Development of pointing as a social gesture. *Developmental Psychology*, *47*, 1148–1158.

Lewis, C., & Osborne, A. (1989). *Three-year-olds' problems with false belief: Conceptual deficit or linguistic artifact*. Unpublished manuscript, University of Lancaster, UK.

Lewis, M., Stanger, C., & Sullivan, M.W. (1989). Deception in 3-year-olds. *Developmental Psychology*, *25*, 439–443.

Lloyd, J.E. (1986). Firefly communication and deception: "Oh what a tangled web." In R.W. Mitchell & N.S. Thompson (Eds.), *Deception: Perspectives on human and nonhuman deceit* (pp. 113–128). Albany: State University of New York Press.

Mitchell, R.W. (1986). A framework for discussing deception. In R.W. Mitchell & N.S. Thompson (Eds.), *Deception: Perspectives on human and nonhuman deceit* (pp. 3–31). Albany: State University of New York Press.

Morgan, C.L. (1894). *An introduction to comparative psychology*. London: Walter Scott.

Moses, L. (1990, May). *Testing the limits of children's belief difficulties*. Paper presented at the Twentieth Anniversary Symposium of the Jean Piaget Society, Philadelphia.

Olson, D.R., Astington, J.W., & Harris, P.L. (1988). Introduction. In J.W. Astington, P.L. Harris, & D.R. Olson (Eds.), *Developing theories of mind* (pp. 10–15). New York: Cambridge University Press.

Perner, J. (in press). *Understanding the representational mind*. Cambridge: The MIT Press.

Perner, J., Leekam, S.R., & Wimmer, H. (1987). Three-year-old's difficulty with false belief: The case for conceptual deficit. *British Journal of Developmental Psychology*, *5*, 125–137.

Peskin, J. (1989). Ruse and representations: *On children's ability to conceal their intentions*. Unpublished manuscript, Ontario Institute for Studies in Education, Canada.

Piaget, J. (Original work published 1932) (1965). *The moral judgement of the child*. New York: Free Press.

Premack, D. (1988). "Does the chimpanzee have a theory of mind?" Revisited. In W. Byrne & A. Whiten (Eds.), *Machiavellian intelligence: Social expertise and the evolution of intellect in monkeys, apes and humans* (pp. 160–179). Oxford, UK: Clarendon Press.

Premack, D., & Woodruff, G. (1978). Does the chimpanzee have a theory of mind? *Behavioral and Brain Sciences*, *1*, 515–526.

Russell, J., Sharpe, S., & Mauthner, N, (1989, September). *Strategic deception in a competitive game*. Paper presented at the Annual Conference of the British Psychological Spociety, Developmental Section. University of Surrey, Guildford, UK.

Selman, R.L. (1980). An analysis of "pure" perspective taking: Games and the delights of deception. In R.L. Selman, *The growth of interpersonal understanding* (pp. 49–68). New York: Academic Press.

Sexton, D.J. (1986). The theory and psychology of military deception. In R.W. Mitchell & N.S. Thompson (Eds.), *Deception: Perspectives of human and non-human deceit* (pp. 349–356). Albany: State University of New York Press.

Shultz, T.R., & Cloghesy, K. (1981). Development of recursive awareness of intention. *Developmental Psychology, 17*, 456–471.

Sodian, B. (in press). The development of deception in young children. *British Journal of Developmental Psychology*.

Sordahl, T.A. (1986). Evolutionary aspects of avian distraction display: Variation in American avocet and black-necked stilt antipredator behavior. In R.W. Mitchell & N.S. Thompson (Eds.), *Deception: Perspectives on human and nonhuman deceit* (pp. 87–112). Albany: State University of New York Press.

Strichartz, A.F., & Burton, R.V. (1990). Lies and truth: A study of the development of the concept. *Child Development, 61*, 211–220.

Vasek, M.E. (1988). Lying as a skill: The development of deception in children. In R.W. Mitchell & N.S. Thompson (Eds.), *Deception: Perspectives on human and nonhuman deceit* (pp. 271–292). Albany: State University of New York Press.

Wellman, H.M. (1988). First steps in the child's theorizing about the mind. In J.W. Astington, P.L. Harris, & D.R. Olson (Eds.), *Developing theories of mind* (pp. 64–92). New York: Cambridge University Press.

Wellman, H.M. (1990). *Children's early theories of mind*. Bradford Books.

Wimmer, H., Gruber, S., & Perner, J. (1985). Young children's conception of lying: Moral intention and the denotation and connotation of "to lie." *Developmental Psychology, 21*, 993–995.

Wimmer, H., & Perner, J. (1983). Beliefs about beliefs: Representation and constraining function of wrong beliefs in young children's understanding of deception. *Cognition, 13*, 103–128.

Zaitchik, D. (1989). *Is only seeing really believing?: Sources of the true belief in the false belief task*. Unpublished manuscript, MIT, Cambridge, MA.

10
The Trust-Value Basis of Children's Friendship

KEN J. ROTENBERG

The role of interpersonal trust in children's friendship is portrayed vividly in various fiction books and magazine articles for children.[1] Those writings include rather "real-life" descriptions of how children's friendships are affected by secret sharing, secret keeping, promise fulfillment, and the underlying perceptions of trust and attributions of trustworthiness. The following are some examples.

The importance of secret keeping in friendship is a theme in books written even for very young children. In Sharon Lee Roberts' (1986) book for preschoolers, entitled *Friendship*, a picture of a boy and a girl is accompanied by the text "friendship is listening to his secrets without telling them to anyone else" (p. 19). This theme is evident in books for older children, as well. Susan Beth Pfeffer's (1980) book entitled *Just Between Us*, depicts a girl who has difficulty keeping secrets and therefore has serious problems in her relationships with peer friends and her mother. At the beginning of the book, a friend threatens, "I am never going to speak to you again" (p. 1) because the protagonist had revealed the friend's secret. The book further depicts how the mother, who is a psychology student, attempts to use behavior modification to rectify her daughter's secret-breaking behavior.

The theme of promise keeping behavior in children's friendship is portrayed in a book entitled *A Promise is for Keeping* by Ann Wade (1979). This is a story about two girls who are friends and who find a bracelet on the beach. They agree to alternate the possession of it each week. One girl fails to give the other the bracelet after the week expired and receives a note from the other girl stating, "I know you are hiding from me. You broke your promise. We are not friends anymore" (p. 16). At the conclusion of the book, the girl gives the bracelet to the other, stating that she will never break her promise again.

---

[1] The term *children* is used to denote a conventional period of childhood and adolescence.

The role of trust per se in friendship is articulated by Gail Kessler (1984) in the *Seventeen* magazine article entitled "Can You Trust Your Friends?" In the article, Kessler discusses the pitfalls of adolescents' revealing secrets to friends. The article begins with the description of an incident in which one female adolescent revealed another adolescent's secret. The latter responded by saying "What matters is that I told you something in strict confidence—and you couldn't keep it to yourself. How can I ever trust you again?" (p. 155). The article continues by emphasizing that the secret breaking resulted in a decline in the quality of friendship. Kessler also discusses the problem of being the recipient of a friend's secret. On this issue, she cited Dr. Jane Anderson, a child and adolescent psychiatrist in Boulder, Colorado, who recommends that "if you tell a friend she can trust you, then you must be trustworthy no matter how hard it may be" (p. 156). One of the arguments advanced at the conclusion of the article is that the revealing of secrets does not have to destroy a friendship if the individuals are willing to work at reestablishing trust in the relationship.

Of course, fiction books and magazine articles for children are not definitive evidence for psychological processes. These must be established empirically. It is worthwhile to keep in mind, however, that the writings probably reflect the authors' recall of their childhood or their personal observations of children. Kessler actually drew on specialists' observations. Also, we should not overlook the possibility that the books and magazine articles may shape children's understanding of friendship; the books and magazine articles I have described are quite popular.

One important role of these writings is that they are a source of valuable hypotheses. The writings converge with my own theory and research in suggesting three fundamental hypothesis regarding children's friendship. First, secret sharing, secret keeping, and promise fulfillment are behaviors that affect friendship. From the present perspective, these are essentially communicative behaviors that are important for friendship because they entail some risk, in which either the communicator or recipient of the communication is in the position of depending on the person to keep his or her word (see corresponding definitions of trust by Rotter, 1967, 1971; Schlenker, Helm, & Tedeschi, 1973). By necessity, the willingness to engage in the risky behavior varies as a function of the confidence that the person will keep his or her word. If the person keeps his or her word, then this increases confidence in him or her, by the communicator or recipient of the communication, and permits joint activities. Both the resulting confidence and joint activities foster friendship. This is clearly demonstrated in promise fulfillment. Imagine that a peer promises to meet a child at the movies. Initially, the child's willingness to undertake the somewhat risky activity of going to the movies (potentially standing around alone and even wasting a trip or day) depends on his or her confidence that the peer will keep his or her word. If the peer shows up at the movie on time, then that enhances the child's confidence in the peer to keep his word–promises and results in joint activities, both fostering friendship. This principle is slightly more complicated in its application to secret sharing and secret keeping. When a child reveals personal information as a secret, he or she risks incurring negative consequences (i.e. criticism) directly from the recipient and *most* importantly, if divulged, secrets result in negative social consequences from others. In most interactions, the recipient has promised, either at that time or over the course of their relationship, that he or she will refrain from criticism and, most importantly, maintain secrecy of the communication. The child's willingness to reveal a secret depends on his or her confidence that the recipient will keep his or her word. If a peer keeps a secret, then he or she enhances the child's confidence and permits the joint exchange of personal information, both fostering friendship.

The second hypothesis is that the effects of secret sharing, secret keeping, and promise fulfillment behaviors on friendship are mediated, in part, by their effects on the children's perceptions of trust and their attributions of trustworthiness. From their confidence that the other person will keep his or her word, children generate perceptions of how much they can trust the person. As a result, children attribute an underlying personality dimension of trustworthiness to the person. By making that attribution, children form a well-defined orientation toward sharing secrets with the other person or depending on his or her promises in future or other situations. Furthermore, that attribution shapes the children's decisions about their formation or continuity of friendship. Theoretically, after children are able to generate attributed trustworthiness, it serves as a core person-perception construct that plays a powerful role in their decisions about whether they should form a friendship with a given peer and whether an established friendship should continue.

It should be emphasized that the hypothesis is *not* that all the effects of secret keeping and promise fulfillment on friendship are mediated by attributed trustworthiness. Specifically, the breaking of a secret and a promise have consequences for children that affect their interpersonal relationships independently of attributed trustworthiness. For example, if a friend breaks a promise to go to a movie with a child, then he or she may go to the movie alone or not go at all, both likely aversive. If a friend reveals a child's secret "crush" on a certain boy or girl, then this could jeopardize the development of an opposite-sex relationship. In response to these events, children often experience anger or sadness that attenuates friendship without the mediating factor of attributed trustworthiness.

The third and final hypothesis generated by writings is that trust between individuals has a strong mutual or reciprocal component; a child's trust in a peer affects and becomes "locked on" to the peer's trust in that child. This is guided by principles of reciprocity of communication in dyadic interactions (see Miller & Kenny, 1986) and also by self-fulfillment processes associated with trust. In particular, a child's attributed trustworthiness to a peer affects the opportunity for engaging a behavior that could foster confidence and enhance trust. Imagine, for example, that David distrusts John (a peer) and attributes untrustworthiness to him. Under these conditions, David will *not* share secrets with John and thereby remove the opportunity for John to keep his word to maintain confidentiality, which would maintain the initial attribution. Also, David's lack of secret sharing with John prevents the development of any reciprocity of secret sharing. If John does not have the opportunity to share a secret, he cannot establish confidence that David will keep his word and, therefore, attribute trustworthiness to him. Other concomitant behaviors could foster the emergence of this distrusting relationship, such as David insulting John (calling him a liar or cheat). During the course of relationships, attributions of trustworthiness dictate the opportunity for reciprocal word keeping and other concomitant behavior and thereby cause locked on or mutual trust.

In previous articles, I have referred to the preceding pattern (Rotenberg, 1986) as the trust-value basis of children's friendship and to the mutuality of trust (Rotenberg & Pilipenko, 1984). (I will refer to both of these as the trust-value basis of friendship in this chapter.) The primary question of interest is whether trust-value is a basis for friendship in children. Before discussing the research relevant to that question, I want to point out the practical and ethical problems encountered in the investigation of the trust-value basis of friendship.

It is my belief that the limited investigation into the trust-value basis of friendship in children is due, in part, to the great number of practical and ethical problems. First, naturalistic observations of secret sharing, secret keeping, and promise fulfillment are difficult to obtain. Simply, those behaviors, particularly secret activities, are private in nature and potentially low in frequency when compared to other behaviors (e.g., aggression, prosocial). Second, because of the probable adverse consequences, researchers are very reluctant to manipulate the trust-value behaviors and observe their effects on peer friendship. Obviously, if the trust-value basis prevailed, then a child's friendship with a peer would be in jeopardy when a researcher convinced one of them to reveal a secret they had shared. As a result of those constraints, researchers have depended in large part, on the use of two methods: (a) judgments of hypothetical events and (b) self-reports of behavior. Unfortunately, both methods have limitations, notably, whether the findings can be generalized to, or are accurate reports of, naturally occurring events.

Research indicates that trust-value is a basis of adults' friendship and other intimate relationships (e.g., marriage, counseling) (Merluzzi & Brischetto, 1986; Rempel, Holmes & Zanna, 1985). To what extent is this the case for children? Research has documented, rather well, one facet of the trust-value basis of friendship, that of the role of sharing secrets in children's friendships. This has emerged in the literature primarily (although not exclusively) in the research concerning children's understanding of the role of the sharing of personal information or intimacies in friendship. It should be pointed out that a distinction can be made between secrets and personal information and/or intimacies. Sometimes secrets are not strictly personal information, in that they do not pertain to *personal* attributes or behaviors. For example, some secrets pertain to the activities of others that the child has observed, such as the behavior of brothers or sisters. Moreover, secrets are conceptualized as information that the *sender* views as confidential to the receiver (i.e., the promise to keep it a secret). This may not always be true for personal information. In this context, it is interesting to consider whether the *recipient* of the secret viewed the information as confidential. It may be that this represents one common way that children (and adults) break secrets; they do not understand that the personal information or intimacies they were told were meant to be kept confidential.

A wide variety of studies yield evidence for the role of secret sharing and trusting in children's friendship. For example, Furman and Bierman (1984) investigated the qualities that second-, fourth- and sixth-grade children expected for friendship. These researchers employed a multi-method approach that consisted of children judging stories, responding to open-ended questions on friendship, and responding to a forced choice questionnaire on friendship. Furman and Bierman found that children from all three grades expected secret sharing (termed *behavioral intimacy*) for friendship; this expectation did not vary with age on the story judgment measure. Furthermore, those authors found that children expected trusting (termed *dispositional intimacy*) for friendship, but that expectation increased with age on all three measures. In some studies, researchers assume that sharing secrets and trusting are intrinsic aspects of children's friendship. An example of this is Sharabany, Gershoni, and Hofman (1981), who used children's reports of the degree to which they shared intimate information with female and male friends as a measure of the *quality* of friendship.

A more behavioral approach to the phenomena of secret sharing was adopted in the study that Dave Sliz and I carried out on children's restrictive disclosure to friends (Rotenberg & Sliz, 1988). This study is relevant to the extent that high-personal information serves as a secret. If secret sharing is an important facet of children's friendship, then they should be more willing to disclose high-personal information to peer friends rather than peer nonfriends. Because low-intimate information is not a secret, then children should be willing to disclose to friends and nonfriends, equally. Generally, we referred to this pattern of disclosure as *restrictive disclosure to friends*. In the study, we required kindergarten, second and fourth-grade children to provide, on audiotape, a message on topics varying in intimacy to a classmate who was a friend and a classmate who was not a friend (nonfriend). We found that children from each grade showed the restrictive disclosure to friend pattern. They disclosed more high-personal information in their message to a friend than to a nonfriend. Also, the children did not differentially disclose low-personal information in their messages to the two types of peers. The findings are consistent with the notion that secret sharing is an important facet of friendship for children of those ages. Whether these patterns are strictly the result of the trust-value basis of friendship remains to be examined, however. For example, it is not clear whether the children regarded the high intimate information as secrets and whether their tendency to reveal that information to a friend than a nonfriend was due to greater attributions of trustworthiness to the former peer.

Although researchers have explored the sharing of secrets or intimacies as a basis of children's friendship, they have all but ignored the role of secret *keeping* as well as that of promise fulfillment. One exception to this is the study I carried out on children's friendship (Rotenberg, 1986). This was guided by the expectation that if children adopt the trust-value basis of trust, then their peer friendship and attributed trustworthiness to peers should be correlated and each should be correlated with the extent to which the peers keep secrets and fulfill promises. In this study, fourth-grade children reported, at two intervals (a) the number of secrets they told their classmates (secrets); (b) the number of secrets their classmates kept (secrets kept); (c) the number of promises their classmates made (promises made); and (d) the number of promises their classmates kept (promises kept). In addition, they rated on 5- or 6-point scales how much they trusted their classmates (attributed trustworthiness) and how good or bad a friend each classmate was (friendship). I calculated two additional measures in the study. First, I divided the number of secrets kept by the number of secrets told, to yield the proportion of secrets kept by each classmate. Second, I divided the number of promises kept by the number of promises made, to yield the proportion of promises kepts by each classmate. These measures were necessary to assess secret keeping and promise keeping while controlling for the total number of secrets told and promises made, respectively.

The following correlations were consistent with the trust-value basis of friendship: (a) For girls and boys, attributed trustworthiness was correlated with friendship. (b) For boys, the number of secrets was correlated with attributed trustworthiness. (c) For girls, the proportion of secrets kept was correlated with attributed trustworthiness and friendship. (d) For boys and girls, the proportion of promises kept was correlated with attributed trustworthiness and friendship. Also, consistent with the trust-value basis of friendship was the finding that, for boys, the proportion of secrets kept was correlated with friendship. Contrary to the principle, however, the proportion of secrets kept for boys was not correlated with attributed trustworthiness. This was interpreted as suggesting that secret keeping between friends in boys may be a product of coercive behavior rather than the attribution of a personal characteristic of trust-worthiness.

The preceding study (Rotenberg, 1986) yielded one additional set of data. Teachers of the children were required to identify the pairs of children who were friends. The teachers apparently succeeded in identifying "mutual" friends, because their selections corresponded to the children's friendship ratings. Consistent with the mutual notion of trust, perceived trust, secret sharing, proportion of secret keeping, and the proportion of promise keeping were greater between members of those pairs than between them and other same-sex peers.

The purpose of the present study[2] was to examine some implications of the research and, in particular, the preceding study (Rotenberg, 1986). It was reasoned that if fourth-grade children base their actual friendship on trust-value, then they should use that as a basis of friendship preferences. In more specific terms, if fourth-grade children view peers who keep secrets and keep promises as good friends, then the children should *prefer* peers who exhibit those behaviors as friends and therefore (a) desire them as friends, (b) view them as potentially good friends, and (c) want their company. This should be mediated by their perception that they trust those peers, indicating an attribution of trustworthiness.

The present study was designed to test those hypotheses. In addition, the study was guided by the hypothesis that the play-value of peers would have some but clearly less of a role in fourth-grade children's friendship preferences. Play value concerns how much a peer can contribute to the child's play activities, such as having many toys or liking the same games. The study was guided by the notion that having many toys is a rather superficial attribute. Although the children may desire to have peers as friends who have many toys, the children would not view this as contributing to the preferred *quality* of friendship (e.g., how good they would be as a friend or want their company in other activities). Finally, it was expected that the food preferences of peers would serve as a neutral value and not play a role in friendship preferences.

Subjects

The subjects were 40 children (20 boys and 20 girls) from fourth grade. The children had a mean age of 10 years and were obtained from two metropolitan schools in West Lafayette, Indiana.

[2] Portions of this study were presented, with Gary Ladd and Tracy Tidwell as coauthors, at the Southeastern Conference on Human Development, April 1984. Thanks are extended to Russena Comer, Bill Watkins, and Paula Watkins for their assistance in the study.

Stimulus and Apparatus

Four pairs of stories were used in the study, and they were the following. One pair of stories depicted the protagonists as varying in food desires. In one story, the protagonist was described as "likes to eat hotdogs" (arbitrarily coded as high level) and in the other story, the protagonist was described as "likes to eat hamburgers" (coded as low level). These stories were used to depict a "neutral" dimension that was, theoretically, unrelated to friendship preferences.

The second pair of stories was designed to depict play value and showed this in terms of play possessions. In one story, the protagonist was described as "having lots of fun toys to play with" (high level), and in the other story the protagonist was described as "not having any fun toys to play with" (low level).

The third and fourth pairs of stories were designed to depict trust value. One pair of stories showed sharing secrets, and in these stories, the protagonists were told by another child his or her liking for an opposite-sex peer. In one story, the protagonist was described as "never told another child" (high level—secret kept), whereas in the other story, the protagonist was described as "told the secret to another child in the class" (low level—secret broken). The other pair of stories showed promise–behavior consistency and were identical to the promise "all" and promise "some" stories used by Rotenberg (1980). In both stories, the protagonist was shown as carrying out some kind of a helping activity. In one story, however, the protagonist was described as stating that he or she would do *some* of the helping activity (high level—promise kept) while in the other story, the protagonist was described as stating that he or she would do *all* of the activity (low level—promise broken). The examiner presented the stories in a randomized order with the restriction that stories depicting the same value (neutral, play, or trust) were not presented sequentially. Also, there were two sets of stories, one depicting boys and the other depicting girls; subjects were presented stories depicting protagonists who were of the same sex.

The subjects made judgments of desirability of friendship and preferred company on 5-point scales ranging from 1, "not at all," to 5, "very, very much." The scale was depicted by a series of black columns of increasing height. The subjects also made judgments of the quality of friendship on a 7-point scale, ranging from 1, "kind of good," to 7, "very bad." This scale was depicted by a series of yellow and black columns that were descending and then ascending height.

Procedure

The examiner tested subjects individually. Initially, the examiner provided each subject practice in the use of the scales and the judging procedure. This entailed presenting the scales until the subject was able to identify the labels of the 5-point and 7-point scales correctly and then requiring him or her to judge a pair of practice stories. Subsequently, the examiner used the following procedure, for each of the four stories: First, the examiner presented the story verbally and pictorially until the subject achieved complete recall of it. Second, the examiner asked the subject to judge on the 5-point scale "how much you want the protagonist [by name] to be a friend?" (desirability) and to give his or her reasons for that judgment. Third, the examiner asked the subject to judge on the 7-point scale, "If the protagonist [by name] was a friend, how good or bad a friend would he or she be?" (quality). Fourth, the examiner asked the subject to judge on the 5-point scale, "If you had a chance to go to the movies, then how much would you want to go the movies with the protagonist [by name]?" (preferred company).

In addition, after all the stories had been judged, the experimenter reviewed each story and asked the subject either why he or she made his or her judgments for his or her view of the protagonist. The examiner required the subject to choose between one of the following four answers, "like, do not like, trust, or do not trust."

Results and Discussion

The three friendship-preference judgments were scored from 1 to 5 or 7, with larger numbers corresponding to greater values of friendship preference. The judgment scores were subjected to a 2 (sex of subject) $\times$ 4 (type of story) $\times$ 2 (level of story) multivariate analysis of variance (MANOVA) with repeated measures on the latter two variables. The analyses yielded a significant main effect of story type, $F(9, 332) = 2.70$, $p < .01$, and a significant main effect of story level, $F(9, 332) = 66.93$, $p < .001$. Both of these were qualified by the expected two-way interaction, story type $\times$ story level $F(9, 332) = 16.75$, $p < .001$. Univariate ANOVAs yielded this two-way interaction on desirability, quality, and preferred company, $F(3, 114) = 48.68$, $p < .001$; $F(3, 114) = 37.08$, $p < .001$; and $F(3, 114) = 16.75$, $p < .001$; respectively. The means for these interactions are shown in Table 10.1. Tukey a posteriori comparisons indicated that, as expected, the subjects did not differentiate between the two food-desire protagonists on the friendship-preference judgments. As expected, though, the subjects showed some differential preference of the play-value protagonists. The subjects judged the protagonist who had fun toys as more desirable as a friend than the protagonist who had no fun toys ($p < .05$).

TABLE 10.1. Means of friendship preferences for the story by level interaction on the three measures.

Type of story with corresponding value	Level of story	Measures		
		Desirability	Quality	Preferred company
Food desire	High (1)	3.53	5.30	3.28
(neutral value)	Low (2)	3.10	5.38	3.18
Play possessions	High	3.90	5.65	3.50
(play value)	Low	3.05	5.18	3.20
Sharing secrets	High (S-K)	4.75	6.70	4.35
(trust value)	Low (S-B)	1.68	3.13	1.80
Promise–behavior	High (P-K)	3.63	5.63	3.48
consistency	Low (P-B)	1.95	3.53	2.03
(trust value)				

S-K, to secret kept; S-B, secret broken; P-K, promise kept; P-B, promise broken.
Note. Higher numbers correspond to greater friendship preferences.

As anticipated, though, the subjects did not differentiate between these two protagonists on the other two judgments, that of quality and preferred company.

As predicted, the subjects differentiated between the protagonists in the two pairs of trust-value stories. Specifically, on all three judgments (desirability, quality, and company) the subjects had higher friendship preferences for the protagonist who kept secrets than the one who broke secrets and for the protagonist who kept a promise than the one who broke a promise (all $p < .01$).

Two naive raters coded the subjects' explanations for their friendship-desirability judgments. Initially, both raters coded 25% of the protocols, and interrater reliability of 90% (agreement/total) was achieved. Each rater coded a separate 50% of the protocols for analysis. The following dominant patterns were found, and these conformed with expectation, to a large extent. For the play-value stories, 33% of the subjects gave "having toys" as an explanation of the high-level story and 18% of them gave "not having toys" as an explanation of the low-level story. For the secret-keeping trust-value stories, 88% of the subjects gave "keeping a secret" as an explanation of the high-level story, and 83% of the subjects gave "breaking a secret" as an explanation for the low-level story. Finally, for the promise-fulfillment trust-value stories, 18% of the subjects gave "keeping a promise" as an explanation of the high-level story, and 63% gave "breaking a promise" as an explanation of the low-level story.

The subjects' selections of the four alternatives as explanations–attributes were subjected to a 4 (type of story) × 2 (level of story) × 4 (type of descriptor) log-linear analysis. The frequencies are shown in Table 10.2. The analysis yielded main effects and two-way interactions that were qualified by the expected three-way interaction, story type × story level × descriptor type, $X^2(9) = 23.47$, $p < .01$. Separate log-linear analyses for

TABLE 10.2. Frequencies of the four descriptor types of level and story.

Type of story with corresponding value	Descriptor type				
	Level of story	Like	Not like	Trust	Not trust
Food desire (neutral value)	High (1)	25	6	8	1
	Low (2)	25	10	3	2
Play possession (play value)	High	28	5	6	1
	Low	20	11	6	3
Sharing secrets (trust value)	High (S-K)	7	0	33	0
	Low (S-B)	0	3	2	35
Promise–behavior consistency	High (P-K)	9	3	23	5
(trust value)	Low (P-B)	2	4	2	32

S-K, secret kept; S-B, secret broken; P-K, promise kept; P-B, promise broken.

each pair of stories yielded main effects of descriptor type for neutral and play-value stories, $X^2(3) = 56.62$. $p < .001$, and $X^2(3) = 49.03$, $p < .001$, respectively. Subjects primarily gave "liking" as explanations–attributes of both high- and low-level protagonists in both types of stories. The analyses of both the secret keeping and promise fulfillment trust-value stories yielded two-way, story-level × descriptor interactions, $X^2(3) = 86.27$, $p < .001$ and $X^2(3) = 45.32$, $p < .001$, respectively. As expected, the subjects primarily gave "trust" explanations–attributes of the high-level stories in which the protagonists kept a secret or fulfilled a promise. Also, the subjects primarily gave "not trust" explanations/attributes of the low-level stories in which the protagonists revealed a secret or broke a promise.

The findings conformed to expectation. As anticipated, the neutral value played no appreciable role in the friendship preferences. Also, play value had an effect on the desire measure only and not on the qualitative judgments. In contrast, trust-value had substantial effects on all friendship preferences. Moreover, the children's explanations or attributes support the hypothesis that those effects were due to (a) the secret or promise keeping versus breaking content and (b) greater attributed trustworthiness to those who kept rather than broke secrets and promises.

Directions for Future Research

Although not exhaustive, these are some of the questions that should be addressed in future: (a) When does this trust-value basis of friendship emerge in development? (b) Assuming that it is acquired with age, what factors account for that development? (c) Are there stable individual differences in the trust-value basis of trust, and if so, what socialization practices contribute to them? (d) Are there other facets of the trust-value basis of friendship?

Some speculations on the possible answers to the preceding questions may be useful as a guide a future research. It seems probable that some facets of trust-value basis of friendship emerge in children during pre-school age. The research by Rotenberg and Sliz (1988) may be taken to suggest that secret sharing in friendship emerges at least by kindergarten. Other facets of the trust-value basis of friendship may emerge later. For example, research indicates that children's ability to understand promises and use them as a basis of trust is acquired with age (Astington, 1988; Rotenberg, 1980). A moderate degree of sophistication in those appears to emerge around second to third grade (8 to 9 years of age), and as such, promise fulfillment could play a role in friendship only by that time in development. Also, there is some debate over when children acquire the ability to understand personality characteristics or dispositions of others (see Eder, 1989). Whenever this develops, however, it should have con-siderable impact on children's trust in that it will permit them to attribute trustworthiness to others. This should alter children's friendship in two ways. It should foster greater generalization whereby children adopt a dis-tinct trusting or distrusting orientation toward others. Also, once achieved, attributed trustworthiness will serve to guide how children *select* peers as friends and their *decisions* to continue friendships.

Considerable research reveals stable individual differences in children's trust (Imber, 1973) and adults' trust (Rotter, 1967, 1971), as measured by their beliefs that others will keep their word or promises. Nevertheless, researchers have not yet addressed whether there are stable individual differences in their *value* of promise fulfillment and the complete trust-value basis as a criteria for friendship. Potentially, secret keeping, promise fulfillment, and attributed trustworthiness are more valued for friendship by some children than by others. Parental practices may play a role in determining such values, as they apparently do in fostering children's belief that others fulfill their promises (see Katz & Rotter, 1969). One would expect that parental preaching, values, and behavior would shape children's adoption of the trust-value basis of friendship.

Finally, as revealed in this book, chidren's sensitivity to other cues affects their interpersonal trust. I have examined the role of secret keeping and promise fulfillment as a trust basis of friendship, but actions such as lying and deception also may serve in this capacity. In effect, children's friendships should be negatively affected by the extent to which the peers engaged in lying and deception, and those effects may be mediated by attributed trustworthiness.

References

Astington, J.W. (1988). Promises: words or deeds? *First Language, 8,* 259–270.

Eder, R.A. (1989). The emergent personologist: The struture and content of $3\frac{1}{2}$, $5\frac{1}{2}$ and $7\frac{1}{2}$-year-olds' concepts of themselves and other persons. *Child Development, 60,* 1218–1228.

Furman, W., & Bierman, K.L. (1984). Children's conceptions of friendship: A multimethod study of developmental changes. *Developmental Psychology, 20,* 925–931.

Imber, S. (1973). Relationship of trust to academic performance. *Journal of Personality and Social Psychology, 28,* 145–150.

Katz, H. & Rotter, J. (1969). Interpersonal trust scores of college students and their parents. *Child Development, 40,* 657–661.

Kessler, G. (1984). Can you trust your friends? She let you down. Can you ever confide in her again. *Seventeen,* June, 155, 156, 184.

Merluzzi, T.V., & Brischetto, C.S. (1986). Breach of confidentiality and perceived trustworthiness of counsellors. *Journal of Counseling Psychology, 30,* 245–251.

Miller, L.C., & Kenny, D.A. (1986). Reciprocity of self-disclosure at the individual and dyadic levels: A social relations analysis. *Journal of Personality and Social Psychology, 50,* 713–719.

Pfeffer, S.B. (1980). *Just between us.* New York: Delacorte Press.

Rempel, J.K., Holmes, J.G., & Zanna, M.P. (1985). Trust in close relationships. *Journal of Personality and Social Psychology, 49,* 95–112.

Roberts, S.L. (1986). *Friendship.* Chicago: Children's Press.

Rotenberg, K.J. (1980). "A promise kept, a promise broken:" Developmental bases of trust. *Child Development, 51,* 614–617.

Rotenberg, K.J. (1986). Same-sex patterns and sex differences in the basis of children's friendship. *Sex Roles, 15,* 613–626.

Rotenberg, K.J., & Pilipenko, T.A. (1984). Mutuality, temporal consistency, and helpfulness in children's trust in peers. *Social Cognition, 2,* 235–255.

Rotenberg, K.J., & Sliz, D. (1988). Children's restrictive disclosure to friends. *Merrill-Palmer Quarterly, 34,* 203–215.

Rotter, J.B. (1967). A new scale for the measurement of interpersonal trust. *Journal of Personality, 35,* 651–665.

Rotter, J.B. (1971). Generalized expectancies for interpersonal trust. *American Psychologist, 26,* 443–452.

Sharabany, R., Gershoni, R., & Hofman, J.E. (1981). Girlfriend, boyfriend: Age and sex differences in intimate friendship. *Developmental Psychology, 17,* 800–808.

Schlenker, B.R., Helm, B., & Tedeschi, J.T. (1973). The effects of personality and situational variables on behavioral trust. *Journal of Personality and Social Psychology, 25,* 419–427.

Wade, A. (1979). *A Promise is for keeping.* Chicago: Children's Press.